The Mighty Five

The C...lle of

...u...

THIS is the first book in English devoted entirely to this fabulous group of men who gave shape and form to Russian national music. In this story, we meet and learn and come to love them. Though the book reads dramatically, it is by no means "fictionized biography". It has been prepared with the scholar's fastidiousness for accuracy and devotion to original source materials. Indeed, many of the passages quoted from diaries, documents, and letters are here appearing for the first time in English.

Victor I. Seroff, the author of *The Mighty Five*, is familiar to American readers as the author of a brilliant biography of Shostakovich, published a few years ago, and through his scintillating articles on European music in *Town and Country*, *The New Republic*, *Harper's*, *Collier's*, and other periodicals. He has long been an American citizen, though he is also widely known in Europe as an informed, acute, and witty writer on musical subjects.

THE MIGHTY FIVE

BY THE AUTHOR

DMITRI SHOSTAKOVICH: THE LIFE AND BACKGROUND
OF A SOVIET COMPOSER

A caricature of The Mighty Five, drawn in pastels by Makovsky, when the group refused to give a private performance of Dargomijsky's *The Stone Guest* for Turgeniev, the Russian novelist, who had offended it with remarks about Glinka and Balakirev in his novel *On the Eve.*

From left to right: Cui; Balakirev, with baton in hand; Stassov, dressed in national Russian costume, blowing the horn of fame and beating a drum; Victor Hartmann, architect and artist, whose exhibition of pictures inspired Mussorgsky's *Pictures at an Exhibition,* sitting on Stassov's shoulder; and Borodin.

In front: Rimsky-Korsakov as a crab, with the two Purgold girls as little lap dogs; Mussorgsky leading the whole parade as an arrogant rooster.

The hardly visible head at the right is that of Alexander Serov, looking like Zeus shooting arrows.

The Mighty Five

THE CRADLE OF
RUSSIAN NATIONAL MUSIC

By Victor I. Seroff

6552

Allen, Towne & Heath, Inc. : New York

FIRST PRINTING

PRINTED IN THE UNITED STATES OF AMERICA
BY THE COLONIAL PRESS INC.
BOUND BY F. M. CHARLTON CO., N. Y.

To NELDA R. AUDIBERT

Gut verloren—etwas verloren!
Musst rasch dich besinnen
Und neues gewinnen.
Ehre verloren—viel verloren!
Musst Ruhm gewinnen,
Da werden die Leute sich anders besinnen.
Mut verloren—alles verloren!
Da wär' es besser: nicht geboren.

—Goethe.

THE MIGHTY FIVE

Introduction

"THE MIGHTY FIVE"—"*LES CINQ*," AS THEY ARE called in France—is a free translation of the Russian *Moguchaya Kuchka* ("The Mighty Little Heap"), which was the name for a group of Russian musicians—Balakirev, Cui, Borodin, Rimsky-Korsakov, and Mussorgsky—who founded the new Russian national school at the beginning of the sixties of the last century. The importance of their influence on music can be compared only to that of Richard Wagner's influence. When at the beginning of their rise above the musical horizon they were scornfully dismissed by the critics as "just a little heap of musicians," Vladimir Stassov, a famous writer on art and music of that time and their most ardent champion, remarked, "A little heap—ah, but how mighty!"

Their nickname brings to mind the derogatory term applied to another nationalist group—those noblemen of the Netherlands who in 1566 rebelled against the civil and religious despotism of Philip II, and who were called "Les Gueux" ("The Beggars"), a name which they forthwith adopted as their battle-cry. And in the artistic alliance of their talents and complete unselfishness in

[3]

their mutual work, there is a striking analogy between The Five and the Florentine *"Camerata,"* grouped around Count Giovanni Bardi at the end of the sixteenth century, whose greatest service to music was the creation of the first operas.

The music composed by The Five was a further development of that of their two forerunners, Mihail Glinka and Alexander Dargomijsky. It was the cradle of Russian national music. Though national, it did not embrace all Russian music, because such composers as Anton Rubinstein and Tchaikovsky not only did not join them, but, with their followers and supporters, even formed a decisive opposition.

The two "camps" had their seats in two capitals. The Mighty Five, the advocates of national policy in music and regarded as revolutionary, were in St. Petersburg, while Tchaikovsky presided over the group in Moscow. There is a curious reversal in this situation because, ever since the time of Peter the Great, who "broke the window into Europe" and allowed the European influence to flow into Russian life in a constant stream, St. Petersburg had been the clearing house, as it were, for the outside world while Moscow had remained more conservative and national. Yet the choice of residence of the two groups should be attributed not to any political reason, but simply to the fact that the professional occupations of the members required their presence in one or the other capital.

The prologue to the history of Russian music belongs to the tenth century, when Prince Vladimir of Kiev brought Christianity to Russia. The saga of this event tells that Vladimir had to make a final choice among the religions of the world and adopt it for his people. He sent his councilors abroad to observe "by whom and how God was worshipped." "We did not know whether we were in heaven or on earth," they related to him on their return from the Church of St. Sophia in Byzantium. Vladimir made his choice.

It was the pomp and the splendor of the rituals, in which choral

[4]

singing had no small part (musical instruments have no place in the services of the Greek Orthodox Church), on which the Church had to rely for permanent acceptance among the newly converted people. As the new churches grew in numbers, choirs were formed, and the schools in which the singers were trained for religious services grew in numbers with them. Every prince and every bishop struggled to surpass the others in the extravagance of ritual and the beauty of the choral singing.

But the Church was far from being a secluded organization. It represented the chief cultural force and stood at the head of national development. As its power grew, it took control of every phase of life in the land. In its striving to introduce the new morality and the new sense of responsibility toward God, the Church preached piety, abstinence, and humility, and found a disturbing obstacle in the old pagan spirit which still lived in legends and folk-lore. It was determined to stamp out the last vestige of this spirit. The priests, no matter how important they were in the hierarchy, waged a relentless fight, repressing all innocent demonstrations of happiness. "Laughter does not edify or redeem us. It dispels and destroys edification. Laughter grieves the Holy Spirit, it banishes the virtues, for it causes forgetfulness of death and eternal punishment."

Such was the ecclesiastical precept of disfavor with which the Church regarded every popular amusement. In the following centuries the *Skomoroch* (traveling theatrical groups, such as those portrayed in Shakespeare's plays) and *Guslars* (men who sang and accompanied themselves on instruments), for whom the wealthy Novgorod merchants were ready to empty their cases of gold, were outlawed and cursed as scum and the disciples of the Devil.

The battle reached its peak when in 1636 the Moscow Patriarch, Joseph, not only decreed that all musical pursuits in the home were unlawful, but ordered the confiscation of all musical instruments. Fifty wagons were loaded with instruments gathered from

[5]

the population and brought to the Moscow river. Among the wild cheers of the people, avid for any kind of spectacle, the instruments were burned in big bonfires and dumped into the river, all in the name of God. "At last peace will reign on all the lands of Russia," noted the chronicle.

Secular music in Russia entered its second phase of development when Peter the Great beheaded the Church by taking away the power of the Patriarch—"the second Tsar"—and making himself its virtual head, thus freeing secular music from its yoke. He was the first to introduce military bands (such as they were) into Russia, in imitation of the Germans. He also was the first to establish a theater (on the Red Square), which he subsidized and in which performances were given by foreign actors. From then on, music was subjected to the political orientation of the Russian court.

During the reign of his niece Anna, his daughter Elizabeth, and that of Catherine the Great, court life flourished and became very luxurious. Balls, theatrical plays, and musical entertainments, chiefly by foreign artists, became a regular pastime. The Italians and later the French shared the ebb and flow of court favor. Italian artists, such as Francesco Araja, were imported into Russia at the time of Empress Anna, and men like Baldassare Galuppi and Giuseppe Sarti came during the reign of Catherine the Great. When the latter showed a preference for light French comedies because (as she wrote to Baron Grimm) a serious opera was hard for her to digest, the Italians in order to gain her favor wrote operas that were sung in Russian. Later the French used Russian plots for their theatrical performances. Thus these foreign artists opened the road for Russian opera which would be based on Russian plots and sung in Russian.

Gradually musical life at court reached society-at-large. By the time of Catherine the Great it was no longer necessary, as it had been during the reign of Elizabeth, to send couriers from home to home urging the nobility to appear at the theater by Her Majesty's

[6]

order. Wealthy noblemen and those close to the Crown aped the court and formed their own orchestras and theaters in which the performances were even more splendid in their extravagance than those at the court.

The retarded development of Russian music is due to the whole feudal structure of the Russian state, in which the great bulk of the population had very little to say in art-development entirely controlled by the upper classes. The latter still preferred to speak a foreign language and dismissed their own national music with a shrug and the suggestion that it belonged to the stables and the barns of a mujik.

The smaller nobility in distant parts of the country also had their own musicians, taking their cue from the higher nobility. These expressions of Russian musical activity would have been of paramount importance in the development of musical conscious- ness throughout the land if they had not been just a smaller replica of the performances given by the higher classes. If there were any works created by native Russians, they must have been lacking in any striking originality since they did not survive the test of time. Only a few names are known: Fomin (who is supposed to have written the first Russian opera, *Aniouta*); Volkov, Alabiev, Ver- stovsky, and Bortnyansky (who wrote religious music). If there were other composers, their names lie undiscovered among the annals of the gentry who owned them, just as the gentry owned whatever they produced.

Until the nineteenth century, Russia had no symphonic music of her own to speak of—that is, in comparison with the Western European countries—but in the abundance of her folk-songs she had no rival, although this wealth lay untouched. "Name me the land that has more songs than Russia!" said Gogol.

"Love, jealousy, hatred, gentleness, impatience, eagerness, indif- ference, fear, revenge, pride, humility, joy, laughter, tears, gaiety, sorrow, pomp, poverty, valor, timidity, generosity, honor, nobility, beatitude, despair, storm, calm—yea, heaven and earth, sea and

[7]

hell!" were mirrored in all their songs from the White Sea to the shores of the Caspian and the foothills of Tibet, from the Polish border to the Siberian Taiga. They sang their songs solo; in chorus, accompanied by musical instruments (one, several, or an entire orchestra); or *a cappella*. They sang as they went to war, exile, or hard labor. They sang at ease in their home, on the road, or at work. They sang of birth, marriage, death. With their songs they recorded the burgeoning, the fruition; harvest, quiescence.

Mihail Glinka was the first to realize the immense potentialities of this store of wealth. "We the composers are only arrangers," he said, and it was with Glinka that Russian music made a debut worth of attention. But Glinka became a prophet only after he died. He left two operas, *A Life for the Tsar* and *Russlan and Ludmilla,* the cornerstones of Russian nationalist music and products of a genius that defies logical explanation.

Glinka was mostly self-taught, except for three piano lessons he had with John Field while still a student, and a few lessons in composition with Siegfried W. Dehn at a much later date. At the time when Franz Liszt was thundering across the Continent leaving thousands of admirers aghast, Glinka preferred Field's delicate art of playing and the simplicity and purity of the cantilena in his nocturnes* because they were in accord with his own dreamy nature. Mihail Glinka used to say that shrill notes made him shiver, caused him actual pain, so that he shrank from the Liszt bravura. If Franz Liszt thought that Field was asleep when he played (*"endormie"*), Glinka compared Liszt's drumming on the piano to the chopping of hamburgers.

To Glinka the art of piano-playing was really only a form of poetic expression, and it is certain that he never knew nor was interested in its new forms as revealed in the piano works of Beethoven—the later ones—and of Schumann, Schubert, and Mendelssohn. He had no taste for these. Perhaps this explains why he never composed any piano works of importance, but was en-

* Field originated this form of composition which Chopin made so popular.

tirely absorbed in other fields: the orchestra and voice, the opera and ballet.

The true romantic, Glinka composed songs and informal piano pieces usually inspired by the young woman with whom he was currently in love (or thought he was), until in 1829 at the age of twenty-seven he went to Italy both for his health and because he wanted to study music with Italian masters. The change of climate, however, proved no more beneficial to his health than it was effectual in spurring his energy in studies. Though he realized that he did not know enough to undertake any ambitious musical composition, he lacked the desire, the curiosity, and above all the inner drive to master even the technical skill to express himself in the medium he preferred. After three years in Italy he would have returned to Russia with empty hands had he not devoted so much of his time to attending Italian operas. At La Scala and the small Teatro Carrano he heard Pasta, Rubini, and Orlando sing, as well as the famous basso Galdi, and operas conducted by such men as Bellini and Donizetti. But everything Glinka composed while in Italy convinced him that he could not sincerely become an Italian. While he admired the perfection (*fini*) delivered with natural ease (*grace naturelle*), Italian *sentimento brillante* was alien to him.

"We, the people of the North, feel differently. An impression either does not touch us at all, or it falls deeply into our souls. We are either wildly gay, or we weep bitter tears. Love with us is always mixed with sorrow. . . . There is no doubt that our melancholy, plaintive song, which is the child of the North, has also an oriental strain. Just listen to the Volga boatman's mournful song—one almost feels the Tatars' domination."

Such were Glinka's thoughts, and he was homesick. He planned to write a piece for the theater, but it was to be purely Russian both in subject and in music. He wanted his compatriots to find themselves at home in his music, and he was determined that abroad he should not be taken for "a daw in peacock's feathers."

[9]

Far away from home, seeing his own people in perspective, Glinka perhaps understood them better, understood their spirit more clearly, and saw the potentialities of the Russian songs he had heard at home in Germanized harmonization. Thus, on Italian soil, at the beginning of 1832, there was born to Mihail Glinka the idea of nationalist Russian music.

On his way home Glinka spent six months in the Prussian capital, and here for the first time in his life he studied seriously the theory of harmony and counterpoint with Siegfried Dehn, according to Glinka "the greatest musical doctor in Europe." But Dehn realized the futility of giving a man of nearly thirty his first lesson, and instead he put all Glinka's "promiscuously acquired" knowledge into a sort of organized order.

Back in Russia, Glinka confided to his friends, a group of leading Russian poets and writers of the time—Jukovsky, Pushkin, Vyasemsky, Pletnev, and Gogol—his desire to write a Russian opera. Jukovsky suggested a story from Russian history—the story of Ivan Susanin, who had saved the life of the first Romanov Tsar, Mihail, by sacrificing his own; and this became the basis of Glinka's first opera.

Glinka wrote the overture first (most composers write it last), and incorporated in the score most of the melodies he had already written. The première of *A Life for the Tsar,* on Friday, November 27, 1836, was a brilliant social affair; but the reaction of the aristocratic public—*"C'est la musique des cochers"*—damped Glinka's first enthusiasm. However, the opera ran for thirty-two performances, a fact that spurred him to plan another. This time the subject was suggested to him by Prince Shahovskoy: the great Pushkin poem *Russlan and Ludmilla.* Glinka spent a great deal of time in Pushkin's company, and would probably have had his collaboration but for the fact that Pushkin was suddenly killed in a duel. Instead, it was K. Bachturin, Glinka's old friend, who sketched the plan for *Russlan and Ludmilla.* Though Bachturin, who was drunk at the time, composed the outline in a quarter of an hour, his was the outline on which the opera was written.

The première of *Russlan* was given on Friday, November 27, 1842—in the same month and on the same day as *A Life for the Tsar* five years earlier. The applause was very mild, and Glinka heard booing, most of it coming from the stage and the orchestra. *"C'est une opéra manquée!"* was one comment. And it was reported that Grand Duke Mihail said he was going to punish his officers by sending them to *Russlan* instead of to the guardhouse. Even Count Vielgorsky, a musician himself and Glinka's friend, told him: *"Mon cher, c'est mauvais!"*

The *Russlan* libretto was very poor. The charming Pushkin poem was overburdened, overdone, and—as people jested—"In every act somebody on the stage went to sleep, and the audience slept through all the acts!" But the music was better than that in *A Life for the Tsar,* and for the first time in an opera the Orient had been presented in all its rich colors.

Whether or not successful at the time, both experiments showed how the wealth of Russian native material could be exploited. And if Glinka did not fully rise to his opportunity, the reason lay largely in his own personality, the key to which he left in his memoirs. Only his adoring sister could have encouraged him to persist in this ambitious autobiography, written two years before his death. It astonishes us by its picture of a shallow man of limited interests. It puzzles us: How could such a man have been capable of creating such masterpieces? Glinka would have done better not to attempt a self-portrait. It does, however, set forth his reason for refusing to study the art of composition seriously: "Who knows? Perhaps after all it was for the best. The severe German counterpoint is not always good for the free imagination." It was these fighting words that the "Mighty Five," some twenty years later, were to pick up and use as a slogan in their fight for Russian national music.

Glinka also describes the formation of "The Fraternity," fore-runner of the Mighty Five. His closest friends—the writer Kukol-nik, the painter Brullov, the singer Petrov, and the actor Kara-tugin—along with Glinka himself used to meet at Kukolnik's home where they sang, recited poetry, talked and argued far into the night about the future of Russian art. Everything Russian was praised to the sky and everything foreign treated with sarcasm and contempt. This fraternity differed from the Mighty Five in one respect, however: though the trend of its thought was nation-alistic Russian and patriotic, its method was frivolous and roman-tic. Vague ideas were mooted heatedly, but the criticisms were not seriously analyzed, and the discussion almost always ended with Kukolnik's characteristic remark: "Mihail, I don't agree with you! Let's have a drink."

The history of any evolutionary movement, whether cultural or political, comes closer to us, grows more vivid and easier to un-derstand, when the chronicles of the men involved in it embrace all the details of their lives, even when bordering on gossip. It is to their surroundings, to the whole mold in which they were cast by heredity, that the Mighty Five owed the power and the weak-ness in their art.

1

JUST AS THE AUDIENCE IN THE IMPERIAL THEA-
ters in St. Petersburg watched the Tsar for a cue—whether to
approve or to disapprove of a performance—the eyes of the audience in the provincial town of Nijni-Novgorod were fixed on a
little, middle-aged, fat man with rosy cheeks, neatly framed by a
thin gray beard, who sat in the first row from the entrance to the
right. Dressed in a loose tweed coat and gray summer trousers, no
matter what time of the year, he took his place on every "theater
night" of the week.

It was known in town that he paid two, sometimes three, and
even ten times the regular price of admission for his own ticket
and the box that was occupied by his family, depending on the
degree of his admiration of the actor. Usually he sat alone, watching the stage through his gold-rimmed glasses and looking like a
professor, though his actions betrayed the wealthy landowner who
knows his worth. If he liked the scene or the actors he would ex-
claim aloud so that everyone could hear: "Bravo! Bravo!" and
even "Attaboy!" and the whole audience followed him with enthusiasm. But sometimes he was bored and fidgeted in his seat, or

became intensely irritated, and then one would hear: "Bad, very bad!" or "What a bore! What an idiot!" Then the audience, embarrassed, would keep silent or sometimes take his lead and even dare to boo, though gently, since real booing might bring the police, and who knew what trouble *that* might create? After all, it was in the early 1830s, the gloomy time of ferocious despotism in the reign of Nicolas I, and the public watched its behavior.

Alexander Dmitrievich Ulibishev was a provincial bigwig, one of the last links between the generation that had thought and spoke only in French and the generation brought up on the best century of Russian literature. He was the author of a biography of Mozart which aroused no small discussion and even controversy not only in Russia but also abroad.

Neither a Frenchman, nor a musician, nor a writer, Ulibishev wrote a literary composition, in French, about music and a musician. His choice of subject could probably be explained by the fact that, up to the age of sixteen he had been educated in Germany, where at that time (the beginning of the 19th century) Mozart was the Alpha and Omega in music.

Ulibishev was only thirty-six years old when in 1830 he suddenly retired from his post in the Ministry of Foreign Affairs, throwing to the winds a most brilliant career. He had just rejected an invitation to become ambassador to Persia, and moved to his country estate at Lukino, about thirty miles from Nijni-Novgorod. But he did not retire, as one might have expected of a wealthy landowner, to lead the usual life of a country squire of that time—reading the reports of his estate managers while lying on a couch and smoking a pipe, or planning elaborate menus for dinners while resting from exhausting lunches, or playing cards every night at the Noblemen's Club. Instead, he devoted his life at Lukino to the study of the theater and, above all, of music.

His work on the Mozart biography indirectly had an invaluable influence on Russian music. For Ulibishev, who started the book as a young man and thought of finishing it in a couple of months, realized, as he progressed, how little prepared he was for the subject he had chosen; and for the next decade, therefore, he spared no effort to acquaint himself through every possible means with the necessary knowledge. He assembled in his home a large library of books on drama, philosophy, history, and music, and also of orchestral scores, and to study these last he organized his own orchestra. Ten years had passed before he completed the Mozart work; he had started it as a young bachelor, and finished it as a man with a large family. But in these ten years, through his constant musical and theatrical activities, he developed the musical life in the small provincial town to the level of that in the capital.

As a great patron of art, he kept open house in Nijni-Novgorod. Ulibishev, who himself sang and played violin and viola, drew into his circle those members among his neighbors, all wealthy landowners, who were good and enthusiastic amateur musicians. He also engaged a young Viennese musician, who conducted in the town theater, to take charge of his private orchestra.

Carl Eizrikh was probably the only professionally trained musician in the town at that time. "Musical life in Russia only now begins to live," wrote Rimsky-Korsakov in 1864. Rimsky was doubtless referring to the musical life of the capital, whereas Eizrikh had come to Ulibishev some thirty-four years earlier and to a remote provincial town. Yet it was under this very Eizrikh's direction that parts of Mozart's *Requiem,* Handel's *Messiah,* and Palestrina's *Stabat Mater* were performed at Ulibishev's, as well as such works as Mozart's Symphony in G minor, the overtures to *Don Giovanni* and *The Magic Flute,* and Beethoven's Symphony in C major. In order to accomplish this, Eizrikh summoned every talented and musically inclined person in the town, including the chorus from the military regiment stationed there.

In 1849 Eizrikh also brought to Ulibishev's attention the extraordinary talent of the twelve-year-old Mili Balakirev.

The Tatar connotation of Mili's surname led those who could not find any hereditary explanation for his remarkable musical

[15]

gifts to assume a mixed racial origin. Mixture of blood does sometimes produce unusual traits in a child's character, but in Mili's case the assumption was completely unfounded, for research reveals that the Balakirev name appears in Russian annals long before the Tatar invasion.

Not only the name suggested a Tatar origin: Mili's very looks were Mongolian. He was heavy-set, with a square head growing almost out of his shoulders, short-cropped black hair, and little squinting gray eyes that looked out from behind high cheekbones.

Mili was the eldest child of Alexey Balakirev, a poor nobleman without "title or land" who held a small position in a government office in Nijni-Novgorod, earning barely enough to support his wife and three children. (Mili had two sisters.) The mother was the first to notice Mili's unusual musical aptitude when at the age of four he reached up to the keyboard to pick out melodies he had heard. She gave him his first lessons, but it was beyond both her knowledge and their means to give the boy a musical education. Like the rest of the boys he had to go to school—to the gymnasium—and it was only due to his mother's perseverance that in 1847 he was taken at the age of ten to Moscow for music lessons during one of his summer vacations.

In Moscow he played for Dubuque, the pupil of John Field, and after ten lessons his teacher was so impressed that he offered to teach him free of charge and to make a piano virtuoso of him. But lack of funds prevented Mili from remaining in the capital. On his return he became a pupil of Eizrikh who, besides being a conductor, was a very good pianist. However, Mili himself said later, in one of his rare moments of modesty: "If I can play the piano at all it is entirely due to the ten lessons I had with Dubuque." Mili must have been a born wonder child, for except for these two teachers he was completely self-taught.

Ulibishev was considerably impressed by the talent of the little boy and welcomed him into his home with great joy. The musical life at Ulibishev's provided just the air that Mili's lungs needed so urgently, and the wise guidance of Ulibishev—who treated him as a close friend despite the great difference in their ages—came at an opportune moment. For Mili's mother died soon after their return from Moscow, and with her death he lost the only person at home with whom he could discuss music. His father had neither any interest in music nor any time to devote to the education of his children.

"You know," wrote Ulibishev to Mili years later, "I cannot stand any kind of sentimentality, but I must tell you that I love you as my own son and that I would be very, very grateful to God Almighty if you were really my son."

Ulibishev's home became virtually Mili's school, for here in the rich library and during the long and intimate discussions of music he was learning what had been denied to him when his parents were forced to bring him home from Moscow.

Eizrikh had so much confidence in Mili that when, a couple of years later, he decided to leave Nijni-Novgorod, he suggested to Ulibishev that the young Balakirev take his place. The fourteen-year-old Mili took the baton in his hand and became a conductor.

What Mili lacked in knowledge he made up in courage and self-assurance. From childhood he had had to rely on his own resources, his own ingenuity, curiosity, and energy. Mili was endowed with a clear head and had learned to speak out the truth probably with his first taste of milk. He shrank from compromise as one does from physical pain. These characteristics in the boy made him both authoritative and attractive. And the new post, placing him at the head of a group of musicians, further strengthened his sense of authority, which later established him as a leader among the great musicians in Russia.

Now Mili took the most active part in all Ulibishev's musical enterprises. Ulibishev planned to write another book, this time about Beethoven,* and to acquaint himself with Beethoven's

* Beethoven's Critics and Commentators.

works he organized a series of concerts at which almost all Beethoven's symphonies were performed. Mili studied the new scores, coached and accompanied singers and rehearsed with the orchestra, and thus learned about instrumentation and the forms of composition in practice rather than in theory.

Three years passed, during which Mili Balakirev matured into a full-blooded musician and a brilliant pianist. But the profession of musician in those days was not particularly attractive. Even a post as a minor clerk offered a better social position and a more secure existence, for as yet there were no music schools, and music teachers had to rely on precarious earnings from private pupils.

Balakirev therefore entered the University of Kazan to study mathematics and physics so as to prepare himself for a more practical job. The musical life of Kazan was not so rich as Nijni-Novgorod's. Overtures to Italian operas were much in vogue owing to their noisy and vivacious trombones and trumpets, and individual concerts were given only occasionally by artists who were on their way somewhere else. However, the making of music "at home" prevailed on a far larger scale than in Nijni-Novgorod. Since the young Balakirev received no support from his father, he was forced to find pupils and play in salons in order to earn his living. He also began to compose. In Nijni-Novgorod he had heard and been impressed by the aria "Don't torture me" and the trio from Glinka's *A Life for the Tsar,* and now he composed a fantasy on the themes from this opera in the style of Liszt's transcriptions. This he did without anybody's help, for at that time the only textbooks on composition were in German and he did not know German. For the next two years Balakirev studied at the university, spending only his vacations with Ulibishev on his estate at Lukino.

"No matter how much you love a country life in summer," Ulibishev reflected, "no matter how you adjust yourself to a provincial life in winter, there comes a time when you feel a need of the fresh air of civilization," and he decided he wanted to see for himself the changes that had taken place in the capital during the years of his absence. But above all he must hear some new music. When he invited Balakirev to accompany him to St. Petersburg, it was not hard to persuade the young student of mathematics to give up his studies at the university, for he had longed for just such an opportunity. Late in December 1855, therefore, the two friends arrived in St. Petersburg.

"From his pen came our national music, for the first time worthy of the historical fate and moral greatness of our people." So spoke Ulibishev of Glinka, whose *A Life for the Tsar* he considered one of the greatest works of the time. Now he took his young protégé to meet Mihail Glinka.

Glinka was back from his travels abroad. He had been in France again and in Spain, where he fled from Russia to nurse his wounded ego. Both of his operas—*A Life for the Tsar,* and *Russlan and Ludmilla*—had failed with the aristocratic audiences in the capital; they said that if these were the "Russian operas" they would rather listen to their own mujiks and not go to the theater. At fifty-one Glinka was still the same spoiled, hypochondriacal, disappointed man, very bitter toward his country and very restless when at home. Ulibishev and Balakirev found him living with his sister Ludmilla and her little girl Olga.

Glinka was still toying with new ideas for Russian operas; he even began to work on one, *Taras Bulba* (after Gogol's novel), but he never finished it. During this period his only noteworthy contribution to Russian music was his short piece *Kamarinskaya*— a fantasy on a nuptial song he had composed while in Warsaw, where he liked to live because, as he said, Polish women were so much like the French, and (what was even better) they were kind to aging men, and Glinka felt his age.

Glinka was much impressed by Balakirev. No one looking at the lad's somber Mongolian face, framed by a heavy beard, could have guessed his age. Though only eighteen, Balakirev's erudition and self-assurance were those of a fully matured man. He had brought with him his fantasy on the themes from *A Life for the Tsar*. Flattered and surprised by Mili's compositions and brilliant playing, Glinka took the young musician under his wing. He made him a present of Spanish themes from his notebook so that Mili could compose another fantasy, and insisted that it be dedicated to Ulibishev. "In this way," said Glinka, "our names will be bound together." In his enthusiasm, Glinka told his sister that if he were to die she must trust no one but Balakirev with Olga's musical education. "He is going to be a second Glinka," said Mihail, thus bestowing on the younger man his own majestic mantle—that of Patriarch of Russian music.

Glinka's encouragement of Balakirev's work almost made up for the hardships the young provincial musician was to encounter in the capital, since he had decided to stay on after Ulibishev's departure. His only means of subsistence were private pupils, and he was completely unknown.

However, he soon had chance to show his ability when he played a movement from his own concerto (the Allegro from the F-sharp minor Concerto) at one of the university concerts, which were noted for their progressive tendencies. He was mentioned in the press, and when in the spring of the same year (1856) V. A. Kologrivov, with whom he was staying, arranged to have him give a recital in a small hall (its purpose being to raise funds for Mili's subsistence), he proved himself a musician worthy of Glinka's praise. They began to talk about Balakirev in the capital. But he had no ambition to become a concert pianist. While he was often asked to play in salons and concerts, Glinka's home was his favorite resort.

Ludmilla Shestakova, Glinka's sister, did not have a salon. She and her brother were visited only by old and close friends of his and by singers who performed his songs and sought his advice. He led a retired life, having ceased even to frequent musical homes.

[20]

Glinka's beneficial friendship with Balakirev was of very short duration, however, for Mihail was restless; he had never forgiven his country for the ungracious treatment his two operas had received. "I don't want to have anything to do with Russian music —any more than with Russian winters. I don't want any more Russian drama—I have had enough trouble with it."

Though past fifty, he wanted to study again, and in April 1856 he once more started on a journey abroad. Ludmilla and his friend Vladimir Stassov accompanied him to the boundaries of the capital. There Glinka took his leave, warmly embracing them both. He looked for a while at the distant outlines of the capital, spat on the ground, exclaimed, "May I never see the damned country again!" and stepped into the carriage that was to take him to Berlin.

Providence granted Glinka's wish. Within less than a year he died in Berlin.

For Balakirev, Glinka's death was a great loss. Mili was then taking his first steps in the musical world, still "looking for the right direction," and Glinka's advice and encouragement had been of paramount value. It was therefore very fortunate that he had met Glinka's friend, Vladimir Stassov.

The name of Vladimir Stassov (1824-1906) has a unique place in the history of Russian art, especially in its music—unique because he was most intimately connected with it for more than three-quarters of a century. He knew Glinka, and he knew Alexander Scriabin.

When Balakirev met him, Stassov was doing research work and ghost-writing for Baron Korf, Director of the St. Petersburg library. Alexander II had asked Korf to write a series of historical articles; but Korf was apparently a baron only, and so he asked Stassov, who was always working on something in the library, to "help" him. The consequence was a curious arrangement: Stassov was officially attached to the Baron's office, was to receive salary and rank, but was to get no decorations. In less than seven years he had a civil-service rank equal to that of a general, his salary permitted him to live and occupy himself with the work he was most interested in—and, as for the decorations, the Baron could have them all.

Stassov came from a family belonging to the Intelligentsia. He lived with his family: four brothers, his sister, the wife of his brother Nicolas and their three daughters, two aunts, and an adopted girl with her governess. All these were very active in social life in various fields, and the house was always full of their friends. The cream of the Russian Liberals came to see his brother Alexander, whose advanced ideas caused him trouble with the police; the musicians, among them Anton Rubinstein, came to see his younger brother Dmitri; and Vladimir himself knew everybody in St. Petersburg. Here in this hospitable home the younger generation met to discuss new ideas, talk politics, exchange opinions on the latest theatrical event, or hear Anton Rubinstein play. Here they grew into manhood, their ideas and convictions took shape, they chose their professions, fell in love, married.

Stassov's interest in music had begun at his school bench, when he struck up a friendship with a somewhat older boy, Alexander Serov. It was a romantic friendship formed at a time when the world seemed a happy place with only a few defects, which they two would correct. They could not live without each other. They read together, played duets, went to all the concerts, and when apart wrote detailed diaries to each other. Of the two, Serov was the better musician, better schooled, and a better pianist. As a very young man he had already decided his career, while Stassov's interests were still scattered, and he was still learning, still interested in everything. Alexander Serov became one of the leading musical critics and one of the first Wagnerites in Russia, whereas for Stassov this branch of art alone was too narrow. They drifted apart, particularly after Stassov went abroad for several years.

[22]

Like the rest of the members of his family, Vladimir Stassov fell in and out of love periodically. At one time he was in love with Serov's sister Sophia, then Sophia fell in love with his brother Dmitri, then she would not have any Stassovs, and Vladimir turned his interest to others. He did not believe in matrimony, certainly not for any Stassov, though sometimes his credo was upset by an act of God and Stassov just had to go abroad. . . .

He traveled about Europe, saw and learned a great deal, and lived for some time in Italy, where he took part in every phase of Italian life. He heard their operas, saw their museums, danced on the street during the Carnival. In Vienna he saw *Lohengrin;* he tasted French cooking. But all this was not what he wanted to do in life, and it was high time to decide what he did want. Stassov was *"zu alt um nur zu spielen, zu jung um ohne Wunsch zu sein."* He knew he did not have the talent to become a musician, yet music was one of his chief interests. What eventuated was that, on his return to Russia, because of his energy and his love of Russian music Stassov supported and guided it for the next thirty years.

Balakirev met Stassov at just the right time. In his schooling at home as well as at the University of Kazan, he had been occupied with practical education—whether the art of playing the piano, or studies in higher mathematics, or even conducting an orchestra. His interest in literature and history was slight, and he was hardly touched by the complexity of the historic events unfolding right before his eyes in his own country; his knowledge of these was that of the average man. Ulibishev—a liberal and acutely aware of everything around him—probably never mentioned these subjects with his young friend. Not so Stassov.

Though Stassov was some fourteen years older than Balakirev, he respected him in everything that concerned music—who would not? Balakirev's knowledge of classical and contemporary music was fabulous, his memory so remarkable that he could quote at will, his pianistic capacity almost equal to Anton Rubinstein's. Stassov marveled, as they played both old and new music four-hand, at his younger friend's interesting and clear interpretations, listened to his enthusiastic comments on Liszt and Berlioz, and was carried away by his vision of new music. In classical music, however, Stassov was himself an expert (the years spent with Alexander Serov had not been in vain), he knew Italian music much better than Mili, and when it came to general education he was Mili's master.

Stassov recognized Balakirev's potentialities, saw his future, and visualized the part he would play in the future of Russian music. He knew that the provincial Mili needed a wider general knowledge and wider concepts of life. They spent nights reading together. Mili liked reading aloud, and Stassov read very well. They read Homer and Shakespeare, Gogol, Nekrassoff, Herzen's magazine *The Bell,* and the famous socialist Chernishevsky's novel *What Is To Be Done?* which so stirred Mili that he considered making an opera of it. But above all they read and discussed everything that touched on the subject of "Narodnichestvo"—a cultural movement originated by the Intelligentsia, who urged their members to "go to the people" and share with them their knowledge.

"I am handing you command of the country in a poor state," said Nicolas I in 1855 to his son Alexander II as he lay dying while Russia was losing the Crimean War. Public opinion blamed the state for the humiliating defeat and the loss of Russia's prestige as a military power. Public opinion, which for the first time had made itself felt not so much in the abortive one-day revolution in December 1825 as in its indignation over the cruel measures Nicolas adopted to punish that revolt, was, during his reign, ruthlessly crushed by police and censorship. But Alexander II was a weaker character than his father. The peace treaty put an end to Nicolas's foreign policy, and the people clamored for reforms, demanding a new code of law, the institution of the jury, and—above all—the abolition of serfdom.

[24]

"Better that the reform come from above than wait until serfdom is abolished from below," said even the Emperor himself.

"Hamlet's dilemma—to be or not to be—is facing us—sinners," wrote Ulibishev to Balakirev from Nijni-Novgorod, one of the oldest nests of Russian nobility. "All the owls, bats, and vampires flew into our town from eleven districts with great screams and cries that rend your heart, for it seems someone wants to tear from their claws the human prey on which they have fed for so long. Alas, alas, alas!!! It is impossible to suck from the peasants the last drop of their blood, and then sell their flesh. 'We don't want it, we don't want it!' scream our noblemen." (Ulibishev had already told his peasants of the coming reform, but he did not live to see them freed.)

All this was bewildering to Balakirev, whose roots lay deep in the Nijni-Novgorod middle class with its traditions, religion, and prejudice. "Go to the people, learn about people . . . people . . . people . . ." was all he could see as he read the newspapers, articles in periodicals, and the latest novels by Russia's best writers, or looked at the latest works by painters and sculptors. What about this "people" who seemed to have all the virtues except one —that they don't know what they want, or, if they do, are so silent? Mili was a musician, an individualist. The masses did not attract him, yet he loved his own country. Stassov believed in people, and Balakirev did not, but they agreed on one thing: the future of Russian music must be national.

It is particularly at the time of one's country's disaster that the national spirit is aroused. In 1812 the glow in the skies over burning Moscow had summoned all Russians to stand together. It was good to see that one was ready to perish rather than give in. It was good to feel one's own strength. But national feeling is surrounded by a romantic halo when the people are fighting for their freedom from a foreign yoke, whether political or cultural. This is why it has always been so poetic and admirable in Poland, and was so vulgar in Germany. The fancy aristocratic claims of race superiority and blood purity, the rights of "national self-determination" and "territorial integrity," are nothing but an inflation of the simple idea that any nation prefers its own individuality rather than another's. Better to have one's own, if it is no more than a *Kamarinskaya* or the church bells from *Slavsya,* than the whole sum of songs, arias, and symphonies written in Russian but with a foreign accent! No more borrowing from abroad, no more Italians and Germans. It was high time for Russians to create their own music.

Stassov realized the dimensions of this task, but he also believed that Russia would not be lacking in talent. Balakirev was there; others would come, join, follow.

By chance, at a chamber-music concert in 1857 at the home of Fitzum von Ekshtet, Balakirev met a young officer, César Cui. This young man was of medium height and seemed to have nothing seductive about him at first glance. His brownish hair, parted correctly on one side, the well-trimmed beard and whiskers that framed his delicate features, and his grayish blue eyes which blinked as he looked through his glasses, all made him seem to be just what his uniform indicated—an Army Corps Engineer. But as one heard his voice, soft but penetrating, dominated by gentle authority, one could discern a double personality. Outwardly cold, peaceful, patient, a man who could control his emotions, and with a measure of wisdom in his philosophy, methodical, positive, and precise, Cui was capable of very simple, intimate, warm relationships. Ready with confidence, he was given to a gaiety that bordered on the infantile, was the enemy of banality and fond of all sorts of dreams and fantasies. His was the imagination of a poet.

Balakirev talked to him about Glinka, of whom Cui knew nothing, and Cui told him of Moniuszko,* the talented Polish

* Stanislas Moniuszko (1819-72) wrote many operas of which the best-known is *Halka,* songs, religious music, and piano pieces—polonaises and mazurkas.

Balakirev

pianist and composer who had generously offered to teach harmony and counterpoint to the little fourteen-year-old César, free of charge, after seeing his first composition.

Cui's sincerity and warmth drew Balakirev to him, and the exchange of their ideas on music bound them together. Soon Mili learned the story of his new friend, which was no more sensational than his uniform. He had been born in Vilna in 1835 of a French father and a Lithuanian mother. Apparently the oath that Alexander I took at the beginning of the war with Napoleon—"We shall not lay down arms until the last Frenchman has left Russian soil"—had not affected Antoine Cui. César's father was in Napoleon's Grande Armée, but was wounded at Smolensk and, half frozen, was unable to rejoin the Army in its retreat. Like so many of his compatriots he stayed behind in Russia, where he married and started a new life, first as tutor to children of rich families, and later as teacher of French in the Vilna gymnasium.

Though Antoine Cui's occupations were peaceful and cultural, he must have retained admiration for military glamour, since he named his three sons after three great generals of history—Alexander, Napoleon, and Caesar. (Cui's first name is spelled so in Russian.)

When Balakirev sat down at the piano to play duets with Cui, he realized at once what poor schooling his friend had had. At the age of ten (in 1845) César had taken piano lessons from his sister, and later under a teacher who was really a violinist, but with excellent taste. Before this, he had tried to pick out march tunes on the piano, with one finger—sometimes right and sometimes wrong. But neither teacher in the little provincial town had done much to develop him into a pianist. Indeed, he never became one. His playing had a certain amount of intelligence and charm, but no real technique. True, he did not particularly care for it even when he grew up. When he met Moniuszko he knew very little of musical literature. He admired Chopin, but knew only his mazurkas, since his parents were too poor to buy him music, and he had to copy it on ordinary paper which he ruled out himself. Unfortunately, after six months with Moniuszko, he was sent by his parents to St. Petersburg, where he joined his two brothers. Alexander and Napoleon were studying architecture and painting at the Academy of Art, but César entered the Military Academy.

When he was graduated and received his officer's rank and could live alone, he was free to spend more time with music. Meeting Balakirev at this moment was most opportune. It was not only his mature appearance (Balakirev was in fact a year younger than Cui) and his self-assured manner, but his immense knowledge that made him the indisputable authority in their relationship.

However, he was not going to teach Cui to play the piano. With Stassov's constant prodding, he had more important problems on his mind: to create Russian national music, to follow Glinka, to make the Russian people conscious of art—and, above all, of their own art. To the general public music was an acquaintance, as it were, with whom one shook hands while passing on the street, not a friend with whom one shared one's life. Literature, painting, and sculpture had already become a part of the national wealth, already marched side by side, and music must be made to take its place along with them.

And Cui was to be Balakirev's first fellow-champion in the new cause. The two young friends met almost daily, to spend three or four hours reading music or playing duets, or Mili at the piano explained compositions or illustrated his ideas. All of the old literature and everything obtainable in the new went through their four hands. In the evenings they discussed and planned the future of Russian music. From the close bond between these two men, Cui and Balakirev, Russian national music received a new impetus, and a new school of thought in music was born.

2

A YEAR PASSED. CUI'S KNOWLEDGE OF MUSIC
through his association with Balakirev began to reach solid
ground. His musical interests broadened, and his acquaintance
with Petersburg musicians was extended, after he found his way
to Dargomijsky's house.

Alexander Dargomijsky, the Russian composer whose role in
the development of Russian music was as substantial as Glinka's,
was then in his early forties. Unfortunately the early period of
his musical development was concurrent with that of Glinka's
popularity, when every composition in the Russian style was compared with Glinka's; and Dargomijsky admitted that the competition was too stiff. Yet it was Glinka's example that changed him
from mere dilettante into serious musician, Glinka's opera *A Life
for the Tsar* that turned his interest from composing songs and
brilliant piano pieces to creating music drama. But both of his
operas, *Esmeralda* and *Russalka* (The Sea Maiden), were complete failures, and Dargomijsky gave up his twenty-year struggle
for fame and recognition. "While there was still time" he turned
again to composing songs and to coaching, and retired to his own

world, to his salon where he was surrounded by his pupils and admirers.

"Here [in his home]," he used to say, "meet all who love art, who are not bound by any job, career, little position in the government, or government opinion—in fact, all the independent musicians of St. Petersburg."

Alexander Dargomijsky never married. After his mother's death and his sisters' marriage, he continued to live with his father, a man of great wealth. The old patriarchal hospitality reigned in their home, and Alexander was a perfect host. While he himself did not drink anything except wine with his dinner, he saw to it that his guests had plenty of everything. Twice a week his friends would gather at his home. Early in the afternoon, after tea with meat pies and pastry had been served, the musicale would begin, with his pupils and friends performing Russian numbers mostly, including some Italian music only as a joke. Since in this circle the most popular composers were Glinka and Dargomijsky himself, a good part of the program was devoted to the latter's own compositions.

Clad in a sky-blue jacket with a bright red waistcoat, Dargomijsky hardly cut a prepossessing figure as he acted as pianist, accompanist, and singer. He was a little over five feet tall, not particularly well built, with a large, wide head out of proportion to his size. His slightly turned-up nose, full lips with little thin mustaches, curly dark brown hair which he carefully combed·down, and sallow complexion gave him a sickly look. But as one observed him, one could not miss the expression of a thinking man with a strong will. Even his unpleasant squeaky soprano voice did not mar his impressive and vivid phrasing and dramatic delivery.

For these musicales Dargomijsky would take great pains in rehearsing all the previous week. If the performer was a man, he would have him at his house every day working on details; if it was a woman, no distance was too far to go to coach her. "I prefer the company of women singers to any other. If there were no women singers, it wouldn't be worth while to compose," said Dargomijsky, and he even wrote most of his songs for the female voice. He prided himself that in the whole of St. Petersburg there was not a single famous or talented woman singer who either was not his pupil or did not profit by his advice.

At his house the years passed in almost routine sequence, with new members joining Dargomijsky as regularly as the enrollment at the universities. Cui was still a freshman at the musicales when in 1857 he met there an officer even younger than himself.

The young man belonged to the élite regiment in the Russian Army, the Preobrazhensky. Dressed as befitted a lieutenant in such a regiment, he produced at first the impression of just another fop. He spoke as if opening his mouth were too much of an effort, and he broke repeatedly into French, though what he said would have sounded just as well in Russian. The slight, seventeen-year-old artillery officer's name was Modest Mussorgsky. As he presented himself he put a definite stress on the first syllable of his name and swallowed the G. He offered his small hand with its carefully polished nails, slightly bowing his head on which every hair was in its place, and noiselessly bringing together his little feet dressed in pointed shoes that shone like mirrors. From the dignity with which he carried his head, and the way in which he carelessly and wearily, with his feet pointed outward, glided through Dargomijsky's salon, anyone could have divined that the newly arrived visitor was a man of the world. The ladies smiled on him.

He spoke to Cui, his friend in arms, but not about fortifications, for he himself was also a musician. No one else at those gatherings—except perhaps Balakirev, who came very seldom—was so good a pianist as Modest Mussorgsky. Cui and Modest found a great deal in common. This was Modest's first visit to Dargomijsky's, and he was very curious, very anxious to learn. He looked up to Cui, while Cui's attitude had a touch of condescension in it—Cui who, poor as a church mouse, had to count the contents

[31]

of his purse twice before he dared enter a shop, while Modest's uniform implied his association with the "golden youth" of Russia, whose major occupation was squandering fortunes. And it is remarkable that condescension was to remain the keynote of Cui's attitude toward Mussorgsky.

Cui soon introduced his new friend to Balakirev, and Modest on his first visit to Balakirev's showed him a youthful composition, *Souvenir d'enfance,* which he had composed only a few months before. Mili brushed it aside, bidding Mussorgsky bring him something more important. Impressed by Mili's manner, Mussorgsky expressed the wish to become his pupil; for, like Cui, he had had very little musical training.

True, Modest was an excellent pianist. For this he was indebted to his mother, who early recognized his musical talent and herself taught him to play the piano. He made such remarkable progress that at the age of seven he could already play small pieces of Liszt's, and at the age of nine gave a worthy performance of a concerto by Field at an evening party in his parents' home.

Like Balakirev, he must have been a wonder child—there could be no other explanation of such a phenomenon. His mother was somewhat *exaltée,* inclined to romantic dreams and poetry (she wrote amateurish verse), and she played the piano as such ladies do, and therefore neither she nor the German governess who followed her in teaching the boy was equipped to create a pianist. Nor was there anyone in the family whose musical talent little Modest could have inherited. His father was a passionate lover of music, but no performer. It is easier to trace Modest's relationship back to the Rurik—the first Russian dynasty (862)—than to find through all the thirty-two generations a single musician.

All of Mussorgsky's ancestors were wealthy landlords with estates in the provinces of Smolensk, Pskov, and Yaroslav which they had inherited or had been granted for government service. Since the middle of the 17th century Modest's family had owned "Karevo" in the Tropez district of the government of Pskov, with all the neighboring domains, farms, and villages. Here in 1839 Modest was born. He was brought up like the rest of the children of Russian nobility. Governesses—German and French—took charge of his education as soon as he had outgrown the care of his old *nyanya.*

Though Peter Mussorgsky, Modest's father, a retired Senator from St. Petersburg, acknowledged his young son's musical talent, there was no question of changing the family's plans for the boy: he was to follow the same routine and the same career as all the Mussorgskys—that is, enter the Preobrazhensky Regiment.

After two years at the secondary school of SS Peter and Paul and a year in the Army Training Establishment, Modest entered the Guards Cadet Academy. Soon it became obvious that a military career was ill chosen for his temperament, and that the school's atmosphere and environment did not suit either his interests or his character.

"What kind of officer, *mon cher,* are you going to be?" The director of the school shook his head on learning that the young Modest was spending his free time reading and studying German philosophy. He did not like his pupils to do much thinking, and was only annoyed with them if they drank plain vodka instead of champagne, or arrived at school in a cheap droshky instead of a carriage drawn by their own pure-bred trotters.

While in this school, Modest for the first time worked with a professional musician. He studied piano privately with Anton Herke, who in the course of four years managed to give him a very sound basis for his piano technique, but did nothing to introduce his pupil even to the rudiments of musical harmony and counterpoint, which was far more important since Modest was interested in composing. However, Herke was responsible for the publication of Modest's first composition—a *Porte-Ensighne Polka* (Ensign's Polka)—a piano piece that he dedicated to his cadet comrades at the school. Later Mussorgsky was very impatient with this work, just as he was impatient over his attempt at an opera

[33]

whose libretto he himself had compiled from Victor Hugo's romance *Han d'Islande*. "Nothing came of it," he remarked later, "for the simple reason that nothing could have come of it—the composer was seventeen years old and knew nothing."

Mussorgsky claimed that he had learned a great deal from the Divinity Master of the Academy, Little Father Krupsky, whom he visited not only for religious conversation. According to Mussorgsky, this teacher introduced him to the old church music of Russia as well as to Catholic and Lutheran music; though if one takes the Little Father's word, he had very little to do with this chapter of Modest's musical knowledge because he himself did not know much about it. And so in 1856 Modest was graduated from the school, not too overburdened with either scholastic or musical knowledge, and joined the Preobrazhensky Regiment.

Thus Modest seemed to have reached the point from which his life should have rolled on according to the well-established rules of a military career with promotions, decorations, and a distinguished rank with which he could retire. What else could a young, moneyed aristocrat desire? But social position and a military career were the last things that interested him.

As in a dream Modest walked home after his first visit to Dargomijsky's. Modest, who knew next to nothing of Glinka's and Dargomijsky's works, now suddenly realized that Russian music was being composed in the very room he had just left.

"We perform Russian music simply, without any sort of affectation"—he recalled Dargomijsky's words. "In fact, we perform it the way our late friend Mihail Ivanovich [Glinka] would have liked it performed. . . ." But Modest remembered that Dargomijsky had also said: "I am not fooling myself. My artistic position in St. Petersburg is not to be envied. Most of our music lovers and press scribblers don't find inspiration in me. In their routine interests they look only for sweet little melodies. I have no desire to lower music for their fun . . . I want music to express the spoken word . . . I want the truth."

What Modest did not know was that Dargomijsky's being considered only a talented amateur did not discourage him in the least from following his ambition to find a way to express the spoken word in musical sound; or that at the beginning of his musical career he had ventured on his first experiment when he composed a scherzo which he called *Ardor and Composure* with the subtitle—"Written from an actual conversation." The subtitle is more significant than the fact that this first attempt was unsuccessful; it indicates how early Alexander Dargomijsky conceived the idea of "truth in music," "truth in sound," which underlay all his vocal composition. "I did not expect you to soar so high," remarked Glinka to him after hearing his *Russalka.* "There is a lot of truth in it, but the public will not understand, and you will create no effect with it."

"He was right," related Dargomijsky, "but why should I care about the 'effect' when there is real thought and truth in it? The teaching of Christ had also only truth, but it reaches the hearts of a few hundred only while the Tsars, the great of this world, and the masses prefer the Church because of her 'effect.'"

Modest was young. He knew nothing of Dargomijsky's disappointment and his bitterness, and the word truth—truth in music —puzzled him. That word was so often spoken: truth in music, truth in painting, truth in literature. It was very bewildering, and Modest was to wait long before he found a clear explanation for the problem of truth. Meanwhile he attended Dargomijsky's musicales because their artistic atmosphere was so attractive to him.

If he did not see Cui at his home he was sure to find him at Dargomijsky's, for Cui was attracted to these evenings by more than just the music. Presently he took Modest into his confidence, told him he was in love with one of the Dargomijsky pupils, a poor German girl named Malvina Bamberg. It was a lyrical, sentimental attachment that suited Cui perfectly. There was no great stormy passion, no drama, no clash of characters with irresistible attraction which conquers and sweeps everything out of the path to happiness. It was all very quiet. And the awakened affection found its expression in Cui's composing two symphonic scherzos. The first (Opus 1) took as its musical basis the letters BAEG from the name of his betrothed, and his own initials, CC; and the second (Opus 2) was labeled *à la Schumann*. No doubt the idea for both came from Schumann's early *Variations on the Theme of Abegg*.

Cui was a poor young man who, after suffering early from deprivation, had now set foot on solid financial ground purely by chance, and he intended to keep to it. It was his characteristic (so derided by admirers of the artistic temperament) never to spend two rubles when he had only one. His only extravagance was tea with jam. "I think," Cui once said to Modest, "that I should be happy even in hell."

In all his twenty-one years of living, Cui had never gone on a spree, had never been drunk, nor had loose women hanging on his arm. He betrayed his officer's uniform only in this respect: he was not reckless with his affections. In fact, his eyes were completely controlled by the knowledge of what he could afford, so that his life remained unscarred by useless alarms. The shy Cui would melt as he watched the prima-donna of Russian opera, Latishova, on the stage, but she was unaware of the loud beating of the heart under the poor officer's tunic.

Cui's passion for the young Malvina Bamberg was very serious, but the exuberance of his love was well measured by the thrifty economy and the modest surroundings which were all he could offer her. However, the prosaic question of finances did not intrude on the poetic raptures with which he told Modest all the details of their betrothal. Modest knew the hour and the day of their first kiss, the exact moment at which he had proposed, the

[36]

words with which she accepted, and the particulars of his confer-
ence with her parents.

As a careful citizen, Cui used common sense in regard to the
most minute purchases. With cautious circumspection he had
chosen the apartment in which they would live. The same consideration was given to the furnishings, which were bought not
haphazardly nor hurriedly, but after long deliberation, since they
would have to last a long time.

Cui and Malvina observed the conventional period after their
engagement, and then were married in a Protestant church. The
best man was Mussorgsky, who composed and dedicated to the
bride a song whose German words he himself had written, *Meines
Herzens Sehnsucht*.

Stassov, whose feeling toward the group of young musicians
was that of a mother cat toward her kittens, fumed. This was
the end of Cui's career as a composer! Marriage at twenty-three
was a crime! "One should marry after one has worked, lived, and
even become a little tired. One goes to sleep after a day's work.
Otherwise there is no point in the sleep. It is the same with marriage. But of course there is no use arguing. Cui will not listen to
me."

As for Balakirev, he was interested only in Cui's compositions,
but his friendship with Mussorgsky was of a different nature. The
two did not meet so casually or so often as did Cui and Mussorgsky, probably because Mili was not so frequent a guest at
Dargomijsky's, nor did he go about visiting friends just for the
sake of visiting. At first the relations between him and Mussorgsky were rather formal. Then in the fall the latter began to
study with Mili.

Strictly speaking, Mili Balakirev's teaching was something like
a course in musical appreciation, except that it was on a much
higher plane, since serious technical analysis went along with the
discussion of form and interpretation. Since he himself had never
gone through a regular course of training in harmony and counter-

point, Mili oddly enough actually thought that the composer did not need any preparatory studies in orchestration and counterpoint, and that the development of a sense of form and technical skill were to arise from one's own composing experience. Apparently he did not realize that what he was doing was equivalent to teaching a man how to swim by telling him to jump into the water, assuring him that if he drowned he would at least find out how deep it was. Mili himself was a most acute critic of every technical defect, but he denied to his pupils the fundamental studies which should have been the foundation for their criteria of right and wrong.

What Modest now needed was a teacher who would introduce him to the fundamentals of composition. But Balakirev never bothered with such trifles—he just told Modest to compose a scherzo for orchestra and to write a sonata, when Modest hardly knew the difference between the two. After many months, Modest confessed that the scherzo was not yet ready and that he was tired of it.

Moreover, the lessons were very irregular, because time and again Modest either had to attend a parade or must be on duty at court. In any case, the sort of life he led as a member of the Preobrazhensky Guard sometimes left his mind not so clear as it should be. Finally, despite his blind and adoring belief in Mili, Modest was slow in grasping and following his teacher's ideas and instruction. Mili, whose mind worked with the speed of lightning, grew irritated with him, preferring to work with the methodical and well-organized Cui.

But he liked Modest, thought him a good fellow, and soon their lessons turned into friendly exchanges of opinion. Either they met at Mili's, or Mili came to visit Modest, who was living with his mother and his brother Philaret. (The elder Mussorgsky had died in 1853.) Those evenings were charming. Mili played cards with Modest's mother, who was proud to have such an illustrious friend of her son's in her home; he drank tea with them, played

[38]

on their new piano, and shared with them his visions of a new music, voiced in a language they hardly understood.

All this fed Balakirev's ego, but it did Mussorgsky little good except as it fulfilled his desire to find a responsive friend willing to listen to his very complex ideas and with whom he could discuss the emotions that had troubled him since his schooldays. Modest was far from being well, and he had an extremely sensitive nature. In his childhood, his *nyanya's* stories had fascinated his imagination and held him in terror at night in his little bed. The supernatural, the unknown, crept into his mind as he grew up on the old country estate where among the plain people reality and pure fantasy were confused. At school his tendency toward mysticism was nourished by the books he read on religion, the existence of a future life, and the fate of the soul. And he took no small part in his comrades' drinking parties, with the result that his nerves were considerably disturbed.

For the next two years, whenever Modest was not seeing Balakirev, he wrote him either short, nervous notes or long dissertations in which he analyzed himself and "poured out" his soul.

"Remember [he wrote once] how, two years ago, we were walking down Garden Street together—you were going home—it was summertime. We had just been reading *Manfred.** I was so wildly excited by the sufferings of that lofty spirit that I cried out: 'How I wish I were Manfred!' I was quite a child at the time, remember! Fate thought fit, apparently, to grant my wish—I became Manfred for the time, literally—my spirit slew my flesh! Now I must have recourse to every kind of antidote. Dearest Mili, I know you are fond of me— then for God's sake keep a tight rein on me when we are talking together, and don't let me kick over the traces! For the time being, too, I must give up all my musical activities and avoid every kind of work that tires the brain, if I am to get better. My rule must be: 'Everything must be done for the physical cure, even at the expense of the intellectual development. The reasons for my nervous excitability are clear to

* Byron's poem.

me now. It was not only the consequence of onanism (this is almost a secondary reason). The chief causes are as follows: youth, an immoderate capacity for enthusiasm, a strong, unconquerable desire for omniscience, exaggerated introspection, and an idealism that even goes so far as to take the dream for the reality. I see now that, at the age of twenty, the physical side of me is not sufficiently developed to keep pace with my forced intellectual growth. The latter got the upper hand and stifled the former. (Here the reason for underdevelopment—onanism.) We must now come to its assistance; distractions—yet as much rest as possible—gymnastics, cold baths, these must be my salvation. . . .

". . . Today we [Modest and his brother] have been to the ballet, very charming ballet with many beautiful pictures. But the music, Mili, the music was terrible! The ballet made a strange impression on me—I was very nearly ill in the theater. When I got home and went to bed, I was at once assailed by painful dreams, by hallucinations so sweet, yet terrible, so intoxicating, that to die in such a state would have seemed an easy thing. That, fortunately, was the end of my sufferings; I now feel much better—at any rate I am perfectly calm. . . . Mili, I feel as if I had awakened from a heavy dream."

At another time he wrote:

"You reproach me with two peculiarities that you assume to be present in me. I will begin with the first—the mysticism—or, as you rightly express it, the mystic strain in my nature. Two years ago, as you know, I was in the grip of a terrible illness, which attacked me with extraordinary violence while I was staying in the country. This mysticism, aggravated by cynical thoughts about the Deity, got much worse after I came to Petersburg. I managed to conceal it from you, but you must have noticed its effects upon my music. I suffered greatly and became fearfully sensitive, even morbidly so. Then—either as the result of distractions or thanks to the fact that I gave myself up to fantastic reveries, which held me captive for a long time—my mysticism began gradually to disappear, and when my reason had gained the upper hand, I took steps to get rid of it altogether. I have made a great effort of late to conquer the thing, and fortunately I have succeeded.

At present I have put mysticism far from me—I hope forever, since it is incompatible with a healthy intellectual and moral development."

Or he would write that he was busy translating Lavater's letters about the fate of the soul after death:

"A very interesting subject. As you know, I was always drawn to the fantastic world. These letters are very interesting. Lavater was a physiognomist, meaning that he could judge a person's character by observing his face. Here is his remark about the image of Bacchus: 'A very sanguine temperament, yet he is more material than divine.' He is right. This does credit to an artist. Here is what he says about the state of the soul: The soul of the deceased transmits its thoughts to a man who is capable of clairvoyance and of informing the friend of the soul's present locality. Please note the correlation of the two souls. But you will read all this when I finish the translation."

But Mussorgsky was also capable of reading at the same time popular books on geology, and hastened to inform his friend that this also was very interesting. "Just imagine," he wrote, "Berlin is built on ground of infusorial earth, some of which is still alive!"

Reading all these notes and letters, Balakirev—whose head was preoccupied with the practical problems of life—only raised his eyebrows. "What utter rubbish! And how does he manage to reconcile faith in immortality of the soul with infusorial earth?" He advised Modest to make a piano arrangement of the Persian Chorus from Glinka's opera *Russlan and Ludmilla* and to get on with the sonata he talked so much about.

Without saying a word to Mili or his other friends, Modest would suddenly leave the capital and go to stay in the country. Later, letters would come from him, telling where he was and saying that he was "thinking . . . thinking . . . thinking," that he had had to go off in order to solve some of his problems, but that he was composing, that the idea of writing music to Sophocles' tragedy *Oedipus* had never left him, that he wanted to dedicate it to Mili, that he was writing on the side another little sonata, and that he was going to bring with him some new musical ideas that he had written down at a country fair.

Little was known to his friends, even to Mili, about any love or even affection he may have felt for any woman. Modest, who expressed his emotions so spontaneously and freely, kept this subject to himself. He took the mystery into his grave. Only once did he mention the words "woman affairs" in a letter, adding that he would tell Mili about it when he next saw him. But he never did.

I should like to refer here to a story that has appeared in our time, written in the form of a novel.* If one can give it credence, the action must have taken place at about this period in Modest's life. According to this story, Modest fell in love with a singer prostitute from a cheap night club along the river bank. He was going to marry her and make an honest woman of her; but when once in his absence from home (he supposedly lived alone) another woman of his own class came to see him, and the two women met, the singer knew that her dream of becoming his wife could never become a reality, and she left him. He hunted for her everywhere—so the story proceeds—took to drink, and eventually heard that she had drowned herself. But her image haunted him for the rest of his life. Thus the novel. It reads like a movie script that combines Dostoevsky's Raskolnikov and Sonia Marmeladova (from *Crime and Punishment*) and Tolstoi's Katusha Maslova and Prince Nechludov (from *Resurrection*). The

* The novel *Le pauvre amour de Moussorgsky*, by Ivan Sozontovitch Lukash and adapted from Russian by Nadine d'Oblonska, published in France in 1939. On the first page appears an author's note: "This is not a biography of Mussorgsky. This is a novel, but it might serve as a key to the mystery of his existence. A letter dated 1883 was found among the papers of a painter in St. Petersburg which gives reason to believe in it. [This is just as mysterious as "the mystery of his existence." The author does not give the name either of the painter or of the writer of the letter.—V.S.] Once more a legend could be closer to reality than reality at its most exact accuracy. The contemporaries of Mussorgsky always spoke of the presence in a cheap night club of a street singer who accompanied herself on the harp." (In my reading of all the documents, letters, and biographies concerning Mussorgsky and his close friends, I have never seen a reference to the above-mentioned person.—V.S.)

[42]

most that can be said of the tale is that it is possible, though hardly plausible.

It is true, however, that among the guests at Dargomijsky's musicales Modest met Maria Shilovskaya. The young woman was an amateur singer, had a pleasant mezzo-soprano voice, and was strongly inclined to a fiery gypsy manner of interpretation. But, as Dargomijsky once remarked, "Who cares? Look how beautiful she is!" This she was, and scores of young men trailed after her— not excepting Modest, despite the fact that she was ten years older than he, and married. Her husband, Stepan Shilovsky, an officer of an aristocratic Guards regiment, was one of the richest men among the country nobility in the district of Moscow. They lived in a style that was markedly luxurious even for people of that class. On their estate near Moscow they had their own theater where, for their guests, they gave performances of whole operas, no doubt so that the young wife could act on the stage. For those performances a special chorus was brought to sing from Moscow, and the Shilovskys' own orchestra was augmented by players from the city.

Modest not only visited them whenever they came to St. Petersburg, but also went often to their country place. At one time he even helped to coach the chorus for a performance of *A Life for the Tsar,* with his hostess as the star and the rest of the cast from Petersburg. In one of his letters to Mili he spoke of the beauty of the place and "how rich that scoundrel Shilovsky is"; but one felt his slight disappointment, particularly when he wrote that at last he is getting well, that his brain, which had been weak and irritated now grew stronger, that he had turned to reality, that the youthful fire had cooled, and that "there was not even a half-word of mysticism left." This and a song, *What are the words of love to you?* which he dedicated to his hostess, were all that remained from this obviously unsuccessful romance.

Suddenly in the spring of 1859, Mussorgsky declared that he

had decided to leave the military service and devote himself entirely to music. He had been thinking of this for the past year and had even talked about it to Stassov. Both Balakirev and Stassov tried to dissuade him, reminding him that Cui, since his marriage, had opened his own preparatory school for the Military Academy besides continuing with his regular army service, in order to meet expenses. Stassov pointed out to Mussorgsky that the Russian poet Lermontov had also found a way to combine his military service with his work as writer and poet. But Modest was stubborn. "That was Lermontov, and this is I," he replied. "My military duties interfere with my music." And when in the summer of that year he found he was to be transferred into a battalion of sharpshooters—away from his friends and the life of the capital—he retired from military service and went to Moscow instead.

During the past few years Modest's mind, crowded with new impressions and struggling with complex theories about life, would now and then focus on the subject of nationalism, and he would feel a strong urge to see his own country. Petersburg was too cosmopolitan; he was only awaiting an opportunity to go to the older capital. And now at last he saw the city with his own eyes.

"As I approach Moscow," he wrote Mili, "I at once noticed a very remarkable thing. From the belfries and domes of the churches was wafted the breath of the olden time, long since gone by." He walked to the Red Square—the heart of Russia—and stood there as in a trance at the sight before him! The Red Square, "which had seen so much muddled confusion"—those very stones of the pavement on which the history of Russia had passed by. Everything around him was a silent witness of Russia's life through the ages. On his left the old market street, "dark and ugly"; but the Kremlin and the Church of Basil the Blessed—"those were the holy past." With awe and reverence he approached the Kremlin. Queer and mysterious thoughts suddenly passed through his mind. He expected at any moment to see a boyar go by in a long kaftan and a high fur cap. As he walked under the

Spassky Gate he took off his hat—an old custom that he liked. In the old seat of the Tsars he stood in Granovitaya Palata, the banqueting hall in which the trial of Patriarch Nikon had taken place. In Archangelsky Cathedral he walked among the tombs of men who had occupied the throne of Russia—tombs which

> ". . . tell sad stories of the death of kings:
> How some have been deposed; some slain in war;
> Some haunted by the ghosts they have deposed;
> Some poison'd by their wives; some sleeping kill'd;
> All murder'd. . . ."

He recalled Glinka's *A Life for the Tsar.* Moscow transported him to a different world, the world of the past—"a filthy world, but somehow attractive to me. Such beggars and frauds the world has never seen. And they use such weird gestures and manners." He watched the fidgety convulsions of their bodies, watched the grimaces they made; was startled, impressed, and amused by the nicknames they called each other. The plain Russian people, he reflected, have an unerring sense of characterization; indeed, the founder of his own family, Roman Monastirev, had been nicknamed "Mussorga"—the Foul-mouthed. For a moment he savored this kinship with his own people. Then he went on to Samarin's, where he ate excellent *Botvinya* (a cold soup of beets, leaves, pot herbs, and fish) and saw the "waiters in clean white blouses." He climbed the belfry of Ivan the Great and marveled at the beautiful view of Moscow. It felt good to be a Russian. "Do you know, I *was* a cosmopolitan. Now everything Russian is close and dear to me, and I should be much annoyed if Russia were not taken into proper consideration in our time. It seems to me that I begin to love her."

Not all of Mussorgsky's impressions of Moscow were of so lofty a nature. He stayed longer than he had planned, but not because he wanted to study the relics of old Mother Russia. He was having a good time. He hired a piano, talked of composing, but for the most part visited with his friends. "I am surrounded here by a very decent sort of people, all of them former students. They're lively fellows and very capable. In the evenings we shake down to their foundations history, the administration, chemistry, the arts—everything. But oh, Moscow! Such people as my friends are forced to form a separate little circle. However, good people everywhere are on the side, and it's better that way. 'Blessed is the man who doesn't go to the unfaithful for counsel.'"

But Balakirev was greatly concerned over Modest's staying away so long. He did not care very much for the kind of life his friend was leading in the city. He had never approved of Modest's friendship with the Shilovskys, nor did he now approve of this enthusiasm for his new friends—three young students who "are sympathetic to me intellectually. I like to breathe their atmosphere, and they," he assured Mili, "like to breathe mine."

Balakirev even tried to influence Modest through his brother Philaret, asking the latter when he expected Modest to return; but Philaret only knew that Modest was happy in Moscow and might stay there another couple of weeks. Mili was losing patience with Modest; it was not in his nature to coddle a child, and certainly not a problem child. He tried to reason with him, tried to guide him out of the depths of his mental chaos, but his remarks only hurt Mussorgsky's ego and pride.

In a letter, Mili underlined the narrowing atmosphere in which Modest was living. Modest snapped back: "In regard to the fact that I am sinking and that somebody has to pull me out, all I can say is that, given talent, a man does not sink if his brain is working. If he has neither the one nor the other, there is no use pulling him out, like an old splinter. It is about time you stopped treating me like a child who has to be guided so that he won't fall.

"What you say about my being attracted to limited people demands just one answer: 'Tell me whom you love and I'll tell you who you are.' Logically, I am very limited."

Mili did not think he was limited. Mili thought he was a driveling idiot.

[46]

3

THERE WERE OTHER MUSICIANS WHO FORMED A
close circle around Mili Balakirev. Like a Don Juan always falling
in love in his search for the perfect woman, Mili fell in love with
almost every young promising talent that crossed his path. At no
other time had Russian youth been so active in every form of life,
particularly in literature and art. Like an old and dormant vol-
cano, Russia began to eject from her depths all that had been
stored in her for centuries. But since the country had no properly
organized schools of art, most of these young talents remained
dilettantes. Some of them appeared on the musical horizon, shone
for a while, and vanished.

At one time Mili was much attached to an extremely gifted
young man, Apolon Gussakovsky. All of Balakirev's friends had
great hopes for this musically endowed student of chemistry and
geology, who surprised them with what seemed to be an inex-
haustible amount of melodic material. He preferred to compose
for the piano—usually scherzos, owing doubtless to Mili's influence, for at that time it was Mili's favorite form of composition.
Gussakovsky's personality—the gaiety and frivolous bohemianism

that made him so attractive—was also responsible for the fact that he never progressed beyond the dilettante phase, and, since he did not possess either the stamina to endure the difficulties of a musician's career or the true creative urge, he returned to his profession as geologist. And Balakirev needed men like Gussakovsky, for Mussorgsky was talented but unreliable, while Cui's life had been set in its final mold when he was twenty-three.

Small wonder, then, that in 1861 Mili turned all his interest to a boy of seventeen, a midshipman at the Naval Academy—Nicolay Rimsky-Korsakov. At one of the regular Wednesday sessions when Balakirev's friends met at his home to talk music, Feodor A. Kanille, an old friend of Mili's, brought a pale boy with girlish features, to whom he had been teaching piano for the past two years.

Very shy (this was his first meeting with a group of real musicians), Rimsky showed by his manner and his speech those aspects of his character—a strong sense of self-criticism, common sense in reasoning, and, above all, impeccable honesty—which were both inherited and imbued in him by family tradition. To Mili, the greatest crime in human relations was a lie, no matter how small or how unimportant it might be; this constituted the basis of his own relations with others. Nicolay's respect for truth was therefore far more important to Mili than was the fact that his new protégé had almost no musical training and could hardly play the piano.

Learning to play the piano—as Rimsky had so laboriously tried to do since childhood, first with one teacher, then with another—was dismissed by Mili as unimportant and, without even so much as testing his knowledge of harmony and counterpoint, he told Nicolay to start immediately composing a symphony, and handed him for models Berlioz' *Instrumentation* and two symphonies that happened to be lying on his piano. From their first meeting, Nicolay had looked up to Balakirev with the adoration of a young

[48]

girl for her first hero; and because he thought Mili capable of even the impossible, he now did not dare disobey. But he realized that the task was way above his head, for what did his musical wealth consist of, beyond a love of music that was developing into a passion?

Nicolay belonged to a family most of whose members traditionally served in the Russian Navy. The Rimskys, who lived in the small provincial town of Tichvin, regarded music merely as a pleasant pastime, preferable to cards or drinking, and Nicolay Rimsky-Korsakov would have ended as just another navy officer if it had not been for the unusual difference in years among the four members of his family.

When Nicolay was born (1844), his father was already sixty years old, his mother forty-two, and his only brother Voin a twenty-two-year-old navy officer—practically three generations in one family. The duty of parents toward their children, and the duty of children toward their country, these governed all their thoughts and the way the Rimskys lived. "To be his creator, his father, and his friend"—such functions Nicolay's father could fulfill only in part since he was too old by the time his authority and advice were called for. Voin took his father's place almost from the moment of his brother's birth. His letters home from the capital, where he was in service, contained detailed instructions for the upbringing of young Nicolay. A man of wide knowledge, with an unusually developed taste for the fine arts and an interest in philosophy and psychology, Voin was also interested in educational problems. When Nicolay learned to read and write Voin wrote to him direct, in language that a little boy could understand, impressing upon him the need for self-discipline, for the ruthless criticism of one's own defects, and for honesty.

To teach the boy orderliness, Voin insisted that the parents have a little desk made for Nicolay where he could keep all his letters and papers; and one can now almost see Rimsky-Korsakov sitting in the same position and attitude at the age of five as he does in the picture of him that is most familiar to us.* Nicolay's future career was already mapped out for him by Voin in accordance with the traditions of the family. As for music, Voin was delighted to discover Nicolay's talent, and encouraged every manifestation of it.

At the age of twelve, Nicolay was taken from home to become a student at the navy school. Thus far he had only played with building ships and read and listened to the exploits of men of the sea, but now he was taught stern discipline and given practical courses in mathematics to prepare him for professional seamanship. This was his first year away from home, and he was homesick. He wrote long letters to his mother, for, unlike his elder brother, he was drawn closer to his mother's gentleness than to his father's methodical mind. In these letters, in which he speaks of all the home pets, the dogs, the birds, asking about every one of them, reminiscing about country life, the garden flowers, his mother's daily occupations, one finds a portrait of a gentle boy who has no cares.

But Voin's watchful eye was near by. Having always urged his parents not to coddle his small brother, he now devoted his attention to Nicolay's development into maturity. Voin thought that the boy was too carefree and without any sense of responsibility. He hoped that some day Nicolay would either lose his pocket-book or have it stolen from him; and when little Nicolay, during practice, fell from the mast—"seven stories high"—into the water, Voin thought this might teach him to be less absent-minded. In short, Voin wanted his brother to get all the lessons of hard reality while *he* did the moralizing.

However, it was Voin who engaged a piano teacher for Nicolay, and himself supervised the boy's practicing, beating time like a metronome and giving his own advice on interpretation. By the time that Nicolay met Balakirev, his musical knowledge had reached about the same level as that of Mussorgsky and Cui when

* The famous painting by the Russian artist, V. A. Serov, which is used so often in books on Rimsky-Korsakov.

[50]

they had met Mili. He had heard the same operas as they, had tried to play them on the piano by ear, had played whatever scores he could buy, and had done a little composing on the side without any knowledge of writing, using the printed music as a model.

"You cannot imagine," he wrote his mother, "how I love to play the scores of operas and how, on the contrary, I do not like pieces written for piano. They seem to me so dull, so dry. But when one plays an opera score, one imagines oneself sitting at the opera and listening or even acting and singing oneself; one imagines the décors—in short, it is a lot of fun." And this was exactly what his parents and Voin wanted music to be for him— just a lot of fun. "You certainly would not want him to become an *artist!*" his father exclaimed to his mother.

But Balakirev did not intend to let Nicolay just play with music. He drew him closer to his group, had him attend the Saturday meetings at which they performed their works as they composed them, where they listened to Mili's criticisms and discussed music into the small hours of the morning.

Mili opened a new world to Nicolay, a world from which there was no return. The taste of the circle leaned toward Glinka, Schumann, and Beethoven's last quartets. As Rimsky remarked later:

"Nearly all the fundamental ideas of the eight Beethoven symphonies were thought weak. Chopin's melodies were considered sweet and womanish. Balakirev likened him to a nervous soicety lady. The beginning of his Funeral March in B-flat minor aroused them to rapture, but the rest was deemed utterly worthless. Some of his mazurkas found favor, but the greater part of his compositions were looked upon as pretty lacework and nothing more. Mendelssohn was considered sour and bourgeois, except for the *Midsummer Night's Dream* Overture. Mozart and Haydn were considered out of date and naïve, and Bach was held to be petrified—yes, a mere musico-mathematical, feelingless, and deadly character, composing like a very machine. Berlioz, whose works they were just beginning to know, was highly esteemed. Liszt was comparatively unknown and was adjudged crippled and perverted from a musical point of view, and often even caricatured. Little was said of Wagner.

"The attitude toward contemporary Russian composers was as follows: they respected Dargomijsky for the recitative portions of *Russalka;* his three orchestral fantasies were considered a mere curiosity; on the whole he was not credited with any considerable talent and was treated with a shade of derision. Lvov, the composer of the Russian national anthem *God Guard the Tsar,* was deemed a nonentity. [Anton] Rubinstein had a reputation as a pianist, but was thought to have neither talent nor taste as a composer."

It is often the case with young people that, once their own critical opinions find kinship with those of men they admire, they fall completely under the latter's influence and follow them without ever again examining these criticisms on their own. Nicolay had begun to criticize from the time he heard his first opera and first symphony. It is a part of every artistic development. It is such fun to criticize. It gives one a sense of his strength, even though one does feel a bit uneasy about it. Nicolay preferred the *Freischütz* Overture—"the best in the world, equal to those of *Don Giovanni* and *The Magic Flute,* perhaps even better." He shoved Italian opera into the background. Verdi's *I Lombardi* seemed, according to sixteen-year-old Nicolay, to have "nothing in the whole opera but clatter and thunder." He preferred Meyerbeer's *Robert le Diable*—"Oh, how I like that!" He began to enjoy Russian music. "Italian music is more elegant, but Russian is more agreeable to listen to. It reminds one of our little Russian mujiks or the Slavs of the Middle Ages." Glinka's music took hold of him without anybody's introduction. He thought *A Life for the Tsar* the greatest opera of all. Naturally Nicolay was ready to absorb the tastes of his new friends without reasoning or examination, and repeated their opinions as his own, often without even knowing the composition thoroughly—since, as was Balakirev's way, only fragments were analyzed.

Just as Mili did nothing to help Nicolay learn to play the piano

—a thing which as a pianist he could easily have done—so he did nothing to teach him harmony and counterpoint, but just worked with him on his symphony, for the most part simply rejecting fragments which did not appeal to him and writing in his own in their place.

While his devoted pupils accepted his authoritative advice without question, Balakirev knew how to conceal his own shortcomings from them. For instance, Nicolay had no idea of trumpets and French horns, and would become confused when writing for natural-scale and chromatic-scale instruments. He had only vague notions of how double notes, legatos, and chords were played, and in case of emergency he merely indicated them, blindly following Berlioz' *Table*. But at this time Mili himself had only confused notions of the same matters, and therefore whatever was unfinished and unskillful he would change and complete so that the composition might be made ready for performance or publication.

For all his inborn intelligence and brilliant ability, Balakirev failed to see that what was right for him might not necessarily be right for his pupils, who came from entirely different surroundings, who had different natures, and whose developing talent was bound to take a different course. Instead, he despotically demanded that their taste correspond to his, and he criticized and censored severely the slightest manifestation of individual personalities. Usually he insisted that each pupil bring in his composition practically in embryo; then Mili would take the opening phrase and immediately make corrections, praising the first two bars and ridiculing the rest.

However, it was Balakirev who urged on Nicolay the importance of a general education, of the knowledge of literature and history in particular. Nicolay soon realized this for himself, since the circle usually discussed other than musical problems. Stassov—at last seeing the materialization of his ideal of a group of Russian musicians working together—was always at these meetings, prof-

[53]

fering advice, suggestions, and lavish encouragement. He read aloud fragments from the *Odyssey,* or made Mussorgsky read Kukolnik's *Prince Kholmsky* or Gogol's novels. Religion was not discussed, for Mili seems to have been an atheist at the time and Mussorgsky had just declared himself a free-thinker like Stassov, though the touch of mysticism never left him and one did better not to start such discussions with him. Nicolay himself, though he came from a profoundly religious family, had in his childhood gained a very realistic point of view, probably as the result of his own boyish pranks, such as uttering blasphemies while standing at prayer and thus testing the very existence of God, for which he should have been punished by the God he denied.

Nicolay's general views were based on a very liberal upbringing. Even at the time when serfdom was in existence, the Rimskys had only hired servants in their house. When his father was offered three hundred souls* as a reward for one of his services to the government he declined, saying that he did not know how to take care of even one soul—his own.

Nicolay found at Balakirev's a different atmosphere from that of the Naval School, where one could hardly point to any intellectual tendencies in the students. "Horseplay that was not altogether decent, rough protest against the authorities, rude intercourse with fellow students, prosaic obscenity in conversation, a cynical attitude toward the fair sex, a disinclination for reading, contempt for foreign languages and for subjects outside our special studies, and, in the summertime, even drunkenness—these were the characteristics of the school spirit of those days," Rimsky wrote in his memoirs. Now, at Balakirev's, he was among men whom he admired for their knowledge, with a common interest and goal, and who treated him as their equal.

At the end of the school year Nicolay's contact with the Balakirev circle reached a crisis. Having graduated, he was now required by the rules of the school to sail on a world cruise for a

* I.e., serfs.

couple of years. This news threw Balakirev into despair. He was just recovering from the loss of Gussakovsky, who had suddenly gone abroad, leaving behind a score of unfinished but promising compositions. Nicolay had taken his place. Besides, Mili's nature was far more complex than he let people see, and his devotion to young Rimsky bordered on love. Here was a young man whose character was not yet developed, was soft as wax, whom Mili could mold into his own creation. To have him go away at this time for such a long period and into a new world where Mili could exercise no influence over him seemed a major catastrophe, and he did everything he could to prevent it. He exploited all his connections at the Ministry of the Navy, but to no avail. There was only one solution: Nicolay must resign from the Navy. Mili found no support in Cui, who thought that such a voyage would benefit Rimsky's general development; and even Mussorgsky, who had faced just such a problem a few years ago, agreed with Cui.

But the final decision was made by Nicolay's family. Both Voin and his mother looked askance on his new friendship with Balakirev and, while they were very tactful about it, this was their opportunity to turn the young man from the side road his life had taken. Nicolay's mother, now a widow after forty-one years of happy married life, was focusing her devotion on her younger son, since her relations with Voin, though cordial, were always distant. With anxiety she had watched the growing influence of Balakirev on her son and the place he was taking in Nicolay's life. She strove to convince Nicolay that it was all just a passing infatuation with music—"which is no more than a pleasant pastime"—and reminded him of his real duties.

Even Nicolay realized that to renounce his career in the Navy was impossible for practical reasons. His father had left only a small pension for his mother to live on. If he resigned, Voin would have to support them all—Voin, who had hardly enough for his own wife and two daughters. As for Voin himself, he thought that, aside from all the other arguments, two years of absence would be an excellent test of Nicolay's love of music.

Balakirev had to accept the inevitable. But he was far from giving up Nicolay for good. He was determined to keep fast the ties that bound young Rimsky to him, through a continuous correspondence while his protégé was absent.

4

BALAKIREV HAD BEEN IN PETERSBURG FOR FIVE years, and his financial status had not changed a bit. He still lived from hand to mouth, depending entirely on what he earned from piano lessons. He wasted his time running from one rich house to the other. He had to smile and be nice to people he should never have met. He was underpaid. From pure negligence, his rich customers sometimes did not pay for all the lessons, and he dared not mention it for fear of hurting their feelings and losing pupils. It was all very humiliating. But this part of his life he accepted, for his mind was preoccupied with his main goal— Russian national music, which, so Stassov assured him, was his true calling.

As a pianist he made no name for himself beyond the salons, where he played in order to make music and not to earn money. He never sought a career as a mere virtuoso; as a conductor there was not yet an opportunity for him in the capital; as a composer he did not compose enough, and the fees he got for his published works were too small to keep him alive. It was Balakirev's peculiarity that—with all his knowledge, with his remarkable talent in advising, in correcting, in improvising almost a new score while working with others—where his own music was concerned he was extremely slow at composing. With amazing speed he could give life to someone else's composition, but it took him years to finish his first symphony. "One should throw on the paper only completely matured and finished ideas"—this was his precept for his own work. And he brooded for years over his own compositions.

Balakirev was now twenty-five and—except for a few songs and his Fantasies (one on Glinka themes and the other on Spanish themes, which he later rewrote)—he had managed to finish only the music to *King Lear*. Beneficial though the friendship with Stassov had been for his general education and as an introduction to new ideas on the aims of art, it actually retarded Balakirev's development as a composer.

His analytical mind and critical feeling often stifled his creative spontaneity. Influenced by the writings of men like Chernishevsky, Dobrolyubov, and Belinsky, he had made a credo for himself: to value above all the strength of a thought. "The picture created by a poet must contain an idea which should point to a definite direction in life." But though this was his credo, he completely failed to follow it in his own music. The events taking place around him, the forthcoming reforms, the emancipation of the whole country, the creation of a national art—these stirred him to unbounded enthusiasm, but he was impotent to reflect it in his music. He instinctively felt that such music needed new forms, new means of expression; yet he himself was powerless to escape from the classical way of composition, or even from his two favorite keys of D-flat major and B minor.

"With every year the subject of Glinka's *A Life for the Tsar* becomes out of date," Mili wrote to Stassov on the 19th of February, 1861—on the very day that Alexander II abolished serfdom. At the very moment when all Russians were pinning their hopes on the young Tsar's manifesto, Mili considered *A Life for the Tsar* a hymn to the monarchy and "out of date." He had no definite

Borodin

political views. Even his long friendship with such a man as Stassov did not really influence him politically. He sympathized with the liberals—but very mildly, and only when he himself was thrown among provincial officials, as he was on his visits to Nijni-Novgorod.

In 1858 Ulibishev died and left Balakirev a thousand rubles and his music library. Ulibishev's children were willing to part with the library, but as for the money—which was far more important to Mili—they wrangled over when and how he should get it. Also, Balakirev's father was again out of a job and his sisters needed help. To get a scholarship for one of his sisters Mili had to go to Nijni-Novgorod, see the Governor, play at his home, be nice to his wife, bow and click his heels before the tawdry provincial aristocracy—gray-haired rascals and venerable nonentities, bribees, and embezzlers. All of this was revolting to Mili. "I am very poor," he wrote to Stassov, "and feel very low. To find any work for a musician in the province is even harder than in Petersburg." During his years of absence from Nijni-Novgorod he had lost all his useful connections; the former theater director was gone, the new one did not know him, and he got no position as a conductor.

"*King Lear* is silent. I have started on the last entr'acte . . . but I don't even think of music any more. I am surrounded by such petty nastiness that it seems strange to remember that there are quintets, Schumann, Shakespeare. It is impossible to compose in Nijni-Novgorod. . . . I need complete freedom from all worries to write sensibly." Balakirev's nerves were disturbed; he became overanxious about his health, misanthropic.

Stassov called his friend back to the capital, promising that there "he would be mended again, not like a toothless broken-down horse which the Tatars eye from afar. No, but mend him, mend him as one does a young, impatient, full of fire and vigor, pure-bred Arabian stallion who has hurt his 1000-ruble foot scratching against a cobblestone on the road, so that he may race away magnificently with his mane and tail waving in the breeze and flashing fire from his nostrils, making everyone gasp to look at him."

And when Mili returned, Stassov brought new plans, new suggestions, applauded Mili's every beginning, acclaimed as superb everything he managed to finish. Mili resumed his Petersburg life, gave lessons, orchestrated Cui's new opera, *The Prisoner of the Caucasus*, corrected in despair Mussorgsky's compositions, took a trip on the Volga and wrote down some sixty songs that were to form the first volume in a collection of Russian folksongs, went for a cure to the Caucasus where he dressed himself in the colorful native costume like a hero from Lermontov's poem, and started on his composition *Islamey,* which made his name immortal.

Balakirev's talent required a larger field than merely the sporadic instruction of promising composers. His private pupils and even his circle were all too scattered, too lacking in definite basis or method. What he needed was a school, either to direct or to have some part in. Such a school was being organized at that moment, but Mili was not invited to join it.

Anton Rubinstein's long dream of creating schools in Russia on the model of the Western European conservatories was coming to reality. As a pianist already world-famous, he had close connections at the Russian court. The Grand Duchess Elena Pavlovna was his devoted friend, and she was an outstanding personality at the court. German by birth, she had been well educated in both Germany and France. She surprised the Russian historian Karamzin by her familiarity with his works in the original, for she knew Russian before ever, at the age of seventeen, she had set foot on Russian soil. Not completely devoid of feminine charm, she had more energy and organizing talent than most of the men at the court. It was even rumored that Tsar Nicolas I was afraid of his new sister-in-law.

Elena Pavlovna loved music passionately, but her large plans for raising Russian music to the level of that in the Western countries were slow in developing. It was only when her nephew, young Alexander II, succeeded Nicolas I that she felt herself free to act. Anton Rubinstein—"the first pianist in Europe," as he was called at the court—was naturally her choice as the champion of her ideas. She had helped him organize the first Russian Musical Society, and since 1858 he had presented its symphonic concerts. Now she was to help him to start the first music school in Russia.

While the members of the Russian Intelligentsia were calling for broader reforms in education for the people (the abolition of serfdom being considered a *fait accompli* except for the reading of the Manifesto), Rubinstein came out with an appeal for the future of Russian musicians in an article in *Vek* for January 1861. Here he asked that a music school be founded in order to create Russian musicians, instrumentalists, and composers who could derive from their work not only a living but also social recognition. Rubinstein sought to put an end to the absurd situation in which Russian musicians had found themselves from time immemorial. Catherine the Great had granted the privilege of citizenship to painters and architects, thus raising them to the level of the members of other free professions. Not so with musicians, however. Kologrivov, one of Rubinstein's close friends and the man who had harbored Balakirev in his home and arranged his first concert in Petersburg, was one of the victims of the musicians' plight at that time. In order to become a Musical Inspector at the Imperial Theater he had had to surrender his nobility rights, nobles being forbidden to act in any professional musical capacity. A nobleman who did so was not allowed to wear a uniform or own any serfs, nor might his children attend the aristocratic boarding-schools. Rubinstein himself had suffered from this intolerable state of affairs. When once, after confession in the Orthodox Church, he was asked to inscribe his name in the censor's book, he discovered that the deacon could not classify him

[61]

under any of the established professions: student, nobleman, peasant, soldier, or manufacturer. For the musician had no place, even as late as 1860.

Rubinstein pointed out that the proposed conservatory ought to rank with the universities as an institution of higher education, and grant to its graduates the same social rights. But his simple and logical appeal was misunderstood. As often happens, certain words and phrases in his article were lifted from their context and so misinterpreted that their meaning was completely belied. "Artists should seek fame and financial substance" was interpreted as mercenary and vain. The suggestion that music ought to be in the hands of professionally trained musicians was taken as a personal insult by Balakirev's group, and Rubinstein's remark to the effect that it was not in the nature of a Slav to become more than a dilettante aroused their national feeling.

Stassov, the mouthpiece of the nationalists, wrote vitriolic articles condemning Rubinstein's plan, ridiculing the comparison of a conservatory with a university at which one obtained a general education, and rejecting the idea of teaching composing. He finally attacked Rubinstein personally, as one whose compositions were listened to only because he capitalized on the name he had made as a piano-virtuoso, and implied that as a Jew he was no representative of the Russian people.

Besides, Rubinstein's choice for the faculty—Dreyschock, Madame Nissen-Salomon, Wieniawski, Leschetizky, Carl Davidov—though they were outstanding musicians professionally trained in European schools, was deemed a new foreign infringement and added fuel to the blaze.

Balakirev, reporting it all to Nicolay on the high seas, wrote:

"The Russian Musical Society is trying to fulfill its ambitions to organize in Russia a state music Department for which the Conservatory will develop young officials whose aim it will be to bring all Russian music under the yoke of the German musical generals. (I don't mean

Beethoven or Schumann, but Rubinstein and Carl Schubert, those personified conservatories.) Then woe to everyone who opposes them. The Germans have the superiority over us. They have that loathsome clannishness which easily forces their influence on the uncoöperative Russians."

Even the leading critic Alexander Serov, who had no sympathy with the Balakirev group, remarked that for his part he "would never entrust the education of Russian youth to an uneducated pianist, a complete nonentity as a teacher, and a composer without talent." But then when Serov was asked what his position was, he declared proudly: "My position is opposition." However, his whole thinking was absorbed in Wagner's music, and in his articles he attacked foe and friend alike.

Nevertheless, no amount of criticism or even personal abuse could prevent Rubinstein from implementing his plan. The Grand Duchess herself procured 5000 rubles from her nephew, Alexander II, and permission to go ahead with her plans for the school. In October 1861 the St. Petersburg Conservatory opened its doors.

Balakirev's group, with their weekly meetings for musical discussions, had very little to offer in competition with the trained musicians on the Conservatory's faculty, who now started teaching according to the regular routine of any advanced educational institution. The Petersburg public were hardly aware of Balakirev and his group; all it knew was that they held meetings at which they discussed lofty themes, and that some of them wore military uniforms—which only proved Rubinstein's charge that for them music was but an avocation. However, when the polemic in the press appeared, the people of Petersburg realized that the group around Mili was made up of talented musicians whom they would have to respect. They even received a name: the "Balakirevs."

But Mili was not content with merely criticizing the Rubinstein school. To counteract the founding of the Conservatory, he, with the help of Lomakhin, a conductor of Sheremetyev's chorus, organized a Free Music School. Its aim was to give everyone an opportunity to study music, and its basis was to be the most liberal ideas. There would be no titles or ranks, no tuition payments or teachers' salaries, no homework or examinations, and the lecture hours would mostly be in the evening so that anyone, including persons in other professions, might attend. Here, obviously, was one of those idealistic projects that seldom offer serious competition to a well-organized enterprise. First of all, there was no capital to run the project on. Curiously enough, Rubinstein had the complete support of the Government—Rubinstein, who was branded as "an outsider, an impudent Jew who has nothing in common with Russians," while his whole faculty were similarly branded as foreign—"not a Russian in the whole lot"; whereas the Balakirev group—the nationalists—could not find any support except for 500 rubles contributed by Grand Duke Mihail. In order to raise the necessary funds, Balakirev and Lomakhin gave two concerts and were thus enabled, in March 1862, to open their Free Music School.

Mussorgsky wrote to Balakirev:

"I am delighted with the success of the two concerts, and may the newborn school grow great and prosper! . . . I am far from maintaining that all learning means obscurantism; at the same time I find a free and unforced development of natural aptitude, which is sure to be radically fresh and sound, incomparably more sympathetic than any scholastic or academic drill. . . . Just think what the professors cram into the young head, and what the head has to break before it becomes able to throw away the unnecessary and retain the essential! One is reminded of the conversation between Mephistopheles and Mama's boy.* With what fiendish mastery this Devil frightens the poor freshman with antediluvian and modern doctrines! A true professor indeed—only

* Mussorgsky refers to a scene from the first part of Goethe's Faust in which Mephistopheles, dressed as Faust, talks to his pupil, mocking human wisdom.

[64]

more honest than ours because he frightens his pupils away, while ours lure them on!

". . . Passing now from schools of philosophy to schools of music, in Petersburg they have lately set up two music schools side by side, completely contrasted in character. One is a den of professors; the other a free society devoted to the art. In the one place Zaremba and Tupinstein,* clad in their antimusical professorial togas, caulk the heads of their pupils with every sort of vile rubbish and infect them from the very first. The unfortunate pupils see before them not human beings but a couple of posts with some sort of silly scribble written on them as musical rules. Rubinstein is dull, therefore he conscientiously performs his duty by maliciously stupefying the others. Not so Zaremba—a cunning fellow, that, the very man to take measurements of art by inches. Having been elevated to the dignity of Doctor (he is really more like a cobbler in an academic nightcap), he is not so childish and simple as to base his views and his counsels on musical logic or esthetics. Not he! He has been taught the rules! And with this lymph he inoculates every aspirant against free learning. Down on your knees to Mendel [Mendelssohn]! That is Zaremba's slogan. . . .

"As for Aunty Aleona [the Grand Duchess], I suppose she will not live so long as Methuselah; as a scourge, she is but temporary. But the —— with grizzly hair, already she is a —— ——, very unstable in her adoration and hatred; playful and always amorous, she is famous for her fickleness.

"In the other school we have you and Gashenka.** What more is there to say? You are a genius, and consequently all that is broad and free and strong is yours by nature. Mankind needs such men. All success therefore, and a happy future to your splendid work. Again, 'All hail to the newly born!'"

The two schools differed in their teachings—the Conservatory had classes in every branch of musical education, while the Free Music School had classes only for choral singing; but both gave public symphony concerts. Although the Russian Musical Society's

* Tupinstein: in Russian, *tupo* means "stupid."
** Gabriel Lomakhin.

constitution stipulated that each program include at least one work by a Russian Composer, Rubinstein (its conductor) offered programs of classical music, mostly German, while national music found its stronghold in the concerts of the Free Music School, conducted by Balakirev and Lomakhin.

These concerts were Mili's first appearance as a conductor in the capital. Not since the time of Ulibishev's musicales years ago had he led an orchestra; and now, facing musicians of higher caliber, his inexperience was obvious. Alexander Serov did not fail to mention this in his articles.

Such was the first round in the fight that was to divide Russian musicians into two camps, with the odds against Balakirev.

5

WHEN, IN OCTOBER OF 1863, MUSSORGSKY, CUI, and Balakirev were saying farewell to the departing young Nicolas Rimsky-Korsakov, on the other side of the capital a young man dressed in a light summer overcoat was walking slowly and nonchalantly into the private office of Professor Zinin at the Academy of Medicine. All of Zinin's students had heard of the expected return of this twenty-eight-year-old doctor of medicine. The former pupil had much to relate to his old professor, whom he had not seen since receiving his doctor's degree three years before. There was news about the group of young Russian scientists Sechenov, Botkin, Yunge, and the celebrated Mendeleev with whom he had worked in Erlenmeyer's laboratory at Heidelberg. There was his own work—the long experimental researches that had been published in Liebig's *Journal of the Chemical Society* and Erlenmeyer's *Journal of Chemistry,* and his *Researches upon the Fluoride of Benzol,* one of eight chemical treatises that had just been published. Professor Zinin, an expansive soul, was the friend of all his pupils, but this young man he regarded as his adopted son. There were no scientific projects on which they had not exchanged ideas, and Zinin expected great things from him. The report soon spread among the students that the newly appointed assistant lecturer in chemistry was Alexander Borodin.

To Borodin, the routine of the old and well-organized school was as easy to slip into again as a familiar pair of slippers, for the Academy was his Alma Mater, the school to which he had been brought at the age of sixteen (1850) by his mother who, despite his size—he was over six feet tall—still took him by the hand when they crossed the street. Alexander Borodin was his mother's favorite son. She had two other boys by the same man—Dmitri Alexandrov and Evgeny Feodorov. "Alexandrov" and "Feodorov" were, like "Borodin," the boy's surnames; and the explanation of this family relationship Alexander Borodin would give without the slightest hesitation, as simply as he would explain a chemcial formula. His father, Prince Luka Gedeonoshvili—a descendant of the last kings of Imeretia in the Georgia Caucasus, "where the flora of the East blossoms in the shadow of the eternal snow"— was in his sixties when he fell in love with the charm, intelligence, and wit of the twenty-five-year-old Dunia from Narva. Their three boys, born out of wedlock, were registered under the names of serfs whom no one seemed to know. It was as simple as that.

Besides his appearance—Alexander inherited from his father a pair of dark, deep Oriental eyes that looked, as someone said, like the round flat surface of a filled glass—he owed to his Georgian ancestors the Oriental quality of sleepiness in his whole manner.

Because someone said that the little Alexander had a touch of tuberculosis his mother would not send him to public school, and he was taught at home by governesses and tutors. In his childhood, surrounded entirely by women, he had as his sole playmate his cousin Maria who lived at their home, and young Alexander even spoke of himself as a girl.* The two children played dolls, built marionette theaters for which Alexander made up stories, lived in dreams as children do, and through the window watched the

* Russian verb-endings distinguish between the masculine and the feminine.

young soldiers and cadets drill on the Ismailovsky Barracks court. The military drum fascinated little Alexander. (It was to the same sound of a drum, on the same Ismailovsky court, that Modest Mussorgsky thirteen years later learned his first military exercises.) However, it was with the flute that Alexander started his acquaintance with music. A flutist from the regiment used to come to the house and give him lessons for fifty kopeks each, while the old Prince laid aside the Bible and closed his ears with his fingers.

Years went by with little change in the big house.

The old Prince, dressed usually in a dark blue suit, spent most of his time sitting in the study of his luxurious house reading the Bible. A pair of dapple-gray thoroughbreds stood at the gate from morning till night waiting for the master if he wished to take a ride, while the coachman and the footman drank some twenty glasses of tea in the kitchen, gossiping with the maids. The same drum resounded from the court where the young cadets drilled year in and out. Little Alexander was growing up, falling asleep now and then over books on botany and chemistry, in which he had developed a sudden interest. The house smelled of sulphur, and everywhere there were small containers of liquids with which Alexander made his experiments. His mother had no education, but she wanted her son to be a well-educated man—a scientist perhaps—and so she encouraged these chemical experiments even though sometimes they endangered the very safety of the house.

Alexander was drawn again to music when at the age of nine he fell in love with a young woman years older than he, with whom he liked to dance. She was tall, and so big that it looked as though all he could do was to hold onto her knees. He composed a polka for her, blushed with jealousy when she danced with adults, and by his new affection tormented his cousin Maria, who sulked and swallowed tears. Hadn't he and Maria vowed to marry?

Alexander was twelve years old when music began to take as imperative a place in his daily routine as did his studies in science.

[69]

This was due to his friendship with a boy of his own age, Shchig-lev, who was a sort of musical prodigy. The association of the two boys started in a fist-fight, but led to a more harmonious study of music together. Between their lessons in chemistry, they took lessons on the piano from a somewhat second-rate German professor. They played four-hand the symphonies of Haydn and Beethoven and, to have more variety in their performance, Boro-din took lessons in 'cello and flute while Shchiglev learned to play the violin. They went to concerts together, and through the winter slush and snow carried their instruments from one end of the city to the other to play chamber music.

Though at the age of thirteen Alexander composed a Concerto for Piano and Flute, and later a Trio for Two Violins and 'Cello on a theme from *Robert le Diable,* without any training in compo-sition, his talent was not considered important enough to warrant any change in the plans for his career as a scientist. His mother (whom for some unknown reason he called "Auntie") fussed over him as much as ever, and when the time came to decide upon a school for him, she chose the Academy of Medicine. The universities had recently had serious trouble with their students, and the risk of his encountering new ideas there, to say nothing of bad influences, made her feel that it would be safer to send him somewhere else instead.

When the old Prince died, they moved to a new apartment close to the Academy so that she could have him at home and watch over him. She favored his friendship with German boys, who were orderly, did not drink nor discuss politics, and behaved themselves. She even selected, according to her own taste, a young servant girl, Anushka, to live in their house so as to spare the growing boy the storms of young passion.

"You know, Borodin," said Professor Zinin to Alexander after he had been his student for only a couple of years, "all roads are open to you. There are not many persons in Russia like you and

Mendeleev. You would do well to spend less time on composing songs. You know that I count on you to be my successor, but you think of nothing but music; you make a mistake in hunting two hares at once." And it was true. Alexander did spend all his free time either at concerts or playing chamber music with his acid-burned fingers.

Then in 1859 Borodin was sent to Heidelberg. Professor Zinin cared too much about the young man's career to let him remain just a Doctor of Medicine; he needed him for scientific work in chemistry, and Mendeleev at Heidelberg would straighten him out.

For Alexander Borodin the day in the little provincial German university town started at five in the morning. After long hours at the laboratory, he visted daily a small pension with a squeaky staircase where he met many compatriots. There they spent their evenings talking, playing chamber music, and staging *tableaux.*

"Is that all? . . . How provincial you are!" commended Ekaterina Protopopova, swallowing all the L's, as was then the vogue in Moscow, and slightly squinting her short-sighted eyes, while playfully balancing a parasol. The young woman was a pianist who had just arrived from Russia for her health. She knew Borodin from a picture a friend had shown her, had heard that he was a scientist with a great future, gay and handsome, the "best catch" in Heidelberg.

"What shall I play for you?" she asked him.

"Oh, the same one—that Schumann."

And she played for him music he did not know, music that kept him awake. (Or was he telling the truth?—perhaps it was the performer.)

Days followed each other in precise routine. He called for Ekaterina as soon as he was through with his work at the laboratory, and they took walking trips to the old Schloss near by, wandering through its galleries and dark, deserted *allées,* and creeping

[71]

under the heavy stone arcades, where Ekaterina would clutch him in fright. They listened to concerts in the "Museum" or at Peterskirche, and drank beer at Der Wolfsbrunnen.

Ekaterina Protopopova was a good-looking, sensitive young woman, with a clear vision as to what her husband should be, yet trusting and agreeable in the many discussions they had. She thought, for instance, that the marriage ceremony was stiff and banal, and that to be even engaged was "rather embarrassing." As a musician she surprised Alexander with her perfect pitch and easy understanding of modulations. In Moscow she had taught the daughters of rich noble families, and had left there a friend who wrote her long, drunken letters. She had a very moderate income, derived for the most part from the concerts she gave in Moscow. She gambled at the nearby Kursaal, and Borodin borrowed most of her money so that she should not lose it all.

He was a shy and awkward suitor, so embarrassed when she came once for him at Karpfengasse 2 to take their regular walk that, not knowing what else to do, he showed her his closet full of linen; apparently he had not inherited his father's Georgian skill in courting a lady.

Then late one night in the middle of August 1861, they were sitting on a bench near the Wolfsbrunner fountain. Four sprays of water were spouting from the wolves' mouths, evenly and with endless precision falling into the pool. The trout swam apathetically back and forth. Borodin said to her quietly, "I am going to tell you right now something very funny. Be my wife . . . that is all."

But she was ill. She coughed blood. She was so little, so fragile, and he was so strong. Borodin took her to a famous Heidelberg professor, Friedrich, who did not stand on ceremony with his patients. "She will not live another month unless you take her to a warm climate. Go to Italy, to Pisa. It's warm there now." She was willing to go there . . . but to get married—that was not so simple. They went to Pisa, and while she baked in the sun he worked on the volumetric determination of the azote in organic compositions. In the evenings he played 'cello in the orchestra of a Pisa theater. A few months after their return to Russia, Alexander married Ekaterina Protopopova.

The Academy of Medicine provided the Borodins with an apartment separated from the laboratories only by a corridor, and here Alexander remained for the rest of his life. He spent his days in the midst of his students, whose love and admiration he won the day he returned to the Academy. His even temper and kindness made it possible for them to be on most intimate terms with him without losing respect for his authority, and to approach him with any question without fear of being repulsed or receiving an evasive answer. The only signs of impatience he showed were provoked by their occasional negligence. "Little father," he would then say, "if you continue to work that way you will soon destroy fine equipment!" Or, "How can you make such bad smells in such a beautiful laboratory?"

Most of his students visited him in his apartment, where they ate meals at odd hours and mixed with his as well as his wife's relatives and friends who were constantly in and out. Often they heard the piano being played in another room by their host.

"I am a Sunday composer who strives to remain obscure," Borodin said to Balakirev, whom he met during his first month back in the capital at the house of Professor Botkin, his old friend from Heidelberg. Balakirev invited him to one of his weekly gatherings. "This is chemistry; this is medicine!" Mili told his friends, threatening them with his forefinger. "A man of certain age and position, with a small respectable belly, who wears gold epaulets on festal days."

Mili did not have to introduce Alexander to Mussorgsky, for they had met twice before. Borodin remembered that in the autumn of 1856, when he was a second house-surgeon, he had fallen into conversation with a seventeen-year-old ensign of the Guards

[73]

in the military hospital on the outskirts of the city, that they had found common ground in music as they sat and talked in the guard room, and that later in the evening they had gone to a party at the home of Popov, the hospital's head surgeon. Here Mussorgsky played on the piano, with grace and expression, fragments from *Trovatore* and *Traviata* to an enchanted feminine audience who exclaimed in chorus, *"Charmant, délicieux!"*

He remembered that three years later he had met Modest again at the house of one of the assistant professors at the Academy, one Ivanovsky, physician to the School of Artillery. By this time Mussorgsky was no longer the handsome youth Borodin had known at Popov's. He had grown stout and lost his fine bearing. He had by then left the Army, but he was as careful as ever of his personal appearance. His habits were just the same, and his foppishness had, if anything, grown a degree more marked. Modest had told him that he had resigned from his military career in order to devote himself to music. It was the chief topic of their conversation. When Ivanovsky had asked them to play Mendelssohn's A minor Symphony four-hands, Modest had at first turned up his nose a little, but then consented, and they had played the first movement. Modest, however, asked to be excused from the Andante which, he said, had nothing of a "symphony" in it, but was just one of the *Songs Without Words* (or something on that order) arranged for orchestra.

Modest was already at the time a frequent visitor at Balakirev's and on the track of all sorts of new tendencies in music of which Borodin had no conception. He had spoken with admiration of Schumann's symphonies to Alexander, who was still a Mendelssohn enthusiast. Yet as he had played fragments from the D-flat major Symphony, he would suddenly break off, saying, "Now this is where the musical mathematics begin." It was all new to Alexander, and he was captivated. Encouraged, Modest had played other new works and finally his own *Scherzo;* on reaching the trio he had hissed through his teeth, "This is quite Oriental."

Alexander could not say at first that he was pleased with what he had just heard. The musical forms of these compositions astonished him, bewildered him; but, as he listened further, he began to appreciate them and find in them a certain charm. When earlier in the evening Modest had told him of his intention to devote himself seriously to music, Alexander had taken his declaration for a bit of braggadocio. But after his *Scherzo* Alexander had believed him.

Now, at Balakirev's, Borodin shook hands with a man in whom there was no trace of his former military bearing nor the slightest hint of dandyism. The man was a composer—Modest Petrovich Mussorgsky—even if Cui and Mili did not quite approve of his compositions. Modest had matured and made progress in his work and ideas. His *Scherzo* had even been played by Anton Rubinstein (though not without a little skirmish with the great man at one of the Russian Musical Society concerts), and he had just been asked for the score of his *Oedipus*. It was due to Dmitri Stassov,* Vladimir's brother, that the committee requested another work. But the committee insisted that the chorus from *Oedipus* be played first at rehearsal, with Modest present, so that they and Modest himself could judge whether or not it was ready for public performance. Modest's pride as a composer was hurt, and with elaborate excuses he managed to get his score back.

"Does this inconsistent, sloppy society suppose that it can teach me? I have my chorus back and am heartily glad that a collision with Rubinstein has thus been averted. *Basta!* I have had quite enough of the Musical Society." Modest thought he was behaving as a professional musician should. He would not have them treat him as a dilettante whose work must be "tried out." As long as Rubinstein was the conductor of the Russian Musical Society concerts, Mussorgsky's name did not appear again on their programs.

* Dmitri Stassov was on the Board of Directors of the Russian Musical Society, and was responsible for every conciliatory move on their part.

Borodin was warmly received by Mili and his friends. They talked to him of the work they were engaged in at present, and their plans for the future. Modest played fragments of what he called *The Witches,* a work he had conceived in the autumn of 1860 as incidental music to Baron Mengden's drama of the same title—the work that eventually became known as the symphonic poem *A Night on Bald Mountain.* As Modest explained, he wanted the music to give a picture of the Witches' Sabbath, interrupted by the actions of the various witches and wizards, and of a triumphal procession of all "these hellish wretches," ending in a final glory of the Sabbath. But somehow he was not satisfied with his work and he shaped and reshaped it. He seemed to love the subject.

For Borodin they played Cui's *Scherzo* which, as Balakirev said, he had managed to shake out of a methodical mind preoccupied with his lecturing at the Military Academy. And finally they told him about the absent young naval officer, and Alexander heard what must have been a remarkable performance of parts of Rimsky's First Symphony at the hands of Balakirev and Mussorgsky. Borodin was struck by the brilliance, depth, power, and beauty of this music.

When Mussorgsky asked Borodin to play one of his own compositions, he was so embarrassed that he refused. "I am a chemist," he said. Needless to say, Balakirev could not be put off for long by such an excuse, and after he had heard only a few fragments of Borodin's compositions he told him to write a symphony.

"Our relations," Mili later told Stassov, "had important results for Borodin. He had so far considered himself an amateur, and did not attach much importance to his compositions. I was the first to reproach him for this indifference, and he immediately set to work with ardor to compose his First Symphony."

6

Borodin's musical career began with this meeting in November of 1862. From now on, Balakirev worked with him as he did with Cui and the rest of his disciples. Modest and Rimsky had a better background than Borodin's to reflect the national quality of Russian music. Like Glinka, they were born and bred on soil where for a thousand versts round lay Russia, the motherland, while Borodin had seen nothing of his own country beyond its cosmopolitan and even "German" capital. It was due entirely to Balakirev's guidance and influence that Borodin lost the last traces of his Europeanism—the Mendelssohnian in his music—and that the national character was so strongly marked in his First Symphony. Alexander became a frequent visitor in Mili's and Cui's homes and, through their discussions on music, art and esthetics, he learned of the aims of the new Russian school, of which Balakirev was the god and Cui his prophet.

If in practical musical training Balakirev had very little to offer as competition to the newly founded Conservatory, his group had a quite clear formula as to what direction and what forms Russian music should take. One of the striking characteristics of their thinking was the fact that, though all of them played the piano, like Glinka and Dargomijsky, they were very little interested in writing piano music as Beethoven and Schumann had done, and were scornful even of Chopin. (Modest refused to attend a concert while in Moscow because "Nicolas Rubinstein—a worthy relative of Anton's—let his homemade Moscow pianists play Chopin's *pièces de salon*—the height of absurdity!")

Their interest focused primarily on symphonic and vocal music. The preference for presenting a musical idea through the medium of the orchestra was not dictated by the pure glamour of sound (as it is today in the United States) but was due to the influence of the social thinking that then prevailed in Russia: the idea of the "collective" in every form, whether a workmen's union, a group of scientists doing research together in a laboratory, or a musical performance. The symphony orchestra represented the work of a collective; it played in a large hall, for a large collective audience. The opera was an even fuller expression of that idea, since—besides the orchestra and the actors—a whole body of carpenters, painters, and stagehands was a part of the production.

The Balakirevs had ideas no less definite about the subjects of their compositions and the forms in which these should be treated. They thought that the symphony as a form of composition had reached its final development—thanks to Beethoven, Schumann, Liszt, and Berlioz; but that opera—dramatic music—was still in a transitional stage, the third stage in its evolution. At the end of the eighteenth century, opera still was regarded only as a vehicle for the display of vocal virtuosity. The melody, the cantilena, was written not to suit the text, but to give the singers a chance to show off their voices.

It was Gluck who tried to restore opera to its original status as dramatic composition, but later composers like Rossini once more made it merely music for the concert hall, adorned with scenery and costumes. The influence of Meyerbeer, Weber, Glinka, and Dargomijsky was felt as opera developed further, but their

[78]

efforts were only half effectual. Then suddenly a new reform came in with Wagner; in this the Balakirev group joined, though fundamentally they were opposed to Wagner's ideas. The new Russian school of thought laid down the following principles of reform:

1. *Dramatic music should have an intrinsic value as absolute music.*

The Balakirevs thought that composers who occupied themselves only with pure melody and vocal virtuosity—the road to infallible success—wrote the most astonishing banalities. Everything that in symphonic music would, with entirely justified disdain, have been put into the *Index Librorum Prohibitorum* found a place in opera. The Italians, they felt, were unsurpassed in this respect. Aspiring only to easy success, the latter made of the typical Italian opera a potpourri of ornamentation, bad taste, and the excessive use of B-flats and high C's. Finding themselves in complete accord with the public's poor taste, they not only wrote banal themes but exhibited these in all their nakedness without trying to improve them by colorful harmony. The best among these composers repeated one another (or themselves) in style, harmony, and themes. The Balakirevs argued that it was sufficient to look at some thirty Rossini operas and seventy by Donizetti to prove this. Both of these composers wrote only two or three original operas, of which the rest were pale reproductions. Even non-Italian composers like Meyerbeer—one of the greatest dramatic composers—would (according to the Balakirevs) have gained in prestige had he omitted all the virtuoso effects from his scores.

2. *Nothing should stand in the way of the true and the beautiful.*

Everything seductive in musical art must be enlisted in the creation of opera: the charm of harmony, the science of counterpoint, the richness of polyphony, the color of the orchestra.

3. *The vocal music should match the meaning of the words.*

The text should not serve exclusively as the raison d'être of the vocal utterance. For if this were the text's real function, it could just as well be set haphazardly to any music that might come along. On the contrary, for each phrase of the text there should, in a correct musical declamation, be a sound that corresponds to it. It is from the text's meaning that the musical ideas are derived, since it is the function of the sounds to complete the significance of the words. In his conviction that text and music must, in a sense, be *one,* the Russian school placed a new emphasis on the character of the texts chosen. They looked for "art" in the text itself, and then tried to create a composition that was new in two ways— poetic and dramatic.

4. *The music as well as the libretto—i.e., the structure of the themes—should depend on the individual character and function of each actor as well as on the general sense of the piece.*

The Russian school did not deny a place to chorus and to aria, but it felt that nothing must be allowed to stand in the way of the action. Everything depends on the development of the subject; the music must never take a road of its own. The chorus should represent a mass of people—not simply be there to fill in when the soloists need time to rest.

All these principles were very like those underlying the Wagnerian reform; it was the means of implementing them that differentiated the two schools. To begin with, the Balakirevs considered that the subjects of Wagner's operas had nothing *human* in them; they were personified abstract ideas which, like mannequins, were incapable of inspiring real interest. The Balakirevs believed themselves to be concerned with the human passions that charm and stir, confuse and trouble, the lives of men.

Wagner, they charged, concentrated all his interest in the orchestra, giving the vocal parts a secondary role only. He stated his themes through the orchestra, while the actors had only fragments of recitative which, if taken separately, had neither intrinsic value nor any precise meaning. The Balakirevs regarded this as all wrong, for the actors in an opera are not there merely to complement the orchestra—they are there to create the action. The public watches them, listens to them, and it is therefore they in whom the principal interest should center. The Russian school believed that Wagner was wrong in letting the orchestra get the upper hand. The vocal parts in his operas, they maintained, battle with the orchestra, only to be killed by it. It seemed to them that Wagner did his best to deny his characters all musical expression, whereas—according to the Balakirevs—the composer should, save on rare occasions, reserve for the characters his best musical material and the most important phrases of his score. They considered that Wagner's musical ideas were submerged by the heavy waves that roll one over the other, surcharged with exaggerated harmonics and sonorities, and of a boredom and monotony hardly relieved by the few beautiful pages, which, as Cui said, were "as rare as an oasis in the Sahara." In short, opera should be essentially vocal; Wagner's was symphonic.

As for the Wagnerian *leitmotif,* every character is tagged with one and must wear it like a coat wherever he goes, and all his entrances must be announced by it. Wagner tags leitmotifs even to abstract ideas, like vengeance, or to objects—a sword, for instance. It is sufficient merely to mention the idea or the object for the motif to pop up, as though a spring had been pressed. This childish device, the Balakirevs thought, does not honor Wagner's heroes. Why is each of them condemned to one perpetual leitmotif, without the slightest development and almost without the slightest alteration—which constitutes still another element of monotony—? One of the basic principles of the Russian school was variety of form. They were not satisfied with giving a hero one musical idea only, but insisted that the themes should be multiplied and developed as the action demanded, with different rhythm, harmony, color; in a word, that the characters be painted with all the means at the composer's disposal. Generally speaking, and duly acknowledging Wagner's talent and strong individuality, the Balakirevs thought that his doctrine was false, that he had

[81]

written more annoying music than good, and that the mad Wagnerian cult was more fanatical than sincere.

The Balakirevs also rejected the very essence of the dramatic plot: the progressive development of a conflict, as it was known on the Western European stage. They believed that the real essence of an opera lies in the *idea* of the presented work. Whether this idea was expressed in a series of pictures (dramatic or not in themselves) was not important, as long as the presentation as a whole was vital and vivid.

They felt the same way about symphony, for a symphonic work in "sonata form" is based again on the same idea of conflict. Stassov said once to Balakirev: "I don't know who is going to do this—you or someone else (it would be a pity if it didn't come from the new Russian school)—but symphony must stop being constructed in four parts as Haydn and Mozart conceived it a hundred years ago. Why *should* there be four parts? Why should this never alter? The time has come for this to pass into oblivion, as well as the symmetrical and parallel construction within each movement. We have done away with all the academic forms—odes, speeches, statements, and arias—in dramatic expression. Now the time has come to forget about the first and second themes and the exposition—the *Mittelsatz*—in symphonic music."

Finally, the Balakirevs attached very little importance to the erotic, and even less to the psychoanalytic, as a source of musical inspiration—the two vehicles used to so much advantage by European composers, and of course by Wagner.

All this Borodin heard at the Balakirev meetings, and two years later (from 1864 on) César Cui told it to the Russian public in the form of articles and musical criticisms in the St. Petersburg *Gazette,* and then in *Golos* (The Voice), *Nedelya* (The Weekly), and the *Revue Musicale.* The new Russian school was indebted to Cui not so much for his composing of purely national music as for such literary propaganda.

Cui had an indisputable literary talent and a style of his own. His language was clear and laconic; it had color and piquancy. His mocking spirit and lively whims that were so delightful in the drawing room became, in his articles, bitter sarcasm which he sometimes overused. By nature straightforward and determined, never afraid of a fight, Cui was brutally frank in his writing.

He opened an indefatigable campaign against the old German and Italian schools and welcomed the emergence of a new Russian school, attributing to it such qualities as depth of feeling, force of passion, a realism that expresses itself in a tendency toward recitative declamation, and the new element of humor.

In his articles he lashed out against Italian mediocrities—the works as well as the performers: against the hackneyed *Lucia, La Sonnambula,* and *La Favorita,* and against the vogue of the singer with the "Big I," endless high C's, and staccato, bullet-like runs. He hated virtuosity per se. Like the Italian singer whom he berated for holding high notes interminably, he himself held on to his arguments so long that to a certain extent he was successful. If Italian opera did not cease to be the temple of style, at least it ceased to be the temple of art. On the other hand, owing to his continuous criticism, the repertoire of Russian opera became more serious and began to gain in prestige.

In his propaganda for the music he admired, César Cui was very demanding. He was an aristocrat in what concerned art, and he considered it right to be choosy. "One cannot tolerate anything badly made in a symphony."

Essentially Cui was a man of his time. He passionately loved the work of his contemporaries, although he gave their just dues to the masters of the past. These he regarded as necessary in the amalgamation of the chain of art, and as ingenious and interesting though cold. But he felt that real music had started at the beginning of the century with Beethoven. However, Cui looked only at the content of any work, and not at the name signed to it.

[83]

Cui was widely read, trusted, and admired, and he made more enemies than friends, but he fought alone against the rest for the cause which he adopted. He signed his articles with three little stars in the form of a triangle—the insigne that he wore on his epaulets as a lieutenant in the Russian Army.

The St. Petersburg *Gazette* invariably accompanied Cui's articles with the following editorial statement: "In publishing the articles of Mr. ₊ * ₊, we consider it necessary to remind our readers once again that we are willing to give space to any pertinent opposing opinion, though the editorial staff often considers these articles too extreme, and sometimes too violent."

7

OF ALL THE MEMBERS OF BALAKIREV'S GROUP,
only Mussorgsky was directly affected by Alexander II's manifesto of the 19th of February, 1861, which abolished serfdom.
Since resigning from the Army he had been living with his brother
Philaret and his mother at their home in St. Petersburg, in much
the same way he had earlier on their estate—that is, he was taken
care of by his devoted mother and did not give a thought to how
and where their income came from. Though they were not so
rich as the Shilovskys, they were well off. With no material worries, Modest was free to follow his whims, now going to the
country "to think and strengthen his brain" or to nurse his ill-
nesses or to seek peace for his work on planned compositions,
now visiting his friends the Shilovskys, or occasionally going to
Moscow to have a good time. But this was all changed with the
abolition of serfdom, since most of the family income was derived
from the land they owned and the serfs who worked it. The big
house in Petersburg must now be given up, his mother had to return to their country place, and Modest and Philaret faced the

problem of suddenly adjusting their properties to the new economic regime.

For two years Modest spent his time between the capital and the provincial town of Toropetz, arranging property matters with officials, clerks, lawyers, and solicitors. As he wrote to Cui:

"It is all so tedious, dreary, annoying—the Devil knows what! And the caretaker [of the estate] played such a dirty trick! I had intended to do some decent work—instead of which, if you please, I am to make investigations, get information, run to police and civil courts. . . . If my mother were not here in Toropetz, these fools would drive me quite crazy—it is only on her account that I stay on; it makes her happy to have me with her, and I am glad to be able to give her the pleasure.

"Oh, but what 'planters' these landlords are! They are very proud of the club they have opened in the little town, and they meet there almost daily to get noisy. The proceedings generally open with a speech, followed by some sort of general announcement for the benefit of these 'gentlemen,' and nearly always end in a fight so that you feel like sending for the police. And all this goes on in an aristocratic club, if you please, and these are the gentry with whom one has to associate every day! Day after day they tearfully carry on over their 'lost right' and 'total ruin'—nothing but howling and gnashing of teeth and noisy scenes. If you give nobles the right to meet, they meet; if you give them the right to argue about their business, they argue—and at that with their fists and obscene words. True, the younger fellows are more decent, but I never see them; it is they who negotiate with the peasants and are therefore always on the road. And this is the fetid atmosphere in which I, poor sinner, have to live and breathe. It certainly does not appeal to the artistic instincts! A man has enough to do to prevent the stink from hanging about and choking him. How can anybody think about music?"

Apparently Philaret and Modest were not good businessmen, for their estate shrank rapidly through all sorts of risky financial operations. The two brothers had different opinions about the new reform, and reacted differently to it. Philaret, with an elder brother's superior air, thought that it must enable Modest to see for himself, at last, the fruit of his misguided love for the Russian peasants, his notion that the Russian mujik is a human being. But Modest was completely in sympathy with the peasant class, and his abstract love for his own people, awakened in him on his first visit to Moscow, now took a more realistic form.

"The peasants are far more capable of self-government than the landlords are," said Modest. "At their meetings they conduct matters directly and to the point, and in their own way discuss their interests in a very businesslike manner; while the landlords, when *they* meet, quarrel and show off their ambitions, quite forgetting the purpose of the meeting. This is consoling, for it puts a trump card into our hands."

Though his muse was silent during these years, Modest's intellect and character and his inborn talent for analyzing human nature developed through constant association with people, and he gained a firm basis for his ethical beliefs. From then on his love for truth and hatred of deceit, hypocrisy, and even compromise governed him in life as well as in art. He suddenly found himself on solid ground from which no authority could dislodge him. He could view the past in a clear light and make a bold attempt to estimate the value of what he had accomplished. He now saw that, though he had not shirked his task, still—thanks to his "truly Russian laziness"—he had very litle to show in the way of achievement. Moreover, he had discovered a certain tendency in himself that became more and more evident, something very like instability or excessive softness—what Balakirev had called "doughiness." Modest had just begun to notice it, and it worried him, "for dough takes the impression of dirty fingers just as much as of clean ones."

While in Moscow, Mussorgsky had resented Balakirev's patronizing attitude toward his talent and his work. He now refused to compromise or even listen to the advice of his former teacher when it concerned the public performance of his recent compositions. He confessed that Mili's tepid appreciation of his *Witches* had severely irritated his artistic amour-propre. He was of the opinion —"always was and always shall be"—that the piece in question contained some fairly good music, and that it was important since it was his first independent work of any size. He told Mili that he could perform *The Witches* or not, just as he pleased; but that in either case he himself would not make the slightest alteration either in the general plan or in the working-out, since both were intimately related to the subject of the picture, and the work in it was honest stuff. He said that every composer can recall the mood in which his work had its rise and was thought out, and that feeling—that is, the recollection of former moods—forms the groundwork of the criticism he passes on his own achievements.

To his other friends he expressed even more emphatically his belief in the composition. He said that *The Witches* was a vulgar name and that he had changed it to *Saint Ivan's Night on Bald Mountain,* that the piece was "truly Christian—a composition presenting a true picture of folk imagination, born in Russian fields and nourished by Russian bread; a piece devoid of all somber German philosophy and routine, which doesn't need to be vaguely entitled 'In A minor' or 'In D major.' "

The fact that Mussorgsky was facing poverty increased his self-assurance and already over-sensitive pride. Thanks to his fairly "elastic nature," he had recovered his spirits and now hoped to stand firm. Balakirev offered him financial assistance from his friends, but Modest refused it; poor as the beggar in his song, Mussorgsky was as proud as Peter the Great.

"My income is diminished, it is true, but not to the extent of depriving me of all possibility of preserving my independence. Accustomed as I have been to a life of comfort, and in some respects even of luxury, I have naturally felt anxious about the future, and it is no wonder that I looked glum—so would anyone else, probably, in similar circumstances."

He had to go very carefully into the question of how he could make shift with his diminished income. After the most serious consideration and mathematically exact calculation of his finances, he came to the conclusion that the deficit in his budget would make it impossible for him to take up his residence in Petersburg in September, as he wanted. He would have to wait another month, by which time he would, he thought, be able to live fairly comfortably in the city. It meant that he would have to postpone the renewal of intercourse with his friends for one month, but he readily made the sacrifice for the sake of the financial relief it would afford his friends and relations.

He had no doubt that he possessed a certain amount of talent, and it was his intention to set to work to the very best of his ability. Moreover, the atmosphere of the 1860's, which inspired everyone to do his part in social life, affected him, and he looked for other ways of making himself useful. He hoped to find some government job, but planned to wait until the New Year, when changes were to be made in the personnel of various departments.

When, on his first visit to Balakirev's, Borodin saw Mussorgsky, the latter was just getting accustomed to his new life. Instead of living with his brother Philaret as he usually did when he came to the capital, he chose to live in a community with a group of young men.

The sixties and seventies of the nineteenth century formed a remarkable period in the development not only of Russian culture, but also of Russian social consciousness. With the fall of Sevastopol fell physical slavery, and the Government lost its grip over the people's thoughts and emotions. Once given the impulse of freedom, the Russian Intelligentsia and particularly its younger members were avid to get all the new information, exchange new ideas, develop new theories—sometimes farther than the state of affairs permitted, even to the dreams of the social-revolutionary. Striving to solve the social problems that arose with the recent reforms, they studied economics, history, and science; and this was frowned upon by the Government, which feared that through these channels the "free spirit" (politico-social as well as religious) would affect the people's very lives.

The enthusiastic interest in these fields often resulted in developing materialistic and naïve nihilistic ideas in Russian youth of the period. Positivism and social consciousness were reflected in their everyday life, customs, and morals. The striving toward social and political ideals, based on freedom of thought and equality, was often complicated by the suspicion that the lack of such a foundation might not be entirely the fault of the Government. They saw ahead of them the desired truth, and back of them the dark injustice for which society as a whole was responsible. Young minds were tormented by questions such as whether to follow Western Europe or to turn to their own people, as the Slavophils and nationalists advised. More and more one heard the phrase "smaller brother." The now-familiar "Proletariat of the World, Unite!" belongs to a later period; the tendencies of that time did not go beyond the geographical borders of Russia, and their aims were limited to the Russian mujik and the Russian poor of whatever social stratum. Differences in opinion brought an even more living interest into their lives, more craving for an active exchange of ideas, kept their minds more vigorous, and helped them to progress. Small circles sprang up all over the country, where such coöperation of thought and friction of opinion made men out of mere youngsters.

Modest's group of friends was one of those circles which went one step farther than usual: they formed a community where they all lived together in one apartment, each of the five members having his own room, which except by special permission was closed to the rest. They had a common room in which their meals were served and where they met in the evenings for reading, recreation, and the exchange of views. All the members of this community were from the best society of the capital, all of them had

Cui

a lively interest in art, literature, and social problems, but Modest was the only musician among them.

They brought their friends, among whom were such men as Turgeniev the writer, Grigorovich the novelist, Kostomarov the historian, Pisemsky the critic, and Shevchenko, the Ukrainian poet who was shortly afterwards condemned to exile for his song dealing with the freedom of the Ukraine. While chatting and jesting at supper they exchanged news, opinions, and impressions. Ideas that had been worked out by each became the property of all. And there was nothing significant in any sphere of knowledge, in literature or in any art, that did not come to the notice of one member or another and that was not at once communicated to all.

Flaubert's *Salammbô,* which had appeared in 1862, was read by the little community, and Mussorgsky was so enthusiastic over the novel that he decided to make an opera from it. This was his first attempt since his schooldays to venture into this form of musical composition. It was not only the colorful subject of Flaubert's novel that attracted him; it was primarily the form of the composition—musical drama—which had long interested him.

With a sure hand Mussorgsky set out to write his own libretto. Some of the lines for *Salammbô* he wrote himself, for some he used the verses of other men—Heine, or Jukovsky, or another Russian poet—as long as they fitted his ideas. He also placed great stress on the directions for the settings. From Flaubert's novel he took the detailed descriptions of the costumes and noted all the decorative details, the movements and attitudes of the characters, and even the play of light. He was very fastidious about the scenic representations of all the plastic and picturesque elements in the opera. Modest worked very rapidly and in the course of a couple of months had the first act ready. However, it was to be long before he finished the work, for he now took a position in the Engineering Department of the Ministry of Transport.

Thus Modest, who five years ago had resigned from a career in

Russia's most elite regiment because he could not combine military duties with his work as a composer, now found himself at a desk job that afforded him even less material support and free time. This was hardly the position he was looking for "to be useful"—useful to society as he saw it—for his qualifications could not have been of any value to the department, nor was he interested in the job beyond the meager salary it provided. The fact that he spent most of the daytime at the office and that in the evening he did a great deal of visiting was responsible for his small output in composing at this period.

However, while working on *Salammbô* he composed several songs in the true Russian spirit, one of which—*Kalistrat,* with words by Nekrassov, "the poet of the poor, the wretched, and the forsaken"—showed, both in choice of subject and treatment of musical material, the full originality of his talent, hitherto taken with so much reservation even by his closest friends. Modest marked the score: "A first attempt at humorous music." But his humor was closer to Dostoevsky than to Mark Twain. (Kalistrat, the young peasant, recalls the cradle song his mother used to sing to him: "Kalistrat, you were born to be happy—free and careless shall your life be," and contrasts these words with the sad reality—his own actual poverty, his wife and children in rags.)

This piece particularly pleased Dargomijsky, whom Modest saw quite often. For humor in music was Dargomijsky's original idea, and in spite of the fact that Modest was considered Mili Balakirev's pupil, it was Dargomijsky who had given him the basic ideas for his vocal compositions; it was also he who had first brought to Modest's attention the idea of truth in music. Years had gone by since that first meeting, and Modest had learned its meaning in art. The word "truth" in Russian has a double significance. Besides its usual connotation of verity, it also means justice. Pavel Pestel, one of the five leaders of the December uprising in 1825, whom Nicolas I hanged, called his literary work *Russian Justice,* a sort of Russian Tom Paine's *Common Sense.* And when Russian writers wrote of Russian people, they spoke the truth, in both senses of the word, about the people. As painters painted pictures of Russian peasants' lives and sculptors molded in clay Russian popular types, they were all speaking that truth about the people. *Kalistrat* was Modest's truth about the Russian peasant.

In 1865 Modest's mother died. Though it was not unexpected, it was a terrible blow. She had been more than just a mother to him: in their long and close association she had been a friend in whom he found understanding and moral support. With her death came an end to the last link with his former carefree life. Their estate at Karevo was sold, and there was no more home for Modest to call his own.

"When at my mother's death the cruel blows of fate drove me from home into a cheerless exile, when, weary and embittered by suffering I knocked at the door of your pure heart, hesitating and shy, like a frightened child, begging for admission, craving help — No, I cannot—I cannot go on—" Modest never finished this confession. He was speaking to Nadejda Opotchinina, the sister of his friend Alexander Opotchinin and a close friend of his mother. Whether Modest turned to her seeking a friend to take his mother's place (she was years older than he) or whether he was seeking love and comfort from the woman to whom he dedicated the few love songs he composed, remains a mystery. Not even his closest friends knew for certain their true relationship.

But one thing was obvious: Mussorgsky was very unhappy. He was depressed by his dull job at the Ministry of Forestry where he sat at a desk most of the day, surrounded by officials with whom he had nothing in common, in a bureaucratic atmosphere that he despised. Even the lofty discussions at home did not relieve his gloom. There his friends often needed a sympathetic companion with whom, sharing a bottle of wine, they could talk of their misfortunes, and Modest emptied more glasses than was good for him. At Balakirev's he often complained of his nerves, but now he could not conceal the true nature of his physical condition. Now and again he wrote short notes to Mili explaining his absence from their gatherings or from opera or concert performance. "Mili, my nerve trouble is working up again in a most unpleasant manner, and I am obliged to watch it very carefully. To ward off a bad attack I intend to stay quietly at home for a time and take a rest. . . ."

Yet, when later in the year he wrote his *Detskaya* (The Nursery) in memory of his mother, in one part—*The Cradle Song*—he soared high above all his other vocal compositions. If in this song he complained of his fate, in another song, *The Outcast,* he reflected his own helplessness against the habit which was demoralizing him:

> "Look not on her to despise her,
> Turn not away from her so.
> They are more blessed and wiser
> Who can forgive, for they know."

There were three to four weeks at a time when he was excused from his office because of "domestic reasons." For Modest had delirium tremens despite being only twenty-five years of age. His fellow Balakirevs felt that the situation was too delicate for them to handle, so his brother Philaret took Modest into his house to live with him and his family.

8

IN THE SPRING OF 1865 NICOLAY RIMSKY-KORSAkov returned home after two and a half years at sea. The twenty-one-year-old naval officer had almost lost his interest in music despite the facts that during his first year away he had worked further on his First Symphony, and that Mili had kept him well informed of all the happenings at home through constant correspondence. Nor had he learned to love the sea and his naval career. Now he was stationed at Kronstadt, supervising the dismantling of the clipper *Almaz*. He read a great deal, occasionally played the piano, and even seriously considered entering the Naval Academy for advanced instruction. However, in September, when he was transferred to Petersburg, he again joined Balakirev's group, and this time in earnest. Mili was delighted to have him back, for of all the members of his group, Nicolay's nature was the most suitable for his molding.

The Mili of 1865 was different from the Mili of 1859. He had gained in experience and knowledge, and his qualities as well as his defects and shortcomings had become more pronounced. But the foundation of his nature remained unaltered. He had the same proclivity for new inspiration, new ideas. However, the process of nursing these to their full growth was too slow to keep pace with the rapidity with which they came to him and, his nature being what it was—nervous, impatient, and irritable—he still sought talent which he could impregnate with his ideas and which could bring them to fruition. Yet in his despotic way he wanted that talent to be his image and only his. He tried this with all his disciples, but not one survived the treatment.

"This," Borodin related later, "is why Mili spends so much time with Miloradovich, Pomasansky, and even that 'bottle of perfume' Sherbatchev, when Mili himself knows that nothing will come from Sherbatchev. He has completely ruined Pomasansky, whom he forced to compose a Russian symphony in which nine-tenths are by Mili himself because he would not give him the slightest freedom to do as he wanted to. The overture, by the way, is very good, very interesting in its thematic material, and excellently orchestrated . . . but it is all Mili, Mili, Mili, and there is not a trace of Pomasansky's personality in it."

Gussakovsky had proved unreliable, jumping from one idea to another without finishing any one of them. He was a chemist and geologist, and to make a musician out of him, despite his remarkable talent, demanded more patience than Mili possessed. "Gussakovsky should die," Mili used to say. "That is the best thing he could do." And Gussakovsky did die as a very young man—though not because Mili said he ought to.

Mussorgsky balked almost from the beginning of his studies with Mili. He was much too slow for him, and far too argumentative. It never occurred to Mili that perhaps his method had some flaw somewhere—it never does to any despot. He just attributed it all to Modest's being an idiot.

It is one thing to lead a group by guiding its members toward a goal, each one producing the work that reflects his own personality, and it is quite another to demand that each man's work reflect the leader's personality. Of them all, Rimsky was the one who possessed in his youth that feminine quality which was willing to receive Mili's seeds, so to speak, and nurse them into a full creation of his image.

The group was now definitely classified. As the leader, teacher, and performer of their works, Balakirev stood at the head, along with Cui, composer and ardent propagandist of their music. On the other hand, Mussorgsky, Borodin, and Rimsky were regarded by these two as pupils who needed criticism and advice. Mussorgsky's compositions—as for instance his *Scherzo* and the chorus from *Oedipus*—had to go through Mili's hands. Borodin had only begun on his serious work. He knew 'cello, oboe, and flute, but in orchestration he needed Mili's constant help. Rimsky was a mere beginner, and though he was thought to have a talent for orchestration, his piano-playing had become an object of derision. Whenever he sat with Mili at the piano to try out his composition four-hands, Mili would break off, saying, "Never mind. I'll do that later. I will play it with Modest."

It gave Nicolay such a feeling of inferiority that he played much worse than usual in Mili's presence. Rimsky took piano lessons and spent hours practicing Czerny and Chopin études, but he never told Mili this. In fact, at that time he led what he called a "double life." In the circle of friends whom he knew as a naval officer and through his brother Voin, he was regarded as a man with no particular qualities for a naval career but as a well-educated musician and a very able pianist; while Mili's group considered him not particularly intelligent, not well educated, and, though talented musically, definitely not a pianist.

Cui thought Balakirev a great conductor, and in his articles even compared him to Berlioz (whom at the time he had not yet heard); he considered him expert in symphonic form and orchestration, and a brilliant pianist equal to Rubinstein. Mili, on the other hand, thought that Cui had little grasp of symphonic and musical form and none of orchestration (he was willing to orchestrate his works for him), but that he was a master in vocal and operatic music—though even here he treated indulgently many elements that did not meet his approval, and with a kindly wink attributed them to Cui's French origin.

The group's daily occupations were just as varied as their personalities. Cui taught at the Military Academy and at his private preparatory school. He became an expert in fortification warfare and wrote many treatises on this subject. Often he was sent by the Academy on various missions in connection with his scientific military work, and even abroad. Mussorgsky was just coming to himself again under the beneficial influence of his brother's home life. He lost his job and had to look for another. Of them all, he probably was the only one whose mind was completely occupied by the idea of composing. Borodin proceeded calmly with his work in chemistry, lecturing at the Academy of Medicine and at the Academy of Forestry. He was an ardent advocate of the admission of women to higher education, and he constantly attended meetings with Madame P. N. Tarnovskaya and Professor M. M. Rudnev, who planned the School of Medicine for Women. Rimsky spent his days at the office in the Naval Ministry.

Yet despite the diversity of their characters, talents, and personal lives, they were bound together by one idea. As their powers matured, they soared high into that sphere of pure beauty to which all must look up. Thus the Balakirev group resembled an eagle—not the two-headed emblem of the Russian monarchy, but an eagle with five heads and one heart: Russian national music.

And Vladimir Stassov was the pulse of that heart. Now he had a group of young enthusiasts who were burning with the desire to create new music, even if their first attempts were not yet crowned with complete success. It was he who, years before, after Mili's enthusiasm for Rubinstein's *Ocean* Symphony, unearthed from the archives of the library the old Russian legend of Sadko. Mili had toyed with this for a while, then turned to Cui, who in turn had offered the idea to Mussorgsky—they did not as yet have a seaman in their midst.

Stassov, at the beginning of his acquaintance with Modest, felt like thrashing him for his constant brooding on mysticism, and told Mili not to waste any time on him. But after hearing Modest's *Detskaya* and *The Outcast,* his estimate of Mussorgsky's talent was reversed. Now, with a triumphant look, he would nod at everyone in the room as Modest approached the piano, lean back in his chair, "Oh" and "Ah" in his rich bass voice as soon as Modest lifted his hands to strike the first chord of his composition, and be ready to shout "Hurrah" while Modest was still playing.

But Cui realized that Stassov's enthusiasm alone would not bring them success. Despite all their discussions and plans, there was not a single major work ready for performance, and Cui considered this a period of appalling standstill.

Therefore Rimsky's return was most welcome, since he brought with him enough fragmentary material to complete his First Symphony. Balakirev set to work on it at once, for nothing could have been better for the concerts of his Free Music School than the performance of a serious work representing the group. In October, Rimsky wrote the necessary Trio for his Scherzo. In the same month the whole symphony was reorchestrated and rewritten, and in the following month they had copied out the parts.

Here is what Cui reported on the 24th of December, 1865:

"The audience listened to the symphony with growing interest. After the Andante and Finale the composer was called to the stage, and when he appeared—a naval officer, a youngster of twenty-two—all who believe in a great future for our music, all who don't need an authoritative name (sometimes mediocre) in order to admire a beautiful work, all these got up as one man and hailed the young beginner composer with thunderous applause.

[99]

"The music of young Rimsky-Korsakov is characteristic in its simplicity, health, free development of ideas, and varied form. If one has to compare his music, it stands very close to Glinka's. . . . Rimsky-Korsakov has written the first Russian symphony."

9

AMONG THOSE WHO APPLAUDED RIMSKY-KOR-
sakov's debut was Glinka's sister, Ludmilla Shestakova. After the
death of her only child, the little Olga, Ludmilla had retired completely from the circle of musicians which had surrounded her
after her brother's death. Now she opened the doors of her hospitable home to all whom Stassov brought to her. She became
a second mother to Modest, who soon grew so accustomed to her
that he considered her home almost his own and always had to
return, as he said, like a cat. She met Rimsky, Borodin, and Cui;
as for Mili, he had been her constant visitor even during her retirement. She fed them tea and listened to their wild arguments
till way after her bedtime.

Almost ten years had passed since the death of her brother
when the Directors of the Czech Opera in Prague decided to produce *A Life for the Tsar* (they also wanted to give a performance
of *Russlan and Ludmilla*), and approached Ludmilla to ask her to
recommend a suitable conductor. Naturally, she suggested Mili
Balakirev.

The sudden interest shown by the Czechs stirred the group to frantic excitement. At last a Russian opera was to be performed on the European stage, an opera by Glinka, whose importance in musical history seemed to exist only in the memory of his devoted friends and the Balakirev group. Stassov did not miss the opportunity to write a long article in the Petersburg *Gazette,* announcing the forthcoming event with the exaggerated enthusiasm so characteristic of him.

"On Friday, February 3d (our style), a big festival is scheduled in Prague. The whole town will be at the theater, where the date of Glinka's death will be commemorated by the first performance of his *Russlan and Ludmilla.* During one of the *entr'actes,* a festive ovation will be organized before Glinka's bust, which will be on the stage, and after the performance the bust, covered with wreaths, will be taken in a triumphal procession to the National Czech Museum, to be placed alongside other busts of the great public statesmen and men of Slavonic culture. . . . This is the way other nations celebrate men whose names should shine in our history. They are even ahead of us in celebrating our own great people!"

So began Stassov's long article, in which he described in full detail the forthcoming performances, and not missing the chance to compare and criticize those given at home.

"At last Glinka's operas will be given a decent presentation and conducted by a man who loves and understands Glinka's music. Let us await the news of the first performances in *A Life for the Tsar* and *Russlan.* This should be a vivid reproach to us, a mark on our conscience."

The news was not long in coming. "The performance of *A Life for the Tsar* given by the Czechs was the most horrible nightmare I ever saw. . . . The Board of Directors are a bunch of pigs," Mili wrote to Stassov.

When Balakirev arrived in Prague, he discovered that *A Life for the Tsar* had already been given by the Czechs on their own, and it was some time before he saw the second performance. Though warmly received by a few people who were interested in Russian music, Mili was certainly not treated as an ambassador. He discovered that the press was antagonistic to the whole project, that the Polish group, prodded by the Germans and bitter against the Russians since the quelling of the 1861 uprising, had come out with the statement that the whole enterprise was instigated by the Moscow government, which had spent thirty or fifty thousand rubles (they weren't exactly sure which) on it. And they managed to bring Moniuszko to Prague to conduct his own operas at the same time.

The facts that Mili had only a month's time in which to prepare *Russlan,* and that he was a complete stranger—that is, he knew neither the orchestra nor the singers who would be cast for the performance—did not seem to concern anyone, and the Directors let him just sit and wait because they had other operas scheduled.

Existing on bread and tea—such food as he could afford in Czech restaurants tasted "like the rump of fish cooked in crow's milk"—he lived in a cold room with a stove which smoked but gave no heat. Three pictures on the wall—one of the Grand Duchess Amalia in a décolleté dress clutching a flower to her bosom, a portrait of Emperor Franz with a nose looking like an old shoe, and one of a pretty Turkish girl holding a little boy in her lap with an inscription about the elements of friendship, touching but not illuminating—were the only witnesses of the sad days and troublesome nights when bedbugs crawled out of their homes in the picture frames and mercilessly attacked Mili's body; though he thought they might have been his compatriots— he might have brought them with him in the little basket in which he had carried the tambourines as well as other articles and bits of clothing from Ludmilla's storeroom for the forthcoming productions.

As for the political significance to which the Poles referred, only the small Catholic church, and the Karlsplatz, and the little, dirty, broken-down, gloomy street on which John Hus had started on his road to martyrdom, visible from Mili's window, could have reminded him of politics. Mili was far more concerned over the fact that, after running all over the city, he could not find a decent piano. The tone of the piano at his lodgings would turn the milk sour in his landlady's kitchen, and after he played one in the music shop the Czech proprietor refused to rent it to him because Mili's fingers were too strong.

He spent his evenings going to the theater, watching the actors and listening to their voices. Their best soprano squeaked "like a clarinet played in the frosty air," and their best tenor "should have been sent off to Siberia to hard labor." Mili pleaded for a good cast, but Smetana,* the Czech conductor, did not heed him. He wanted him to make new cuts in the score. Mili used his pencil while talking to Smetana, and his eraser when alone.

Czech students called on him and, addressing him as "Herr Professor," spoke with admiration of his collection of Russian songs. But their teachers at the Conservatory told them that the harmonization was *ganz falsch*. Mili patiently made the students sing them, and explained the natural way a Slavic melody should be harmonized. They sang as Balakirev did, and they understood him; but then they shook their heads—it was against the rules they were taught. "I am pouring out the poison of musical nihilism," Mili wrote to Modest. It was all very dreary.

At long last Mili saw a performance of *A Life for the Tsar,* and what he saw brought a cold sweat to his body. Smetana conducted. He was a Polonophile, hated Russian operas (which he considered Asiatic and Tatar), and if he had wanted to kill the performance he could not have done better. It was not so much what

* Bedrick Smetana was born in 1824 and died in an insane asylum in 1884. From 1861 to 1874 he was the conductor of the Czech National Theater. His *Bartered Bride* was a fiasco in St. Petersburg in 1870, just three years after Balakirev's trip to Prague, and Balakirev was blamed for this, being accused of having written damaging articles against Smetana. Mili never wrote anything for the press in his life.

Mili heard that horrified him—the wrong tempi and the inadequate interpretation of Glinka's music—as what he saw on the stage. It looked more like a Viennese operetta than the first Russian national opera.

Russian peasants were arrayed in a sort of mixture of Polish national dress, Hungarian Dragoon uniforms, and the Czech national costume. In the Coronation Scene, Venetian knights and representatives of the Doges opened the triumphal procession, while what looked like French troubadours and German court pages carried a canopy under which Tsar Mihail—dressed like the King of Sicily in *Robert le Diable*—marched on pompously, elegantly bowing to his people, who at the sight of him fell on their knees and stretched out their arms toward him as though to a holy picture. The Patriarch of the Orthodox Church, in the dress of a rabbi, usually marched close to Mihail, but this time, to save Balakirev's feelings, someone quickly ran backstage and sent the Patriarch out to the nearest beerhall for a drink.

When the Czechs finally got around to rehearsing *Russlan,* Mili resigned himself to the amount of work he would have to do. He had to run to the workshops where the décors were made, show the dancers how to perform "Lesginka," coach the singers, see to it that in the fourth act the illusion was given of Russlan's flying with Chernomor on a white cloud through lightning and thunder rather than looking (as they did) like just two men in tights suspended by ropes fighting in midair, and take care that the chorus should not suggest a party of drunkards at a country fair.

Mili did not know the Czech language and, as Russians do when they hear another Slavic tongue, regarded it as a caricature of his own. The different meaning of the same words amused him but more often infuriated him, for it created so much confusion that he had to use his broken German. He could not understand why the Czechs, who had managed to preserve their language, were otherwise so completely Germanized.

He communicated his misery to his friends, who gathered at

Ludmilla's to hear the news. They wrote him a humorous collective letter, but things were not funny for Balakirev, and Modest, who was more inclined than the others to put his feelings down on paper, wrote him at length.

". . . Your letter to Cui confirms what I thought—that your life in Prague is not very pleasant now, and the Devil knows it was miserable before. I confess that when you left for Czechia I thought (in fact I knew) that the gracious invitations you had received had come from a select group, which was as it should have been. But I was wrong in my judgment of the degree of influence these few had on the Czech people. It seems now that among all twofooted Czech animals one can find only three who have the right to belong to the human race. And as though just to be malicious about your arrival in Prague, Pan Moniuszko scurried there with his Catholic operas. This combination of the Polish clique and German academic stupidity is a fruit that makes one vomit. How delighted I should be if after your conducting of *A Life for the Tsar* and *Russlan* such an impression would be made on the people that all these . . . [Here Mussorgsky changes the names of the Czech composers in such a way that, though the words sound like the names, they represent something nasty in Russian: sour cream,* bad shoemaker, scoundrel, and corruption] . . . would choke on their own works—the Devil take them! However, all this is easy to say or to write, but one doesn't get anywhere that way. . . .

"Is it possible that our music has to be limited by our borders—from the west along the Baltic Sea, Prussia, Galicia, and so on, to the south on the Black Sea and so on, to the east and north—in a word, according to geography? Is it possible that among people of our own race our national music cannot be grafted? Just remember that in all Europe two principles govern music—vogue and slavery. The English import singers and produce works—both of them outrageous—but there the idea is the vogue. The French—oh well, the French have the *can-can,* and 'deliver us from Mr. Berlioz!' The Spaniards, Italians, Turks, and Greeks we can ignore. As for the Germans, the best example of their

*For instance, if the accent is put on the second syllable of "Smetana," the name would mean "sour cream" in Russian.

musical slavery is their adoration of the conservatory and routine—beer and stinking cigars, music and beer, stinking cigars and music *ins Grüne!* The German is capable of producing a whole treatise on the way Beethoven wrote a quarter-note with the tail up instead of down, and how this should have been written correctly according to the rules. Once a German recognizes a genius, he becomes his slave. He cannot imagine that Beethoven, while writing fast, perhaps made a mistake or paid no attention to such a trifle.

"This stupid and dead side of a bear's belly *mit Milch* and *süsse Suppe* is revolting enough in a true German, but it is even more revolting in those slaves of slaves, the Czechs, who refuse to wear their own physiognomy. I spin all this out, my dear Mili, because I am furious over the position in which you are placed among these dumb animals, and enraged by these Germans, Italians, and Jews, who here in Russia bamboozle our honest, open-hearted, naïve Russians. Nobody could characterize the Czechs better than you do; though you look through musical lenses, the point is the same. If you try to force me to sing (not in jest) Mendel's* songs, I will, from a soft and refined man, become a mannerless ruffian. If you try to force a Russian mujik to love any kind of putrefied German folksong, he will never do it. If you offer (not force—because you can force a German Czech to swallow Austrian spittle and he *will* swallow it) to sweeten a Czech's soul with tainted German provisions, he will sweeten it and say aloud that he is a Slav. This is how I understood the Czechs from your description, and these corpses dared to listen to a Slav's creations, dare to demand Slavic music. . . .

"People of society who do not feel those sounds which, like the memory of one's own mother or a close friend, make all the life strings in a human being vibrate, which would awaken them from their deep slumber and make them comprehend their own individuality and the yoke they bear that is gradually killing this individuality— such society, such people, are corpses. And the select members of such society are the doctors who, with an electrogalvanic current, made the members of this corpse jerk before it starts to disintegrate chemically.

"Jews are deeply moved by their own songs, which come down to

* I.e., Mendelssohn's.

[107]

them from one generation to the next. Their eyes burn with honest, not money, fire. I have myself been a witness to this. Jews are better than Czechs—I mean our own Jews, those who come from Bialostok, Lutsk, and Nevil, who live in dirty, stinking huts.

"Could one say that a Slavic sound did not touch the Slavic soul because Smetana soured a sound? A lie! He couldn't cripple the opera to such a point that it wouldn't have one live moment which would stir a living human being. Corpses sat in the theater, a corpse conducted an orchestra of corpses, and you, my dear, went to a Prague party for ghosts. One man alive among corpses! I sympathize with you, my dear Mili, in your sad position, and I should be proud of you if just for an hour you could bring these corpses to life. . . ."

This letter, though partly influenced by the fight that was coming to a climax in Petersburg between the Balakirev group and Rubinstein, expressed the chauvinistic views that were shared by Balakirev himself. But at that time it certainly was of no comfort to Mili. "Forgive me, Europe, forgive forever!" he felt like saying, and taking the first train home; but he did not yet have the money to leave on, and besides he believed in his mission as a propagandist for Russian music. He loved Glinka's music, and once he started work on *Russlan* he wrote to Cui that he considered it greater than Beethoven's Ninth. Fortunately Kubichta, a rich Czech merchant and Russophile, came to his rescue by offering him his purse, and thus saved him from financial embarrassment.

Russlan was a great success despite the fact that at the last moment the advocates of the German party stole the only score Mili had with him. He surprised them all by coaching the singers and chorus, playing everything from memory on the piano, and conducting the whole opera without a score. Mili had sent invitations to Dresden where there was a large Russian colony, but the Russians did not come because the Poles, in their campaign against the performance, threatened that no Russian would be safe that day in Prague. However, *Russlan's* artistic success was turned into a Czech political success. The young Slavophiles felt that they had shown the Germans who oppressed them that they had a strong brother to turn to.

Mili was feasted at a banquet, and the students sang choruses of the new Slavic music (Russian music, thought Mili). The festival was to have been crowned by a triumphant procession carrying Glinka's bust into the National Museum. But the German group put pressure on the local Austrian authorities, the ceremony was canceled, and Glinka's bust was quietly placed next to Shakespeare's.

Mili conducted two more performances of *Russlan*, but, despite all the praise that his conducting received in the press, the symphonic concert that he gave on his own to raise some money was badly attended, and he had to borrow from his rich merchant friend in order to get home.

Despite all the unpleasantness he had encountered in Prague, "Mili Chesky" * (as Modest, in mimicry of Rimsky's name, called Balakirev on his return) brought back with him a new interest— Slavic folkmusic. He spent hours in the library looking up and studying old Czech, Serbian, and Bulgarian songs, and even Hungarian, which he somehow considered of Slavic origin.

At this time, in the spring of 1867, the first Pan-Slavic Committee was organized in St. Petersburg and representatives from the "brethren" states were invited to attend. When they arrived they naturally got into contact with Mili Balakirev, whose name they knew and who seemed to them to be a natural cultural link in the relations between their own countries and Russia. Stassov often found at Mili's home a strange crowd of visitors—Serbs, Bulgarians, and Czechs—who were not even musicians, with whom Balakirev spent most of his time. He made them sing their native songs while he wrote them down. With unusual speed for Mili, he composed an overture on Czech folksongs, and even influenced Rimsky to write a Serbian fantasy.

While Mili was away, Rimsky had started on his own to com-

* In Russian, "Rimsky" means "Roman," while "Chesky" means "Czech."

pose his Second Symphony (*Antar*), but somehow he did not progress very far with it. What he showed to Mili, Mili disapproved of. Rimsky then composed a Serbian symphony—the first composition that he did not allow Mili to rewrite or edit. He wrote it not because he was interested in the Pan-Slavic movement, but because he was enchanted by the Serbian folksongs Mili showed him.

On May 12, Balakirev conducted a program of symphonic music, every number of which was to compliment some member of the large Slavic family. Starting with Glinka's *Kamarinskaya* to represent Russia, and Dargomijsky's *Kazachock* to represent the Ukraine, he played next his own *Fantasy on Czech Themes*, Rimsky's *Serbian Fantasy,* and even Moniuszko's *Polonaise*. The gala performance took place in a large hall bedecked with flowers, and flags of all the Slav nations adorned the galleries and boxes.

The audience greeted with applause each number that was played, and the dark fiery eyes of the southern Slavs shone as they shouted "Zivio!" and "Slava!" They felt that this music expressed their nationality and their legitimate right to independence, and therefore signified their protest against German and Turkish oppression. Mili was presented with laurel wreaths and a conductor's stick carved in ebony, of such exquisite workmanship and taste that Stassov insisted it should have been displayed at the World's Exposition in Paris.

"Let us hope," wrote Stassov in the St. Petersburg *Gazette,* "that our Slavic guests will remember how much poetry, feeling, talent, and ability the small but already mighty heap of Russian musicians has." This phrase was picked up by the press, made fun of, and repeated so often that it became the nickname for the Balakirev group. From then on they were referred to as "The Mighty Heap" ("The Mighty Five" in English).

After five years of directing the Russian Musical Society and the Conservatory which he had founded, Anton Rubinstein resigned. With him resigned almost all the members of the Board of Directors. But Kologrivov (Mili's old friend) stayed on, and through his and Dargomijsky's influence Mili was offered the post of conductor of the Russian Musical Society concerts. Thus Mili Balakirev became the virtual director of all symphonic concerts in St. Petersburg. In his appointment, the Five saw their first victory.

One of the first steps Mili took to improve the quality of the Russian Musical Society concerts was to induce the Board of Directors to invite Berlioz to share concerts with him the following season; and Cui wrote, not without glee, that the season of 1867-68 promised to be by far the most interesting yet in the history of the capital's musical life.

10

ALEXANDER DARGOMIJSKY, AFTER ALMOST TEN years of retirement, suddenly began to clean house. He had watched with the keenest interest both the development of the Balakirev group and the fight between Rubinstein and the nationalists, and had listened with appreciation to their credo in dramatic music, so close to his own. He was tired of the admirers who flocked to his musicals. The abolition of serfdom had cut his income considerably, and Alexander was not the rich landowner he had been. In 1864 his father died, and he himself felt old at hardly more than fifty. He was ill, had heart trouble, and was bitter and sad that his life seemed to have ended.

Almost simultaneously with the death of his father, another chapter in his life came to a sudden close. His friend the composer Engelhardt fell in love with Lubov Miller, Dargomijsky's pupil and his mistress for the past eight years. Dargomijsky felt that the young German woman had given him "the best years of her youth," and now, he reasoned, not without pain in his heart, it was all for the best that, since he planned to go abroad and would not be able to provide for her, she was marrying a young man with an income of ten thousand rubles.

He went to Warsaw and saw Moniuszko. He visited Vienna and Leipzig, but hated the small German towns where "there is no theater, where everyone has dinner at one o'clock in the afternoon and at ten o'clock all the street lights are put out and everything snores, and where the women are *ungeheuer*." He visited Brussels. The Belgians were the only Europeans interested at that time in Russian music, and they knew Glinka's work. Even the waiter at his hotel, said, *"M'sieu, on cause de vous; on dit que vous êtes un homme de talent."* It looked as though all the doors were open to him, but he preferred to spend his time with Fétis, the Belgian musical historian, or with a talented Belgian singer (a woman, of course), rather than to accept invitations from the powers that were.

From Brussels he went to Paris, which left him just as disappointed as had his first visit. He called it *"café-restaurants-femmes-se-promenantes."* "Of course," he said, "their feet do not smell and they do not drag their sabers on the ground to make their presence known, but art here is finished. In the theaters only cheap effects flourish. If the singer sings, the public is cold. If he yells, the public yells too." Dargomijsky did nothing in France to introduce his works, but, as Glinka had done once, he taught French girls how to sing Russian songs, regretting that their faces were not always to his taste.

His travels in Europe did not bring him the peace he had hoped for, and in the spring of 1865 Dargomijsky returned to Russia and joined the Balakirev group. His musicales took on a new aspect. He rid himself of all the "invalids," as Stassov called them, who surrounded him at his musicales. Even Dargomijsky had had enough of their flattery.

Of the old entourage he retained only a few friends, among whom the two Purgold sisters were his most intimate collaborators. Dargomijsky's friendship with the Purgold family was of long standing—he had known them since the early 1840's. The Purgolds were of German origin, with roots in Thuringia, but several generations of the family had lived in Russia and they had become completely Russified. Nicolay Purgold was the father of seven daughters and three sons. This large family, with nurses, governesses, teachers and domestic help, occupied a spacious apartment on Mohovaya Street, just one floor above Dargomijsky's. It was here that Vladimir, Nicolay's brother—"Oncle," as he was called—arranged his "artistic evenings," generally of a theatrical nature.

Although in the government service, Vladimir Purgold preferred the company of artists to that of his office colleagues, for he was an ardent music-lover, had studied voice in his youth, and had been a friend of Glinka. He had a weakness for writing plays based on incidents that occurred in his brother's house. He staged and directed these himself, choosing for the cast all the members of the family.

"The Beginning after an End," "Where to Find a Comedy," "The Arrival of the Aunt," and "Children's Masquerade-Ball"— such were his plays, inevitably marked: "The action takes place in Nicolay Purgold's home." Usually these performances were supplemented by several musical numbers—a trio from an Italian opera, or a group of Russian songs. These were chosen and presented by Dargomijsky.

The artistic atmosphere of the two homes was continued throughout the year, for when in the summer the Purgold family moved to their country place at Murino, they found themselves again the neighbors of Dargomijsky and their friends, who also liked to spend their summers there.

All of the Purgold children were endowed with talent of one kind or another, but the two youngest girls, Nadejda and Alexandra, had a more than usual aptitude for music. At first they were taught by their older sisters. However, Dargomijsky's interest in them made their parents consider their musical education more seriously, and they became pupils of well-known teachers. Dargomijsky himself was not a vocal teacher who knew how to place and develop a voice, nor a piano teacher for beginners. But his advice in interpretation and his constant preoccupation with their musical education (he played with them regularly once a week— duets, usually from his own operas, orchestral works transcribed for piano, and songs) were the paramount factors in their unusual musical development.

The young ladies were now in their early twenties and had grown, under Dargomijsky's watchful eye, into remarkable musicians. More than ten years had passed since the girls had lain on the floor upstairs in their apartment with ears pressed to the carpet, trying to catch the sounds that came from the musicales at Dargomijsky's below. The time when Dargomijsky used to say to Nadejda, "It is too bad that there is no coquetry in your playing," when he told them that every young woman should know music because it was a part of her charm—that time was far behind the years of long, serious musical study. Nadejda was now not only an excellent pianist (she studied for years with Herke, at one time Mussorgsky's teacher), but was a composer with a solid theoretical and practical knowledge of the trade given her at the Conservatory. Her sister Alexandra was a pupil of Henrietta Niesen-Salomon, and had developed into a remarkable singer with a contralto voice of wide range. The two girls were outstanding even in Russian musical gatherings where scores of young talented musicians were making their names at concerts and operas.

"Look at that severe Greek profile," Dargomijsky would whisper to his neighbor. "What innocence and purity are expressed in her face! Darling, talented girl!"

He spoke the truth about Nadejda, his favorite pupil. Alert young life sparkled in every feature of this pretty, graceful, black-haired girl, in the very attitude of her head, her arms, and her neck. A noble mind was expressed in the beautiful eyes which gazed attentively and softly from beneath slender brows. Simply dressed, she moved gracefully about the room as though in contrast with her elder sister Alexandra, a passionate, strong, self-willed nature, whose constant desire to attract and to please imparted to her so much mobility and brilliance.

In January of 1868, Dargomijsky began to write a new opera which was to embody all the principles of the new Russian school. "I am trying to do the unheard-of," he wrote to a friend; "I am writing music to scenes from Pushkin's *Stone Guest** just as they are, without altering one word of the original text. Of course no one will listen to it except my friends."

This time he meant the Five, and indeed they listened. With great pride in the old master, they gathered around him and performed the written scenes almost before the ink was dry on the paper. "Like a magician, he would pull out of his hat new fragments from his opera every time we saw him," Nadejda Purgold used to say, and it was not an exaggeration. This was one opera that Stassov had not suggested. Dargomijsky claimed it had been revealed to him in a dream, and all his friends assured him that it was prophetic.

Dargomijsky was coaching Alexandra in her part as Donna Anna, while Nadejda played the orchestral part on the piano, when he announced to them that he had arranged for a rehearsal of the scene with a young composer, Mussorgsky, to sing the part of Leporello. The two sisters were much excited when they came down from their apartment upstairs to Dargomijsky's flat on the fixed date. They had never heard of Mussorgsky, and their excitement was due merely to the prospect of a new acquaintance and of a performance before a musical authority.

Modest impressed them very much, both with his unusual looks and his manners. His singing enchanted them. He had a small but pleasant baritone voice; what charmed them was the expression, his fine understanding of all the emotional shades, and at the same time the simplicity of his interpretation, his sincerity, and his lack

---

* Dargomijsky used Pushkin's *Stone Guest,* a version of *Don Giovanni* that was different from Mozart's. The Stone Guest is the statue of the Commander, whom Don Giovanni invites to dine with him.

of exaggeration or affectation. They went home much intrigued by Modest's personality. "And it was not surprising," said Nadejda. "There was so much that was interesting, original, talented, and mysterious in him. His face looked as though it were hiding a riddle. His protruding light-gray eyes were almost expressionless, and the features of his face rather ugly, particularly his nose, which was red." (Modest told them it had been frost-bitten on parade.) He soon introduced his friends to them, and "the band of robbers," as the Purgold sisters nicknamed them, found a new home for their musicales.

The father of the two girls had died in the early 1860's and, though most of the members of the large family had dispersed, their musical life at home had not changed, for their uncle took their father's place. Besides, they lived too close to Dargomijsky.

The Five were delighted with their new acquaintances, admiring their talents. Borodin did not think that a song could be any good unless it was sung by Alexandra, and Mussorgsky called her "Donna Anna," while Nadejda was "our charming orchestra." Even Balakirev looked benevolently upon the new addition to his group—he could not deny the exceptional talents of the two newcomers. The charming atmosphere of the Purgold home, where both girls were so enthusiastic and so eager to do their part, soon made it the favorite place for the gatherings of the Five. And needless to say, the additional feminine touch was not amiss. When Ludmilla Shestakova joined their evenings she was startled by the way that Modest—so quickly feeling at home—talked to the sisters. "They are so innocent," he explained, "that they don't understand."

Thus a delightful friendship, its roots lodged deep in artistic understanding, grew up against the background of Dargomijsky's opera. "Nothing can be compared," Stassov recalled later, "with the wonderful artistic atmosphere that reigned at those small gatherings, where every member was a significant talent and brought with him his own poetic atmosphere which exists in the nature of an artist deeply interested in his work and inspired by his creation. Everyone brought his compositions or fragments of whatever he was working on. One would bring a new scherzo, another a new song, the third a part of a symphony or overture, the fourth a chorus, the fifth an operatic ensemble or score for an opera. How rich they were in poetry, fantasy, inspiration! Then the whole group would crowd around the grand piano where either Balakirev or Mussorgsky would play and accompany. And here immediately there were rehearsals, criticisms, evaluations of merit and faults, attacks and defense; and then were played or sung the best-liked compositions—the tragedies of one, the comedies of another—which further spurred their inspiration."

Dargomijsky's operatic ardor was very contagious. Just as Glinka had once suggested to Dargomijsky that he write a comic opera, so now Dargomijsky half in jest and Cui quite seriously suggested to Modest that he make an opera from Gogol's *Marriage*. Even Modest was surprised at first by such a challenge, for naturally they expected him to write it according to their conception of opera, as Dargomijsky was doing. But Gogol's novel was written in prose, and it was a real problem for Modest to set prose to music and yet retain its character. Even Rimsky, the symphonist, was inspired to start on his new work, the *Antar* Symphony, and Cui was quietly and methodically working on his opera *Ratcliff*. The pot was boiling.

The house on Mohovaya Street often resounded with the magnificent four-hand playing of Mussorgsky and Balakirev. But Mili's presence at these gatherings was not so welcome as it would once have been. Both Modest and Rimsky were drawing away from Mili's guardianship. The two younger members of the group had become very close friends since Rimsky's return. They saw each other constantly and together played and discussed their compositions, which they would not show to Mili for fear of his criticism and interference.

Modest's life in the surroundings of his brother's family seemed to have had a very good effect on his health and general mood. He was full of plans for his own future, and generously shared every new idea with his friend. It was then that he suggested to Rimsky that he compose *Sadko*. No one in the group was so well equipped as Rimsky to give this sea saga the salty tang of the ocean. Though in *Sadko* Rimsky still used many devices showing Mili's influence, he had definitely cooled toward Balakirev's guidance and, as he himself remarked, an evening spent *with* Mili was pleasant, but it was even pleasanter *without* him. Rimsky, nearing his twenty-fifth year, was outgrowing his adolescence. The time when he would sit and wait far into the night for Mili to finish a card game just so that he might walk home with him, or escort him all the way to Moscow for no other reason, apparently, than to be his aide-de-camp—that period was now past. Rimsky had learned that Balakirev did not value his time any more than he did anyone else's—except his own. Mussorgsky knew this, too, and felt the same way, though neither of them ever discussed it with Borodin or Cui.

Balakirev was aware of this change. Rimsky's attitude disturbed him not only because it constituted a personal affront from the young man he loved and believed so much in, but also because it was the first blow to come from one of his own disciples. It signified a certain loss of control over his own creation—in this case Rimsky—a loss that might shake to its foundation Balakirev's whole raison d'être.

By now, Mussorgsky also was completely out of Mili's reach. Philaret's affairs were in such a state that by 1868 he had lost all the Mussorgsky properties except the two small estates Shilovo and Minkino. Thus he had to move with his family to the country. Since this left Modest once again without a home in St. Petersburg, he went to Shilovo, where he lived the urban existence of a gentleman farmer. He lent a hand at the harvest, canned and even cooked jam (a dish that no Russian tea table is without), spent most of his time outdoors, and, as he said, "was brought into his stall like the rest of the cattle by sundown," meanwhile watching and studying every peasant with whom he came in contact.

Modest lived in one of the peasant huts, and it was here that, without a piano, he worked feverishly on his opera, *Marriage*. He regarded the new work as a sequel to his songs, and was so possessed by the idea of re-creating human speech in music that he trained his mind, whenever he listened to a conversation, to hear the words as a musical phrase. He wanted his characters to talk like real people in everyday life and—going a step farther than Dargomijsky—he wanted them to speak as Gogol would have wanted them to speak, with Gogol's intonations and gestures, for he believed that therein lay the true picture of Gogol's characters. He wanted to translate the intonation of the voice to music in such a manner that no one could interpret it in any other way than Gogol's.

In the autumn of 1868 he brought the four scenes of the first act of *Marriage* to his friends for judgment. Modest himself sang the leading roles and, with his talent for comedy, was no doubt in part responsible for the success of the performance. "The musical young ladies" were delighted. Dargomijsky thought that Modest had gone far beyond him and his credo. But Cui and Mili considered it a mere curiosity piece.

It pained Mili bitterly that this first crack in their relationship came at a time when he was at last in a position to actually present the new works of the Russian school. For his programs, he needed symphonic music, not operas, and Dargomijsky's sudden influence was, as far as Mili was concerned, ill-timed. He disapproved of Rimsky's enthusiasm for *Antar** and as for Modest's writing an opera on Gogol's novel—"plain mad."

Balakirev was still irritated by Mussorgsky's manner of living and his future plans. Several friends offered Modest their hospitality while he was in Petersburg, but he chose the home of Alexander Opotchinin, for the obvious reason that Nadejda

* A novel by the Polish writer Sienkovsky.

Opotchinina was living with her brother. The Opotchinin house was another center where the flower of St. Petersburg's musical and literary forces gathered. Here Mussorgsky lived in an artistic and intellectual atmosphere that ripened him and made him ready for the kind of work he was craving to do.

"Oh, how many sides there are to the Russian nature that art has not touched! Oh, how much! And so juicy and lovable. Only a part of it all have I recreated for my friends in musical pictures. If God will grant me longer life and force, I will share with my people even more important things. After *Marriage*, the Rubicon will be crossed. *Marriage* is a cage in which I am put until I become tame, and then— freedom. All this is desirable, but it isn't yet there. Yet it should be there. It is terrifying. And it is terrifying because it might happen, and it might not happen, because it isn't there yet."

At Ludmilla Shestakova's one night Nicolsky, an old friend of Modest, suggested that he write an opera about Boris Godunov. Modest dropped everything he was doing and started on the new opera, as though he had been waiting for *Boris*.

For Balakirev this was the last straw. In it he saw Dargomijsky's influence again, and—to make things worse—with his jealousy was mixed an honest skepticism of Dargomijsky's own opera. "All very clever, I'm sure," Mili mumbled to Stassov. "Probably has a lot of good things in it, but he will miss the point."

Mili might have felt, also, that he was not needed at the Purgold gatherings. He began to avoid them, and even those at Ludmilla's home. Perhaps he remembered an evening at her house when, in the presence of many guests and the Five, Stassov reproached Dargomijsky for much that was weak in his opera *Russalka*. Dargomijsky went to the piano and played just those fragments which Stassov objected to, then closed the piano with finality, as though to prevent further discusssion. Mili would hardly have dared to use his pen on Dargomijsky's score.

Fortunately Balakirev had never been so busy with concerts as he was during this season. He presented unusually interesting programs at the Russian Musical Society concerts, always including among the classical works a composition by one of the contemporary Russians, and the presence of such an illustrious guest as Berlioz added to the success of the season. But, while Berlioz received ovations and praise, the Anti-Five group criticized Mili with ever-growing violence. Petty envy, niggling intrigues, and enormous egos—these were embedded rocklike in the character of the opposition group. They had never forgiven Mili for the fact that, at the Slavic concert, he had not included any of their works, and they wrote mean, ugly, slanderous articles against him.

Inwardly on the verge of breakdown, Mili Balakirev steered through all this as though undisturbed. He brought to completion Borodin's First Symphony, which without his constant prodding would probably never have gone beyond the form of separate sketches. This symphony was presented to the Board of Directors for its trial performance, this being the rule with all unknown compositions. At first it made no impression but, through Mili's authoritative and energetic arguments, it was finally accepted for performance in January of the following year, 1869.

And while the group was anxiously awaiting Borodin's début, Dargomijsky was writing the last pages of his opera. In the autumn of 1868 his health took a turn for the worse, but that seemed only to spur his ardor in his work. He was too ill to attend the performance of Borodin's symphony, about whose fate he was just as anxious as the rest because their cause was his own. His friends promised to come to him after the concert and tell him all about it in detail.

It was late at night when, after long discussions of the performance and shaking hands with strangers in the greenroom, Borodin and his friends stopped in front of Dargomijsky's house. Though they saw a light in his apartment, they were not sure it was in his bedroom. They stood for a while, pondering whether or not they should call on him at such a late hour, then decided that it was better not to disturb the sick man, and went home.

It was a few hours later—at five in the morning on January 5th—that Dargomijsky died. In his unfinished score his friends found his instructions: Cui was to finish *The Stone Guest,* and Rimsky was to orchestrate it.

With Alexander's death died the name of his family, for he had no heirs and his sisters were married. The name lasted only one generation. Dargomijsky's father, the illegitimate son of a wealthy nobleman, had been named for Dargomijl, his mother's country estate. But Alexander's swan song, *The Stone Guest,* will live forever—if not as a permanent member of operatic programs, then as a most perfect example of the idea of modern opera. *The Stone Guest* has no additional choruses or dances, and even the two arias were written to fit the exact words of the original songs that were in Pushkin's story.

Rimsky-Korsakov's *Mozart and Salieri,* Rachmaninoff's *The Avaricious Knight,* Richard Strauss's *Salome* and *Elektra,* and Debussy's *Pelléas* and *Mélisande*—all these are the grandchildren of Dargomijsky's *Stone Guest.*

11

IT TOOK FIVE YEARS FOR BORODIN TO FINISH HIS
first symphony. "Do you compose at night when everyone is
asleep, or in the morning when the head is clear, or during the day
between lectures, or in the evenings when you are poetically inspired?" Such questions embarrassed Borodin. He blamed his
tardiness on the amount of work he was doing at the Academy—
lectures, laboratory work, scientific research, and the treatises he
wrote; but the real reason lay in the nature of his character and
his peculiar mode of life. He was a spoiled mama's boy, and
remained such all his life. He never took the first step in any
direction. He was never in a hurry to do anything. He took life
as it came; he took his work and his music the same way.

Five years had passed since the Borodins had moved into the
apartment next to the laboratory at the Academy, but it still looked
as though they had just arrived. A couch and a large wardrobe
closet had been moved into the hall where Eremey, the handyman,
and Mihailovna, the elderly family maid, were waging warfare
against bedbugs, giving the furniture a thorough scrubbing with
hot water and turpentine. In the middle of the sitting-room stood

[124]

the open trunk that the Borodins called the "foreign trunk," half-packed with summer clothes, some of which were lying on the furniture; suitcases were strewn all around, filled with unpacked books and sheets of music. Mihailovna had sprinkled the clothes in the trunk with an odorous powder, but as she could not find the key she just left it open.

The neighbors had reported that the stench from defective sewage pipes in the corridors and bathrooms poisoned the air in their apartments, and the plumbers were still at work. They had ripped the floor of the corridor below apart and dug two big holes for the pipes, but they had forgotten to bring the pipes, and because of the mounds of rubbish on both sides the maids had to go through the windows instead of the doors, and Mihailovna fell down twice and hurt herself. Complaints were sent to the authorities every two months. Though the holes were eventually covered, nothing was ever done about the pipes.

The painters left their brushes and never finished the corridor, and the carpenters were still carrying around doors taken off their hinges. Curtains were lying about waiting to be hung. A second piano had been brought in, but there was no place for it in the sitting-room, and it stood in everyone's way.

Borodin's apartment was spacious and, as has been said before, was supplied by the Academy. This fact was somehow communicated to all their friends and relatives, and they soon found their way there. Distant relatives, nieces and cousins, friends of Borodin's mother, Ekaterina's relatives and a score of her friends whom she admired and who admired her, students from the Academy who needed Borodin's help in their problems, young women who needed medical advice or help in getting a job, an old friend of Ekaterina's mother in Moscow who had brought her little girl to St. Petersburg for an operation, and occasionally a cousin of the cook or a former servant of Borodin's mother's who would drop in with the latest gossip from the country—all of them used Borodin's apartment as if it were their own. "And why not?" they reasoned. The apartment was supplied by the Government, wasn't it? There was plenty of room for everybody. They came at any time of the day or night, alone or in groups, and joined everyone at the table, where tea was succeeded by a late dinner, which grew into a late supper, which disintegrated into tea again. As the day passed, they talked and gossiped and tackled every problem from the personal to the universal with a thoroughness worthy of Henry Thomas Buckle, making everything clear and settling it once and for all.

Borodin would come in from the Academy looking as though he had been posing for Raphael's *Ascension*. A Grand Duke had taken a fancy to chemistry and had begun to study with Alexander, which threw the director of the Academy into a panic. He ordered all the professors to wear their full uniforms. Borodin was wearing his "ammunition," as he called it. His epaulets shone like two suns, the sixteen buttons sparkled like diamonds, the cuffs and collar gleamed as though he were on parade. He radiated brilliance, looked every bit "His Excellency." He would start for the table, but be stopped on the way by those who had come to seek his advice or help. Or the children would interrupt him. (The Borodins had taken two little girls into the family to educate them.) They had just come from the store and wanted him to look at the mushrooms they had bought. Someone else would ask him to pet a kitten that had been hurt in an unfair fight. The Borodins had a weakness for cats, and the cats had a weakness for large families. They all had names, and their biographies were told to every guest. They roamed freely and slept on visitors' laps, on chairs, on the grand piano, even on the dining table.

When Borodin finally reached the table he would find his guests, ignoring the fact that their host had arrived, getting up from their meal, still munching unfinished bits of meat-pie or dessert and still arguing, but now about whether it was better to be a man or a woman. His mother would greet him, much upset because the addition she was building to her house would cost

7000 rubles instead of 4000, complaining that the contractor in charge had turned out to be a fraud, that he had swindled her and the architect and the workmen, and had then suddenly disappeared, that she had to look for another contractor, that she needed Alexander's advice on how to raise more money since she had pawned everything, including the silver and, to make things worse, Vasily Perzov (a painter who claimed distant kinship to Ekaterina) had settled in her home where he had been living for three weeks on her bounty, that he had finally decided to take a room for himself and his son, but that his wife Cleopatra figured that she could just as well stay with relatives in either St. Petersburg or Moscow and that, as her brother Ispalatovsky insisted, of all her relatives, Cleopatra preferred the Borodins. . . .

While Alexander drank glasses of tea like a good Russian, losing count of the number, his brother Yonya,* who had left his job because he could not get a transfer to the south and who stayed with them now and then, would bring in a letter from Dmitri (his other brother), who needed immediate help because he wanted to be transferred to the western provinces where salaries were higher. While correcting a mathematical problem for a student, gently shielding the papers from the cat Vaska, who tiptoed on the table between glasses and plates filled with food, Borodin's sensitive ear would catch the gossip of the guests who whispered that Kirivirurkin was not satisfied with just courting Glafira but that he actually had seduced her and that they had been living together for three months, and that besides, he was having an affair with her mother at the same time, that Elizaveta Zinina had returned to her husband because she lost all her money when she started business on her own, etc., etc.—all suddenly drowned by someone who pounced on the piano and, with both feet on the pedals, gave vent to his suppressed desires.

Not even in his study did Alexander get any privacy. No one

* Nickname for his brother, Evgeny Feodorov.

bothered to ask him whether he was busy, or to keep the door shut while he was working on scientific treatises which had to be copied and corrected and made ready for publication. The fact that his papers and books on the desk were submerged under gloves, sweaters, hats, and magazines which his visitors dropped there as they came in, or that his drawings, sketches for songs, and parts of his symphony were used by Mihailovna in the kitchen to cover jars of sour milk or line cat-boxes did not seem to worry him as long as his two newly acquired objects were still visible on the desk. These were a lighter he liked because he did not need to use matches and "it didn't stink," and a gadget for making carbonated water—"a very pleasant object with which one can make all sorts of fizzy drinks." Both objects were the Government's property and belonged to the Academy, but Alexander thought he might as well bring them home because they were of no use in the laboratory.

Ekaterina had more than one thing wrong with her health. The climate of Petersburg was not good for her lungs, and it also depressed her and she easily gave way to melancholia and general gloom. She was afraid of catching colds, typhoid, and cholera. She was terrified of thunderstorms and dark nights. In her house she dreaded uneven ceilings, flies, cockroaches, and burglars, and outside she was afraid of dogs, horses, cows, chickens, sparrows, mujiks, drunk or sober, peasant women, and little boys. She hated all the students, musicians without jobs, and Borodin's relatives who infested their apartment. Yet she could not bear to be alone. She surrounded herself with all sorts of old women who sat knitting and chatting while she reclined either on her own bed or on a couch in the sitting-room or in Alexander's study, reminiscing and complaining to them while smoking one cigarette after another. She suffered from asthma, due to the stench from the sewage pipes and complete lack of ventilation, developed insomnia and roamed all night through the apartment, stumbling over chairs and the bodies of sleeping guests who, like the cats, slept wherever they found a bed or a couch that could be turned into a bed, or just dozed on chairs in the corridor or on the stairs. She had long since turned day into night, and of course completely prevented any normal schedule on her husband's part.

But Alexander loved her, and in order not to hurt her feelings he arranged his life the best he could. He never knew whether they had already had lunch or dinner, or whether they were going to have it, and if so at what time. Sometimes he ate two dinners, and sometimes just three soft-boiled eggs.

Ekaterina did not like him to wash naked in the morning, to walk about the bathroom without any clothes on, or to use the face towel on his body. She told him to cut his nails, and not to sing aloud or whistle as he walked from one room to another, not to take such big bites while eating that he choked, not to put so much lemon in his tea, not to press it with his spoon. . . .

Borodin's eyes were sensitive to light, and he could sleep only in a very dark room or by putting a piece of dark cloth over his eyes. Noise kept him awake and he liked to cover his ears with blankets, but Ekaterina insisted that he use only the sheet. However, she did not have much occasion to nag him about his sleeping habits because either she was up when he went to sleep, or one of her relatives or visitors got ahead of him and took his bed. Then he would hunt up a pillow and an old blanket or heavy shawl and sleep either on the couch in his study or in the sitting-room.

Despite his robust constitution, Borodin was constantly ill. Nothing very serious was the matter with him. If he did not have a cold he had boils, or toothaches that swelled one side of his face, or such stomachaches (*"locus minoris resistentiae"*) from eating roast goose with cabbage at Cui's (*"c'est si peu français"*) that he could roll on the floor. And when he was so weak that he was incapable of doing anything sensible, when his head was splitting, and his eyes and nose were running so that he needed his handkerchief every two minutes, then, with compresses around his head, he would sit at his piano in an overcoat because the rooms were cold (the stoves had not been cleaned and they smoked), and compose.

Alexander was no better off when Ekaterina would suddenly declare that her asthma bothered her so much and her nerves were in such a state that she could not stay in the house another moment, that she must go to her mother's in Moscow, where she could be quiet and where the climate was dry. Alexander would be left with the elderly maids, Mihailovna and Dunyasha, and Eremey, who was drunk because he was getting a new job, and with guests who hadn't noticed that their hostess had left. His mother would come for dinner and then stay for three or four days. Anushka (now Anna Timofievna) the peasant girl whom years ago his mother had kept in the house as a lightning-rod for his youthful passion, moved into the apartment while waiting for Alexander's mother to give her away to Svyatenko, the bridegroom, who would come to Borodin to ask for "money . . . or poison." Mihailovna was always asleep when she was needed because, after Eremey took his new job at a war factory, she regulated the meals according to his hours; and besides, she said she was not going to work so hard now—the neighbors were astonished that she could combine the jobs of cook and maid. Alexander did not feel like ordering the servants and planning the housekeeping, and so he allowed all these people to do as they pleased. He took most of his meals with his friends, sometimes returning home only to get a fresh shirt.

He was lonely without Ekaterina. He could not sleep well because the house suddenly seemed like a cold cellar to him. At night he felt happy if he could hear someone walking in the corridor, or the floor creak, or—as when the pipes blew up—the plumbers clattering and hammering, working at night so as not to disturb anyone in the daytime. He remembered a German book he had read while still a bachelor, *"Über das Unglück allein zu sein und besonders allein zu schlafen,"* a work which "should have received a prize from the Academy of Happy Spouses." Tortured by insomnia, he reflected that Eve actually was created so that Adam should not be lonely sleeping in an empty Paradise— empty because, except for Adam, there was nobody there but sexless angels and beasts. On the other hand, after she had been created, it was easy to understand that Adam often could not sleep just because he had Eve. So it was a problem.

When he had a vacation from the Academy, he would join Ekaterina in Moscow. His mother-in-law loved him and, with her culinary enthusiasm, gave him no peace. He was engulfed by the troubles of Ekaterina's family: her sister was having financial difficulties, and her sick brother was losing his eyesight and should have been operated on. Besides all this, he had to be patient with Ekaterina. This time Anna Kalinina was the cause of Ekaterina's worries.

While visiting Lodizhensky (an amateur musician who tagged onto the Balakirev group) at his country place at Tarnovo, the Borodins met his sister Anna, or Anka, as she was called. She was then just about twenty, married to Nicolay Kalinin, a rough, peasantlike landowner with a not-too-large fortune. Anka was a good-looking, musical, and very exalted young woman, deeply interested in social problems, the freedom of women, and science, as was the vogue of the day—or perhaps just to please Borodin. She fell in love with him. At first Ekaterina treated the whole affair as one of many infatuations of which her husband was so often the object. But this time Borodin himself seemed also to be interested. And Anka was not the passive type that requires encouragement.

Ekaterina was in Moscow on one of her periodic visits to her mother's when Borodin heard through Lodizhensky of Anka's sudden return to Petersburg from her trip abroad. From the alarming letters Lodizhensky had received from his brother-in-law, it seemed that Anka had been not at all well, that she had developed some kind of nervous fits similar to epilepsy, that

[131]

strange bumps appeared on her skull, that she suffered from sudden attacks that paralyzed half of her body, and had terrific headaches and pains in other parts of her anatomy. Anka, the letter said, was very anxious to come to St. Petersburg, and ten days later the Kalinins settled themselves there for the winter of 1868. Anka got better, but very slowly. She still fainted at the slightest provocation, had nervous fits which were now complicated by hallucinations, had no appetite, and suffered from loss of sleep.

Her manner toward her husband had undergone a marked change: he had become intolerable to her. But Nicolay himself, sensitive to her coldness, grew unusually gentle and attentive, fussed around her to make her happy, tried to fix up a little laboratory for her, and wanted to engage a young student to coach her in chemistry and physics. All this only exacerbated Anka. However, as soon as Kashivarova (a young woman doctor and friend of Borodin's whom Anka consulted) had forbidden her all sexual relations (at least for the time being—they were painful and revolting to her) and assured her that there was no danger of her having any children for some time, Anka began to cheer up.

Borodin saw Anka constantly. She confided all her woes to him, and he in turn wrote every word of their talk to Ekaterina, it being his habit to write her letters in minute detail about everything he did. Though he assured Ekaterina that Anka's attitude toward them both had not changed in the least, he told her in the same letter that Anka must either leave Kalinin or die, that Kalinin was terrified by the prospect of the former, that he was still jealous of Shchiglev (Borodin's former schoolmate) though the affair had been terminated long ago, that he did not suspect "the other" (Borodin meant himself), and that *his* only worry was lest Kalinin become aware of the change in Anka's feelings. For some time Ekaterina had suspected the real reason for the depression that Borodin complained of in every letter. Though he told her "everything," he somehow failed to mention to her the letters he was receiving from Anka. And Anka wrote him seventy, all told, in three languages. Now when Borodin mentioned her name and her return to St. Petersburg, Ekaterina easily guessed the true reason for Anka's sudden return and her hysterical behavior. She felt that she was entitled to know more definitely about the whole affair, and told him so in her letter. Here is what Borodin wrote in reply:

*"Confidential:**

"At first I decided not to write to you about my state of depression and my meeting with Anka—not from lack of sincerity but for fear that it might trouble you and affect your health. Now I see that this wasn't right because I let you allow your imagination to run away with you and picture things as far worse than they really are. While I was in Moscow the sight of your suffering, my taking care of you, my physical weariness, the continual need for a pretense of gaiety, the wheedling on my part—all this covered up my depression. When I returned to Petersburg where I didn't have to control myself for any reason or anybody, it took possession of me more than ever. I used to go to bed at eleven o'clock and wake up at four and even three in the morning. I tried to work at the laboratory. I even tried to work at my music. Nothing helped. There was only a deadly loneliness and gloom. And now I will turn to Anka.

"Last week on one fine day a bell rang very loudly. I opened the door. It was she. First of all she asked about you. Then she said that she had come to Petersburg alone because her husband had to go to Moscow on business for five days. Then we greeted each other and kissed, but very cordially, without any passion, as I kiss . . . [Borodin mentions a few names of casual friends]. And here I remarked that she had changed a great deal, become much thinner, although her face expressed real happiness. I invited her into my study and offered her some tea because she was very cold. But she refused and, as happens in such cases, started to talk, graphically but not consecutively, about her life, her sufferings, and so on. When she finished, I felt it neces-

* Borodin's letters were usually read by Ekaterina's family, and therefore he marked "confidential" whatever he communicated to her personally.

sary to put our relations on definite and solid ground, and therefore unloaded all the statements and arguments that I had thought of and prepared long ago, just in case. I spoke very quietly, but in a positive tone, though not without inner excitement; my head was burning and my eyes were often full of tears. My hands were cold as ice, in fact so much so that A. saw this and with fright asked me, 'What's the matter with you? Are you ill? You have a fever?' I told her that it was all nothing, and then started to unload more arguments—something about fraternité. But here she interrupted me and said with annoyance, 'For heaven's sake! Why do you tell me all this? I know it all myself. And do you think it makes any difference to me whether I am your sister or your daughter? I know that I am happy with you and that I was unhappy without you. I don't demand anything from you, and I have no hope of anything.' Then she looked at me with gay clear eyes, wrinkled her nose, took my hand and passionately kissed it, adding, 'You are so good!' I tried to protest, but she said, 'Oh, stop it! There's nothing bad in this. I have done it before in front of your wife and Shchiglev.' And here our conversation changed. We talked about you. She kept asking about you and sympathized with you, regretting that she had brought you so much unhappiness, and added that the sole reason for her decision to go abroad was your peace of mind, but that, now that she had to stay against her will, she was really very happy. Then we talked about little trifles—about Porovsky and Shchiglev and so on.

"Soon Hlebnikov and Yonya and—imagine!—Shchiglev came in. He must have been surprised to see A. in my home! When they left, A. asked me to take her to 'Belle-Vue' where her sister lived. When I saw that she had only a light shawl with her, I put your little gray woolen blouse on her, and we left. But her sister was not at home, so we stayed at the hotel and had dinner. After dinner we spent the evening with her sister, and I left her there in care of her brother-in-law, who would take her home. When I got home I undressed and went straight to bed. The unexplainable misery which used to make me walk back and forth in your garden or in our own apartment or in the sitting-rooms of our friends suddenly disappeared. Only a clear knowledge of your unhappiness remained, and a sense of guilt—

though there is really no reason for it. A few moments passed and then my old depression returned, this time like physical pain. I put my face into the pillow and wept bitterly, talking aloud to myself. 'Why isn't she my sister, my daughter, or my cousin? How happy I would be then! I could love her without bringing unhappiness to anyone.' But this annoyed me and even sounded ridiculous. But then I realized at the same time that A., no matter where she might be or what might happen to her, would never be a stranger to me. I calmed down and fell into deep sleep until nine o'clock the next morning.

"The next day, as I had arranged with her brother-in-law, we went to A.'s where we spent most of the time having lunch, playing the piano, and talking, and at two o'clock we had to go to her sister's. On the third day A., as we had agreed, came to me so that we could talk to Kashevarova, the gynecologist. Auntie [Borodin's mother] was with me. But Kashevarova didn't come and A., after waiting until three o'clock, wanted to leave, but Auntie persuaded her to stay with us for dinner. The meal was frugal but very gay. A. was very animated and happy to the nth degree and talked without stopping, and Auntie and I naturally were completely under her spell and listened to her, paying more attention to the way she spoke than to what she said. During the dinner I remembered you. I imagined your sitting with us, and here a strange, absolutely new feeling assailed me—I don't know what to call it. It was a feeling of complete contentment. I imagine that a mother must have such a feeling when all her children gather at her table and she looks at them and says, 'Here in my home everything is mine. There, outside, nothing is mine.' I even jumped from the table and ran into the next room so as not to show my excitement and the tears that had come into my eyes. After dinner we chatted and sang. A. ran about the apartment from room to room, examining every little object, talking, talking all the time, even to herself. I kept silent most of the time and watched her with the quiet look of an older brother watching his young sister just home from school.

"When Auntie mentioned N. I.,* A. threw her arms around her neck and interrupted her with, 'For God's sake, don't remind me of him! I'm so happy today. I haven't many days like this in my life. Don't

* Nicolay Kalinin.

[135]

spoil it for me!' Auntie softened and cried herself, and kissed and caressed her. . . . In the whole atmosphere there was something family-like. I felt twelve or fifteen years younger. It reminded me of the old student days when Mary was alive, and Louise.* Finally after tea, A. decided to go home, and I accompanied her.

"Next day we arranged that I would go with her to see Kashevarova, but early in the morning I received a note from her saying that N. I. expected to arrive suddenly today or tomorrow, that she was very disturbed about his coming, and that she didn't want to see Kashevarova. I suddenly felt much depressed. I imagined the rough insults that would again fall on her, and I vowed that whatever might happen, at all costs I would free her from this despot—this behemoth. For the greatest thing one can do for the person one loves is to give him his freedom. I wanted A. to belong neither to him nor to me, but only to herself. Then I would be satisfied.

"Now I feel depressed for another reason. I am sad about you. I feel guilty, though again I know no reason, for neither in Turovo nor here have I promised anything to A. that would damage your interests. I also feel sad about A. It's the sort of feeling that hurts somewhere in my chest. It's the kind of feeling that every good father feels when he has given his daughter to a worthless man and sees her unhappy in her marriage. And at the same time I feel guilty about A.—only for a different reason, of course. For I am firmly convinced that all I need to say is one word for her to be free and happy, and that one word I don't want to say and cannot say. Here you have my naked confession.

P.S. Confidential: I visit the Kalinins twice a week. It is he who annoys me with invitations, saying that A. feels much quieter when strangers are in the house. When she is alone, she cries a great deal and is much depressed. He has started the old story—makes scenes every day which bring her sometimes to hysteria and nervous fits. A few days ago I found out about a little trick he played which almost blew me to pieces. A. is not allowed, under doctor's order, any kind of sexual relations. On the first night Kalinin began to annoy her and demand her, saying that he was a healthy man and that he [here Borodin scratched out a few words] might get a headache from repression. She

* Mary Gotovseva, his cousin, had died in about 1856, his governess Louise in 1853.

[136]

begged him to leave her alone and satisfy himself somewhere else; whereupon he said that, having a wife, he didn't think it necessary to go to any other place, that after all that was why they were married, and so on and so on until she was so hysterical that he gained his way. She developed continual headaches, vomiting spells, fever, and delirium. Then Monsieur got frightened, ran to me, and begged me to bring Florinsky and Krassovsky [gynecologists at the Academy].

"I was there yesterday, Tuesday, but she couldn't get up. Our meetings are extremely beneficial for both of us—a quiet, intimate friendship in which she finds physical and moral support, and I a great relief from my depression. Our relations are like this, and at times she *mi ha bacciato la manina,* and I don't protest. I have become used to accepting this as her gentle gesture—something that is my due. She said that when she gets well she will write you."

Alexander Borodin was a brilliant scientist and a gifted composer, but he was hardly a psychologist. He never grasped the effect his letter had on his wife. Ekaterina refused to resign herself, as other wives have done, to losing the exclusive possession of her husband, and he ignored her view—that she could not share his affection with a newcomer in his life, no matter how smugly he might rationalize his feelings.

A few days later he wrote that he could not leave Anka. It would be stupid and inhuman—stupid because she was a very young woman who might do something desperate, and inhuman because at the time she had no one but him with whom she could be frank and in whom she could find the moral support without which she would perish.

"Don't forget [wrote Borodin], she doesn't even have Shchiglev any more. You must understand that there is a great difference in my feelings for her and for you. I love you as my wife, as a mature, serious woman who, if she needs any help, would need it only because of her physical ailments; and Anka I love as a little girl, a darling, to whom I can (and I feel I should) give all the good I have, who needs my support to release her from the slavery into which she fell because of

[137]

her youth and her extremely weak nature. You must understand that she is not my mistress, not my wife, and if, according to Shchiglev, she blurted out her desire to remain abroad until I would be free,* you must understand that this was a childish hope to which she held as a little girl who didn't have the courage to realize that with her departure abroad every hope would vanish. You must remember that in our relations there is nothing sensual, nothing passionate—nothing but friendship, confidence, and warmth.

"When I am with her I am absolutely tranquil. Not a single sensual thought touches my soul. She supplies, it seems to me, what I need—a childish quality; that is to say, youth, freshness, an unformed element that is dependent on me. . . . In her company I forget all the unpleasantness, sadness, and depression that arise from the serious side of my domestic and social life. With her, if one may express it so, I rest like a father in his children's room, or an elder brother in the room of his younger sister. I love to listen to her stories, full of confidence, truth, and sincerity, which are completely devoid of any passionate or sensual thought, although she is not at all a prude. I love to look at her. I love to listen to her thin childish voice, to look at her light darling eyes, which become alive every time she looks at me. I even like to see her wrinkle her nose. Sinner that I am, I love to have her kiss my hand, which she does simply, naturally, without passion. I don't feel at these moments as a man would from the caress of the woman who loves him.

"Don't forget that from the moment of our first meeting (when we kissed each other) I never kissed her again, though I had plenty of opportunities to do so. She has the element 'de pudeur, de chasteté' to an extreme degree, which makes one forget that she is not a little girl but a woman who has had children.**

"Her feelings toward you are in the highest degree honest, and very warm. She was much touched when I told her that you dislike everyone except her. When I said that you were worried about her relations with me she was much depressed, exclaiming, 'Good Lord! I never wanted to do and have never done any harm to anybody in my life. How could my feelings toward you bring such pain? For God's sake,

* Anka apparently hoped that Ekaterina would die.
** When the Borodins met Anka, she was just recovering from the loss of a child.

go to Moscow, console her, tell her that if it is painful to her I am ready to go away so that she will not suffer. I have a right only to my own happiness, my own life, and no matter how difficult it is, let me suffer the misfortune of having attached myself to you—but not others. Remind her that she herself allowed me to love you as a brother. Am I to blame that I love you so? She ought to understand herself that when one has found such a treasure, one cannot help loving it—that in all my life I never had any thought of taking your love away from her. I don't want anything. I don't demand anything.'

"Will you, Katerinka, understand that in my feeling toward her I don't take anything away from my love for you? I give her what I couldn't give you—my love of children—that is, the element of weakness, youth, hope, and the future. Do you hear me? Don't be jealous. Don't grieve, but understand all this. . . ."

And two days later he wrote to her:

"I have just received your letter, my dove, my priceless treasure. Good heavens, how much unhappiness I have caused you! My conscience is as heavy as lead. And you ask me if I will allow you to come here! Oh, my dove, you should know that everything hurt me so that I became numb. I know that it hurts you, but do understand that it hurts me too. It is all like a dream—it doesn't seem true. I cannot believe that I could be the cause of grief to all of us, and yet it is so. If I were different, nothing would have happened. But I repeat to you, my dear, that you exaggerate. Not only would I like you to come here—I insist on it. It would be much better for you here. You will calm down, probably, when you see with your own eyes what is going on. I have explained to you the difference in my feelings toward you and toward Anka. You can see that one feeling does not exclude the other. Therefore, for God's sake, be calm.

"Today the Kalinins came to see me. They had tea and something to eat. I was in no state to be pleasant and could hardly sit through the evening. Anka saw my distress, though I didn't tell her anything about your letter. But my state of mind was communicated to her.

"You write about my happiness. What kind of happiness, when owing to oneself those who are dearest suffer, innocently suffer, without any reason? And I myself—what am I guilty of? My darling, who would think that I could bring you such grief—so much suffering? And all because you love me so! They say that it is good to be loved by everybody. What utter nonsense! It is hard to be loved by two women, even if one doesn't love them but just treasures their peace and happiness. Come here quickly, my sweet one. And why should you go to a hotel? What utter nonsense! To meet me with tears and so on—that doesn't really mean anything in this case. But for heaven's sake wire me when you leave so that I can meet you at the station. . . . My darling, please come quickly. Cry on my breast, and let me cry with you. Do you hear me? I am waiting. Come quickly.

"*P.S.* About my health—for God's sake, don't worry. I am strong as a bull. Nothing affects my health, thank God."

This sort of daily correspondence between Alexander and Ekaterina could have gone on indefinitely, since both the questions and the answers were so repetitious and led to nothing decisive. Ekaterina would ask for "a few words of love," and Alexander would go into the same detailed explanation of the difference between his feelings for her and for Anka. Ekaterina would say that perhaps he was afraid of her coming back, and he would implore her to come home. Finally she did return to Petersburg, and for a while the subject of Anka was dropped. There was enough going on in their apartment without her, with all their friends and relatives appearing like mushrooms after a rain and as though the hostess had never been away.

Besides, the time was drawing near for the performance of Borodin's symphony (which was played on the night of Dargomijsky's death), and Balakirev had asked for the parts, which had to be copied and corrected. This was a tedious job that Borodin did not relish. He sulked because his symphony had to wait almost three seasons before it could be played, and he was disappointed that it was to be performed at a Russian Musical Society concert and not at the concerts of the Free Music School. The parts were badly copied and carelessly corrected, and the musicians were much annoyed at the rehearsals by the repeated interruptions required for altering their parts, which did not correspond with the score Balakirev had at his conducting desk. The performance was sloppy, and Balakirev saved it only by captivating the audience with the élan he gave to the Scherzo. The composer was called to take a bow.

The next day Alexander Serov wrote in his column that a new symphony by someone named Alexander Borodin was played, and that the audience hissed except for a few friends of the composer's who were in ecstasy.

A month later the critics had a chance to stab again at another member of Balakirev's group. Cui's opera *Ratcliff*, which he had been writing for the past seven years and in which all the members of the group had great confidence, had at last been performed at the Maryinsky Theater in February 1869. But it was not a success, and the chief reason for its failure lay not in its extreme modernism (indeed, it was written in conventional style), but in the public's attitude toward the composer.

In his articles during the past five years, Cui had been offending the public by his criticism of their tastes and habits. He had repeatedly asked, "If one fell ill, would it be in bad taste to get cured by unorthodox methods rather than to die according to the rules?"

Cui the critic was the worst enemy of Cui the composer. When his opera was presented, a regular demonstration was organized. From her box, Ludmilla Shestakova saw men take keys out of their pockets and whistle through them.* After the performance, when someone called for the author, Cui rose in his box (as a member of the Russian Army he was not allowed to go on the stage) and took his bow while people were booing and hissing in his face.

Both the musicians and the actors liked *Ratcliff* and gave seven superb performances of it. But things went wrong at the eighth

* In Russia, whistling is the strongest expression of disapproval.

[141]

performance; the principal singer was ill, and somebody else missed his cue. Cui lost his temper. The next day, in his column, he asked the Petersburg public to refrain from attending the performance of his opera whenever it was announced. Naturally, such unprecedented behavior on the composer's part forced the management of the Maryinsky Theater to take *Ratcliff* off the repertory.

However, Borodin was not so sensitive as Cui. The public performance of his symphony had given wings to his ardor to compose. He was eager to start on a new and important work, and at one of Ludmilla's regular evenings he mentioned his desire to write an opera. The next morning while he was still asleep, Stassov, on his way to his office at the library, left at Borodin's apartment a complete plan, a "scenario," as he called it, for Borodin's *Prince Igor*. He said that he had worked on it all night, and that he would send a messenger later in the day with additional material. But what he left was such a comprehensive plan, as clear as if "one had it in his own palm," that Borodin's mind was as though afire. With an enthusiasm foreign to his phlegmatic nature, he began to study the history and all the documents relating to the epic with which Stassov and his friends could provide him. He wrote down fragments for choruses and ideas for arias, he studied old epic poems—*The Battle of the Don* and *The Battle of Mamai*—he collected original melodies, and even consulted the celebrated traveler Hunfalvi, who supplied him with songs of Central Asia. After a few months he managed to finish the first act.

Borodin was fully conscious that, from the dramatic point of view, he was unlike most of the Balakirev group. Purely recitative style was foreign to his nature and temperament and, though according to some critics he "did not handle the recitative badly," he was far more attracted to pure melody. It was plain in the first act that his opera would be closer to *Russlan and Ludmilla* than to Dargomijsky's *Stone Guest*. But Borodin's enthusiasm was nourished by a weak flame. Presently he fell back into his chaotic life, and only talked about his opera without actually working at it.

After spending the summer with his wife in the country, Borodin returned to Petersburg, leaving Ekaterina in Moscow. The same mass of work awaited him at the Academy, and the same disorder. Nothing was ready in his laboratory. There was no gas, no water, new pipes were lying all over the place, and carpenters and painters were getting in one another's way. The schedule for lectures was mixed up with the schedule for entrance examinations, which were given four times a week—the hours being so confused that Borodin would come to class prepared to lecture to students who were there to take an examination. There were endless committee meetings to work out new regulations for the Academy, and there were meetings at the Academy of Forestry. There was the work he had not finished last year, memoranda which had to be written for immediate publication for the Academy bulletin, and no less important was the news that Kekule,* in his latest paper, had touched on the same field in which Borodin had been leisurely working. Now, in order to anticipate him, Borodin had to feverishly gather together all his research work so that he could present it at the meeting of the Society of Chemists, although his paper was far from being complete.

To all this was added the lack of that indispensable adjunct of a family's happiness—money. The salaries he received from the Medical Academy and the Academy of Forestry "just seemed to go somewhere and into something"—Borodin never knew when and where. He often had to borrow so that he could send money to Ekaterina, who was always ill with fever, colds, headaches, stomach trouble, or weak lungs. She had to consult doctors constantly

---

* Friedrich August Kekule (1829-96), famous German chemist who published a paper on the theory of the constitution of benzene, which has been called "the most brilliant piece of prediction to be found in the whole range of organic chemistry."

and take treatments, and Borodin implored her not to deny herself anything. He even ventured into a few gambling operations on the stock market, but the figures looked much better when he was calculating how easily he would double his income than they did when the operation was completed. "Auntie" came back and had no money. She could not repay the 300 rubles she owed him. To save money she had spent the summer with the Kalinins at their country place, where Yonya had done some construction work. But Kalinin treated everyone in such a way that she was glad to be home, and Yonya was without a job again. Dmitri just missed getting a job at the Samsonyevsky School where there had been a vacancy for a teacher, but now neither of them could get a job because there was a new law that required even a veterinary to have a Gymnasium diploma, and neither of them had one.

The Zablotskys, old friends of Borodin's, moved in to keep him company and run the house for him. He hoped that by having someone in the house he would be able to stay at home more, do more work, and lead a more regular life. Time was flying. When Saturday came, he thought that Monday was only yesterday, and reports for the Academy and orders to be sent abroad and to local drugstores for laboratory supplies were still on his desk. He was growing older. His hair was getting thin. "I shed like a dog. No one says any more that I have a poor shock of hair; they say, 'Your bald patch is not so big,' " though he gave up using the Krankenheil soap for a pomade with phenol —"terribly messy, stinks of coal tar."

He saw the Kalinins. Anka attended the Academy and listened to lectures in mathematics, physics, and chemistry. But there was not a trace left in Borodin of last year's infatuation. Not even the fact that Anka, who had contracted an infection in her eyes, was threatened with eventual blindness, nor that Kalinin had tried to swindle her out of her personal property, awoke in him the feeling of "fatherly care" which he had felt only a year ago. Their squabbles and reconciliations bored him. He was inclined to be-

Balakirev was cordial to her Royal Highness, but kept his distance. Elena Pavlovna, on her part, never cared particularly for Mili. When she had consented to his engagement she was guided not only by the fact that at the moment there was not much choice among conductors, but also by her desire to control the stubborn band of "Balakirevs" who, with their Free Music School and their concerts, were dangerous competitors. She even invited men who sponsored the Free Music School to be on the Board of Directors of the Russian Musical Society, and thought that the mere printing of their names alongside her own would impress them enough to allow her hands to reach the controls of the Free Music School. She thought she could tame Mili, "polish him up," westernize him. It was rumored that she had suggested that he take a trip abroad for this purpose, but that Balakirev turned a deaf ear to the idea. In any case, Elena Pavlovna saw to it that he was not re-engaged for the following season.

Thus two years of comparatively safe existence (Mili received a regular salary from the Russian Musical Society) ended with the last concert in the spring of 1869, and he was left with the Free Music School (which had no money) and the prospect of teaching piano again. To add to his financial distress, his father died, leaving to him the complete care of his two sisters.

The news of the final break between Balakirev and the Russian Musical Society evoked indignation not only among the Five, but from Berlioz in France, and even from those who seemed to be usually in sympathy with the policies of the Grand Duchess. Tchaikovsky, who knew Balakirev personally very slightly but respected him for his ability, wrote an article in which he criticized Elena Pavlovna, and made it plain that he abhorred the fact that Mili should be a victim of her policies and petty jealousy.

He suggested that Balakirev come to Moscow to conduct a series of concerts. Nicolas Rubinstein, concerned over Balakirev's immediate financial needs, offered him a position at his Conservatory. Though Mili was touched by their warm interest, and the 3000 rubles a year that Rubinstein offered him was not a sum he could brush aside, he declined to become a "Professor" at the Conservatory. It was against his principles he had always preached, and he begged to be excused on the ground that he was no teacher. Though he promised to come for the concerts, and later even set a date, one doubts that he ever meant to. Instead he turned all his energy to the concerts of the Free Music School and started to prepare his programs as soon as he left the Russian Musical Society.

But the Grand Duchess was far from being satisfied merely with Mili's removal from the Russian Musical Society. She had only begun to fight him. In this petty wrangle she utilized every means at her disposal, and all her energy. To increase the student enrollment at the Conservatory and to lure pupils away from the Free Music School, she started classes for vocal students, offering scholarships and maintenance allowances, and even serving tea with sandwiches at the choral rehearsals. But, as Borodin remarked, the students of the Free Music School drank the tea and ate the sandwiches but returned for their studies to their own school.

She subsidized Alexander Serov's slanderous articles against Mili, and financed the publication of a new magazine, *Musical Season,* at whose head she put Famintzin, the music critic and arch-enemy of the Five. It was published *de jure* by Iogansen, and *de facto* by her Royal Highness. "You'll pay dearly for this, oh, how dearly," Borodin quoted from Ostrovsky's play, as he noted down how much the fight against Mili cost the Grand Duchess:

"2000 rubles to Max Zeifritz [whom she invited to conduct a charity concert, while Mili was still head of the Russian Musical Society, hoping to have him as Mili's successor in the coming season of 1869];

"5000 rubles to Ferdinand Hiller [another German mediocrity, to conduct a few concerts in the coming season];

"1000 rubles to Napravnik [the talented thirty-year-old Czech conductor who was rapidly making a name for himself, and whom she consented to engage after her failure with her own choice];

"1000 rubles to Czerny [a professor at the Conservatory who conducted the chorus through which she hoped to undermine the prestige of the Free Music School];

"3000 francs to Désirée Artôt * [for one appearance (at the first concert), which she hoped would increase the sale of tickets];

"The expense of *Musical Season* and all the other allurements, not counting the tea and sandwiches."

The Grand Duchess was in a rage when she discovered that Mili had kept his word and was ready with his first concert before her concert series began, and stormed into the Conservatory cursing everyone from the director to the doorman for their negligence in allowing such a thing to happen. When in an article she found a humorous reference to a "Committee of National Defense in the Russian Musical Society," she marked it with red pencil and sent it by courier to Baron Korf. She based her complaint on the grounds that the article would injure the school's reputation and was insulting to her personally. Wasn't she a Romanov? The same night a courier appeared at Stassov's door bringing him a request from his superior to appear *at once,* "or, if impossible, the next morning." The next day another courier came to confirm the order. When Stassov entered Baron Korf's office, he found him looking hurt and annoyed. Hardly greeting Stassov, he pointed to the article on his desk and said that the Grand Duchess had expressed displeasure over the impudent way his subordinate had dared to insult her.

* A French singer who it was rumored was at one time Tchaikovsky's fiancée.

"Have mercy!" replied Stassov. "Did I write this? How can *I* be guilty?"

The article had been written by Cui.

"Glory to God!" exclaimed the delighted Baron. "We are saved!"

"As though Europe had been saved," remarked Borodin dryly when Stassov told him the story.

On hearing of her error, the Grand Duchess dispatched a General to see General Totleben. The poor hero of the Sevastopol campaign, who had never read an article on music in his life, had to wade through Cui's sarcasms so that he could administer proper correction to the young officer. The fiery little Cui, flashing his eyes, said he was ready to offer his resignation. But Totleben valued Cui more than all the music and all the Grand Duchesses in the world, and Cui would have to be a little more careful, at least for a while. . . .

To increase the attendance at the Russian Musical Society concerts, the Grand Duchess considerably reduced the price of admission, and free tickets were given away en masse just to fill up the hall. The audience consisted of high society, the Cavalry Guard, court pages, students at fashionable schools, all those who were loyal to the court of the Grand Duchess, and all sorts of young ladies from private and select institutes with their chaperones and directresses. Low-cut evening gowns, diamonds, epaulets, and sabers glistened in the hall. The whole atmosphere reminded one of an elaborate party, rather than that of a concert hall for serious music.

The programs were chosen to suit just such gatherings. In her desire to make her concerts more successful than those of the Free Music School, and through her influence in the making of the programs, she lowered the high standard to which Balakirev had brought the orchestra. One can lower the prestige of an orchestra by making it play mediocre music, even if the execution is still on a high level. A symphony orchestra can be reduced to the status of a café orchestra, just as the atmosphere of a shrine can be reduced to that of a beer hall.

The Grand Duchess told Napravnik that he must tear out by the roots all the new tendencies introduced by Mili Balakirev. From now on, the programs were to be made up of the old German classics, with a few light numbers performed by singers like Désirée Artôt to attract her kind of audience, and closing with something like the *Marroksky* March (which one was accustomed to hear at Paul's railroad station).

Thus she was destroying Cui's painstaking work of years, by which he had tried to develop the public taste. It was against just such frivolous numbers as an arrangement for voice of a mazurka by Chopin (sung by Artôt) that Cui had been fighting ever since he started his attack on Italian operas and their coloratura effects. Even Elena Pavlovna's most ardent admirers regretted this change, but there was nothing that could be done about it. Such was her Royal Highness's command.

Balakirev's program at the Free Music School, on the contrary, presented everything that was of interest to serious lovers of music, embracing the best classical works as well as noteworthy contemporary compositions. By contrast to the *Marroksky* March, he closed his program with Beethoven's Ninth.

With every concert his popularity grew, but at each success the press criticisms took on a more slanderous tone. Three whole columns in *Musical Season* were devoted to malicious gossip and venomous slander about Balakirev. But nothing surpassed the rage of the opposition when they learned that Nicolas Rubinstein (head of the Moscow edition of the Petersburg Conservatory) had promised to appear with Mili at a concert of the Free Music School.

"Attaboy!" gloated Borodin. "Let them have it."

Cui took on the fight against *Musical Season* single-handed, but he had Stassov's help in lashing back in other ways, too, at every offense directed against Mili's activities. The slander, insult, and vilification had long since passed the bounds of censorship. Lawsuits were threatened and actually brought about.

Mili lived in a fever of excitement. He was working against odds. The Free Music School had no money. No artistic success could hold the organization together against its deficit. The attendance of his concerts was better than at those of the Russian Musical Society, but it was not sufficient, and Mili himself very often paid expenses out of the meager amount he earned by teaching. Despite all this, his exuberance and energy were at white heat.

Perhaps they were nourished by a new interest—this time in Peter Tchaikovsky. When Tchaikovsky took Balakirev's side after the latter's resignation from the Russian Musical Society, Mili sought a closer relationship with both him and Nicolas Rubinstein. While on a short visit in Moscow, just before starting his concerts in the season of 1869, he spent a great deal of time with Tchaikovsky. He saw in him another potential artist whom he could mold to his own design as he had once molded Rimsky. He was attracted by Tchaikovsky's soft, gentle, feminine personality, but probably even more by the prize Tchaikovsky would represent if he could be won from the opposition to Balakirev's camp. Mili suggested that Tchaikovsky write an overture to *Romeo and Juliet,* and when a month later, back in Petersburg, he heard from him that he had begun work on it, Mili wrote him. Characteristically he told Tchaikovsky, as if he were Mili's apprentice, exactly how to go about it. "It strikes me that your inactivity proceeds from your lack of concentration, in spite of your 'snug workshop.' I do not know your method of composing; mine is as follows: . . ." and Mili described in detail the manner in which he himself had worked when composing the music to *King Lear.* And then, as Mili was actually writing the letter, an idea came to him and he wrote four bars of it into the letter, saying: "I should begin in this style. If I were going to write the overture I should become enthusiastic over this germ, and I should

Mussorgsky

brood over it, or rather turn it over in my mind until something vital came of it.

"If these lines have a good effect upon you I shall be much pleased. . . ."

A month later Tchaikovsky's overture was nearly ready for performance, and he sent the score to Mili at the latter's request. Although very busy, Mili found time to look through Tchaikovsky's score, in which the principal and secondary themes were written in Mili's favorite keys. He sent him a letter—another typical example of Mili's instructions to his disciples or would-be disciples, and written in his own hand:

". . . as your overture is all but finished, and will soon be played, I will tell you quite frankly what I think of it. The first subject does not please me at all. Perhaps it improves in the working out—I cannot say; but in the crude state in which it lies before me it has neither strength nor beauty, and does not sufficiently suggest the character of Friar Laurence. Here something like one of Liszt's chorales—in the old Catholic Church style—would be very appropriate (*The Night Procession, Hunnenschlacht,* and *St. Elizabeth*). Your motif is of quite a different order, in the style of a quartet by Haydn, that genius of 'burgher' music which induces a fierce thirst for beer. There is nothing of old-world Catholicism about it; it recalls rather the type of Gogol's Comrade Kunz who wanted to cut off his nose to save the money he spent on snuff. But possibly in its development your motif may turn out quite differently, in which case I will eat my own words.

"As to the B minor theme, it seems to me less a theme than a lovely introduction to one, and after the agitated movement in C major, something very forcible and energetic should follow. I take it for granted that it will really be so, and that you were too lazy to write out the context.

"The first theme in D-flat major is very pretty, though rather colorless. The second, in the same key, is simply fascinating. I often play it, and would like to hug you for it. It has the sweetness of love, its tenderness, its longing, in a word—so much that must appeal to the heart of that immoral German, Albrecht. I have only one thing to say against this theme: it does not sufficiently express a mystic, inward, spiritual love, but rather a fantastic passionate glow which has hardly any nuance of Italian sentiment. Romeo and Juliet were not Persian lovers, but Europeans. I do not know if you will understand what I am driving at—I always feel the lack of appropriate words when I speak of music, and I am obliged to have recourse to comparison in order to explain myself. One subject in which spiritual love is well expressed— according to my ideas—is the second theme in Schumann's overture, *The Bride of Messina*. The subject has its weak side too; it is morbid and somewhat sentimental at the end, but the fundamental emotion is sincere.

"I am impatient to receive the entire score, so that I may get a just impression of your clever overture, which is—so far—your best work; the fact that you have dedicated it to me affords me the greatest pleasure. It is the first of your compositions to contain so many beautiful things that one does not hesitate to pronounce it good as a whole. . . . Send me the score soon; I am longing to see it."

It was just not in Balakirev's nature to realize the effect such insensitive treatment would have on the embryo of what he hoped to make his complete creation. It was this aggressiveness on Mili's part, and his constant desire to have Tchaikovsky with him when Mili was in Moscow, that made Tchaikovsky shrink away from him. He was not as attracted to Mili as Rimsky had been in his youth. He admired him, was very grateful to him for all his suggestions, and even followed them, but he disliked his company. It weighed upon him "like a stone." He particularly disliked the narrowness of Mili's views, the persistence with which he held to them, and he was shocked by his rough language.

Nicolas Rubinstein kept his word and came for his concert. The Grand Duchess was so upset that she postponed the Russian Musical Society concert scheduled for the preceding day. It was a disgrace for the Russian Musical Society not to have him on *their* program when he was in town. And when Nicolas paid her a visit, such being his duty as a member of her organization, she refused to see him.

"Baroness, I presume the Grand Duchess is ill," said Nicolas to Baroness Raden, lady-in-waiting at the court of Elena Pavlovna. "She couldn't be so small, so petty, as not to receive me because I am playing at the Free Music School!"

"And did he play!" exclaimed Borodin after the concert. "— Like a son of a bitch! The Devil only knows what it was. In his execution the Liszt E-flat Piano Concerto reached the heights of perfection. What ensemble playing! How much fire and passion there were in him and Mili! How magnificent the orchestra sounded!"

The Mighty Five, that "Invincible Band," seemed to be winning their fight against the Grand Duchess. Nicolas Rubinstein's brilliant performance of Balakirev's *Islamey* brought storms of applause and calls for the author, who was cheered with the pianist by the audience; the performance of *Islamey* signalized the growing popularity of Mili's concerts. In fact, success was flowing on a sustained crescendo, and both Cui and Stassov, in their articles, cheered the winning champion on his home stretch.

At the party after the concert, Rubinstein offered the first toast to Mili as the representative of Russian contemporary music, and at the "Slavic Concert" on March 11, 1870, he was presented with a laurel wreath while the audience cheered with deafening applause. Standing on the stage, Balakirev looked as though he were in the empyrean.

But the real Mili Balakirev—the man whom Stassov, the Five, and their friends had known—had died a month ago. Some people are born twice, they say; Mili died twice. He died when, at the beginning of the year, he first visited an apartment on Nicolaevskaya Street—when Balakirev, that proud man free from any mysticism or religious belief or childish superstition, turned suddenly and in all earnest to the guidance of a clairvoyant.

[157]

The years of unsuccessful struggle for the idea he cherished above everything else in life—the triumph of progress over stagnation, the accumulation of failures, defeats, and misfortunes in his professional as well as his private life—these had wrecked his nervous system and shaken his belief in himself. Ever since his illness during his first year in the capital, with a consequent inflammation of the brain (he had typhoid fever—everything the doctors were unable to diagnose at that time was called typhoid fever), he had been afraid that he might go insane. He had frequent headaches and, as the years went by, his irritability often broke into hysterical fits. His ego suffered from the loss of his authority over his disciples, and in Rimsky's case his pain took on the proportions of an almost personal drama. He kept no diary and now wrote few letters, and his compositions were never of a personal character, so that if there was (as some writers believe) some intense personal experience in his life at this time, it was sealed in his heart. The seed of his sudden affection for Tchaikovsky fell on barren ground. He became a hypochondriac and grew suspicious. His father's death saddened him, and added the new financial burden of the care of his two sisters.

How Balakirev met the fortune-teller and who she was remains a mystery. Except for Rimsky, Mili told nobody of the furtive visits he paid to the strange woman who seemed to have a hold on him. And even to his old friend he spoke about it unwillingly, mostly by hints and half-finished phrases, and evaded questions. He mentioned to Rimsky that she was a rather young woman with large dark eyes. The wife of T. I. Philipov, a friend of Mili's, said that she was "a real witch"; and according to Ludmilla Shestakova, who saw her once when she came to her house looking for Mili, she was a beautiful young woman who was in love with him. Perhaps she was both. At any rate, she behaved according to all the rules of her profession.

Her séances took place in a semi-darkened room, where Mili

[158]

sat terrified while she called forth images in a large mirror. How much Mili's mind was disturbed is hard to tell, for he never made it clear to Rimsky whether he himself saw the apparitions, or whether he believed the medium who, by describing the characteristics of each, made him think that she saw the Grand Duchess, Napravnik, and other members of the Board of Directors of the Russian Musical Society, simultaneously relating to him their thoughts and intentions. It is hard to imagine that the seeress limited herself to Mili's professional life, and one may easily suspect that "an evil blonde close to his heart and good dark men at a distance from his home" were added to the confusion of information. Thus, as Rimsky said, "Balakirev, who didn't believe in God, became a believer in the Devil."

Whether or not it was due to the influence of her predictions, Mili did not go to Moscow after the close of the season, but planned instead to give two performances—one at the "Manège" (stadium), a gigantic affair, and the other with Nicolas Rubinstein. Both failed to materialize—the first because of police regulations, and the second because Rubinstein's plans had been changed. Discouraged by the final financial outcome of his Free Music School concerts (there was no money left for next season), Mili decided to give a piano recital himself to raise funds for the next season. However, instead of playing in the capital or in Moscow, he chose Nijni-Novgorod, insisting that he was sure to make 1000 rubles there, without which he "might as well jump into the Neva." Perhaps the fortune-teller saw "a diamond interest in the heart's house" in her magic mirror. But Nijni-Novgorod had forgotten Mili, and the concert he gave that summer brought only 11 rubles in gross receipts. "This was my Sédan," remarked Balakirev.

It was an admission of the final blow to his self-esteem. Mili was through with fighting. The last vestige of his belief in himself had been destroyed, and the ground on which he stood, already none too firmly, had been shaken. The surrounding atmosphere of the early 'seventies served as just another goad to drive him to the pit into which he was slowly sinking.

The sudden development of the revolutionary movement, the repeated attempts on the life of Alexander II, the terroristic acts of the "People's Will" Party on the one hand and the brutality of the Government's reaction on the other, brought to an impasse many a representative of the Russian Intelligentsia. Balakirev's never too genuine liberalism was put to a further test and, as the social struggle became more strongly defined, he found himself helpless to fathom the whole meaning of life, and particularly the place of the arts in human endeavor. Music, which had once been to him a "weapon of truth," a medium of artistic realism, a social force, now became a sacred art that he planned to cultivate away from society.

"Many of the most remarkable men between the ages of forty and fifty at that time became recreants and stepped forth on a new and terrible road," wrote Stassov. It was so with Gogol.

"Don't live the way you wish to, but the way God tells you to," became the motto of Mili's life, and he accepted all the dogmas of the Russian Orthodox Church as though through them he could solve his problems. But the catastrophe did not happen suddenly. Like a fog, religion slowly enveloped his whole being and slowly removed him from his old interests and his accustomed mode of life.

The 'sixties—the years of educational and spiritual enthusiasm, when ideological differences were smoothed over by the common creative urge—came to an end. The Balakirev offspring had grown into individual creative figures and, as time passed, Mili saw less and less of his old friends. "Why should I see them? They have all grown up; they don't need me," he said to Ludmilla Shestakova.

Influenced by his close friend T. I. Philipov, a man zealous in the orthodox faith and in all church matters, Mili formed an entirely new group of friends, for the most part among the lower clergy. His surroundings soon began to resemble theirs. In a corner of every room in his apartment there were icons, and the smell of oil from the little icon lamps burning before them gently permeated the air. Mili stopped smoking and ceased eating meat. He ate only fish, and then only the kind that "had gone to sleep," not those that had been killed. He refused to wear fur coats, though he wore shoes. (The Church regulations are so full of inconsistencies that it is hard even for a fanatic to follow them.) His apartment became a refuge for homeless dogs and cats, but he insisted that they observe the Church's rules about abstinence, and was often seen carrying his large watchdog Drujok ("Friend") in his arms so as to protect its morals. Mili's compassion for everything living went so far that he would not kill even a bedbug, but carefully let it out of his window to live a free life in a happy world, always accompanying his action with the words, "Go, dearie, in the Lord, go!"

He was always either coming from matins or going to vespers, and whenever he passed a church he crossed himself. He became a great believer in the power of the sign of the cross; he crossed himself at the rumble of thunder or when he yawned; and probably he could have believed that a man who had swallowed arsenic could save his life by making the sign. He would invariably turn the conversation to religious subjects, on which he had become a very expert. He knew all the saints' names and days, and was practically omniscient on where and in what monastery any given icon was kept, and, closing such a conversation, would beg his visitor to cross himself. "Please, just for my sake, put the sign of the cross over yourself; just once cross yourself. Now, do try!" he would plead.

Balakirev's musical friends were perplexed by his odd behavior, but not one of them dared to take him by his neck and shake him out of it. Religion, curiously enough, has about it a sacrosanct aura that men reserve a special etiquette for and dare not offend. Be-

[161]

sides, with all the medley of Christian meekness and trivialities worthy of an old maid which he preached, Mili retained his usual intolerance toward those who disagreed with him. He still used the same rough language to strengthen his argument and, along with his indifference toward his old friends, managed to hurt almost every one of them.

"I must tell you," said Stassov to Rimsky and Mussorgky, "that Balakirev made the saddest impression on me last night when I saw him. In appearance he looks as though nothing were changed—same voice, same face, same figure, same words, yet— but really it all has changed, and from the old nothing is left. . . . Just imagine that from time to time there was a silence between us lasting for minutes. I tried this way and that way, from this angle and that angle, avoiding very carefully whatever might be unpleasant to him, but I thought, 'Nothing helps.' He would say a few words, and then silence again. When did any such thing happen? It has now been fifteen years that I have known him. No, this is another man; before me was some sort of coffin— not the lively, energetic, nervous Mili."

"Your lines about Mili shocked me," wrote Mussorgsky in reply to Stassov; "though I was not a witness to his state of 'freezing.' Fantastically, I imagined something dreadful. . . . Your words sounded to me like a dirge for Mili's artistic fire. Frightful! If this is real and not a passing phase, it is much too early—it is wicked *how* early! Or is it disappointment? Well, perhaps that is what it is. But where then is the manliness, where the belief in his work and in the artistic aim, which can never be achieved without a struggle? Or was the art only a means and not the aim? Diavolo! Diavolo!"

13

INDEED MUSSORGSKY HAD NOT BEEN AN EYE-WIT-ness to Mili's sudden change. The friendship between the two men, which had already cooled, suffered another blow when Balakirev showed so little interest in the beginning of Modest's new opera *Marriage*. When Modest started work on *Boris* he saw Mili only occasionally.

He lived at the time with the Opotchinins, and whether or not on account of Nadejda Opotchinina's presence in the house, Modest was very bashful about having his friends visit him. No sooner had he moved into the spacious Opotchinin apartment at the "Engineering Castle" that he lost his position in the Engineering Department and had to take another in the Department of Woods and Forests for the Crown Lands. It was the happy atmosphere with which Nadejda Opotchinina surrounded him at home that made it possible for him to work so hard, to "boil" with *Boris,* "to *be* Boris," after days of drudgery at the office where he wrote reports "to protect the Government's interests" and was "making it hot for dishonest keepers and lazy foresters." In less than a year he completed the score. And it was then that he came out of his lair. But Balakirev's scornful attitude toward his composition and his uncalled-for remarks to strangers about it hurt Mussorgsky's feelings and destroyed the last thread of the old friendship and his desire to discuss and share his latest work with Mili.

Mussorgsky now drew closer to Stassov, whose intense interest in Modest's work inspired him. He was in constant contact with Stassov while working on *Boris,* consulting him on almost every bar of the composition. He also saw a great deal of the Purgolds, at whose home *Boris* was first tried out.

But a score has a long, thorny trail to travel from the composer's desk to the stage. While waiting for an opportunity to present *Boris* to the Directors of the Opera, Modest searched Russian history for material that might be useful as a subject for another opera. This led to his even greater interest in Rimsky's opera, *The Maid of Pskov,* since the subject belonged to the time of Ivan the Terrible. Modest not only found and supplied Rimsky with texts and folk-tunes, but took a very active part in shaping the libretto with his old friend.

For the past two years, all the roads of the Mighty Five led to the Purgold home. To be sure, they gathered every week at Ludmilla Shestakova's and occasionally at Stassov's and at Cui's; but the Purgolds' was the favorite meeting place, not only because there, through the Purgolds' uncle's connections with officialdom, were to be met people close to the Directors of the Opera, but also because the two "musical young ladies" were the Five's close collaborators. Here were performed fragments and even the first sketches of Rimsky's *The Maid of Pskov;* Mussorgsky's *Boris* and every song he wrote were played here, and it was here that the final judgment was passed on every aria and song Borodin composed. Even Balakirev, who was reluctant to see his friends, came occasionally to the Purgolds' and played parts of his *Tamara,* a symphonic poem based on Lermontov's verse, on which he was working with his usual deliberation. Here Dargomijsky's *Stone*

Guest was performed after Cui had finished the last act and Rimsky had orchestrated the score, and here the plans were made for its presentation. Alexandra sang all the women parts, and Nadejda played the score, accompanied, copied, and made arrangements for everything that was written.

When in the summer of 1870 the Purgold girls went abroad, they became the accomplices as well as the collaborators of the "brigand band": they smuggled out of the country Modest's *Seminarist,* a composition that was censored in Russia. It was Mussorgsky's contribution to the fight which always raged in the press, and which excited in him a wild desire to take part in it. He created a weapon of his own by writing this satirical work in which he ridiculed the opposition. When the Purgold sisters left for Pilnitz, near Dresden, to visit their uncle, they undertook to get the score published in Germany.

But the two "musical young ladies" carried with them more than just Modest's score; years of association with the two youngest members of the group made the girls' hearts beat with more than an interest in their compositions. Unlike her younger sister Nadejda, who was only just awakening to her feeling for Rimsky, Alexandra was fully aware of being attracted to Mussorgsky, and was much disturbed. Her impetuous nature could not be held in check in her letters, while Modest chose to keep his impersonal. His envelopes were addressed to Alexandra, but he wrote to both sisters, and in a very general, chatty vein as though he were talking to them in the presence of others. There was nothing intimate in them, no hint of a personal message to Alexandra. He even complained that Nadejda did not write often enough. He gave them news of their friends, of Rimsky's going to Finland, and of his own plans to "scare" the Directors of the Opera with *Boris* in the fall—all this very casually, since (as he said) he was "the enemy of advice and the friend of genial conversation."

The Purgold girls must have had a very dull summer. They

smuggled back into Russia the printed score of *Seminarist,* published in Leipzig, and returned home with mixed feelings in their hearts. Nadejda's were recorded thus in her diary:

August 29 [1870]

"It is interesting that in the autumn (at least it is so with me) one has a sort of ferment of thoughts and desire for action. After one thinks things over and finally reaches some conclusion, there comes a desire to put it down on paper. This is the reason why I always begin my diary in the autumn. Just as in the spring one feels a fermenting of the blood, strong impulses of passion, languid longing, and desire for something—in one word, spring is the time of emotion, and autumn, on the contrary, is the time for brain-work and meditation.

"It has been almost a year since I have written my notes. I have read today what I have written, and with sorrow I must say that very little has changed in my situation and in myself except that perhaps my wings have been clipped even more. I have decided not to pursue my studies in botany to the extent of which I dreamed a year ago. This dream collapsed under the arguments against it. My only other interest seems to be music. And this opens up a new sphere for my activities. But as often happens with me, I feel that success will be impossible for me in that field. This question I shall clarify for myself later. My attitude remains the same. It is impossible for me to reach concord within myself, owing to the insufficient balance between the urge and the accomplishment, between the words and the action.

"But I will put this question aside, for I would like today to talk about something else—about Sasha.* The depression that often assails us both has never before expressed itself so strongly in Alexandra; it has now reached dreadful dimensions. I have never seen her in such a state. Her depression began to affect me because I didn't know how to pull her out of it. To my words, 'You must not let it do this to you,' she answered. 'You don't understand what is going on in me.' She is much mistaken—I understand perfectly. It is as clear to me as day. To quote Nicolay,** one could analyze her state in a few words: 'The time has

---

* The diminutive of her sister Alexandra's name.
** Nadejda's brother-in-law.

come.' She needs a husband. Yet the man for whom she could feel great passion* shows her no encouragement, but only coldness. Since she doesn't see in his attitude toward her what she would like to see, she exaggerates and accuses him of feeling almost hatred for her, says that he doesn't even like her singing, and that though he comes to our house, it is not on her account.

"This is the reason for her endless arguments with me: that I am far more attractive to him, that he comes only on account of me and our uncle, that he does not care for her opinion, and so forth and so on. It always happens that if one wants to see more than really exists, one never sees the truth, but somehow less than the truth. She accuses me of being too nice to him, and says that our relations have therefore become closer. She talks so, partly because she is irritated by him, and partly because she wants to show that she is not at all interested in him. That is, she has begun to analyze and criticize him. Much of what she says is correct, but I had to challenge a great deal of it because she now sees in almost every word, every action of his, something bad or wicked. Well, just because I don't agree, it goes on. . . . She says we have changed our roles, that I am interested in him, that I am prejudiced. . . . Now here one is helpless—all arguments are futile, such is her state.

"Actually I don't see that his attitude has changed toward either her or me. But she of course wanted it to change (and of course for the better), and even expected this after her letters to him. Since she didn't find any difference in his attitude, she now sees a change for the worse which in reality does not exist. . . .

"As for his preferring me rather than her, I think that is untrue. I should think that Sasha would suit his character and intellect much better than I would—that is, that he could fall in love with her more easily than with me. This is certain! At one time it seemed to me that he was really fascinated by her. But now, as I ponder it, I don't think this is so, unless he conceals his feelings very well and controls himself.

"I believe that he pays equal attention to both of us even though he treats us a little differently. With me, for instance, he is apt to be more serious. With Sasha he always clowns. He didn't speak to her the last time he was here, but that doesn't prove anything about his change of

* Mussorgsky.

attitude. Sasha was herself at fault; she practically avoided him the whole time.

"His reserved manner is due to his extreme pride. He never starts a conversation, but waits for someone else to begin. He wants to talk only with those who consider this a special pleasure and privilege. . . . It is the same with his other actions. Because of that extreme pride, he will never first offer to bring his new songs; though he knows what great pleasure they would give, he waits until he is asked. For the same reason he never asks Sasha to sing (though I am convinced that he appreciates her singing very highly), particularly when he comes alone. (When we are all together he has asked her; this has happened many times. Though Sasha insists that it isn't so, I remember quite well that it did happen.)

"But when he comes alone it is with the intention of performing one of his new compositions, and therefore he wants all the attention focused exclusively on him. He alone wants to fill the whole evening. In a word, it becomes clear (at least I have come to this conclusion) that the most typical characteristic in his being is his 'amour-propre.' Now that I have started to analyze him, I might as well continue. As for the opinion that he is not intelligent, as some people think, I don't agree. He has a very original mind, a very sharp wit. It is this wit, indeed, that he abuses. He does so either from his desire to show off, or to show that he is not like others. I think he likes to show off. He has too much 'pepper,' if one may express it so. 'Humor,' the nickname Sasha and I gave him (we have a nickname for each of them), I consider very appropriate, because humor is the chief characteristic in his intellect. What he lacks is warmth and softness, of which there is so much in dear 'Sincerity.'* And it may be possible that he isn't capable of being fascinated or falling in love.

"Another reason for Alexandra's depression is that she has not been singing publicly. For her it is a necessity to sing in public at such musicales as we have at home. She needs success and admiration, needs praise—not compliments, but real, true, genuine praise. I think that she was born to be in the public eye and to attract. Knowing that she fascinates others not only with her singing but also with her personality, she

* Rimsky-Korsakov.

[168]

feels very unhappy when she doesn't have the opportunity. This is why she sang so little in Pilnitza—there was no one of interest to fascinate.

"Two o'clock in the morning

"I wanted to continue today about Sasha, to compare our two natures and characters (not a simple problem, because one shouldn't lie a penny's-worth to oneself, and that is something one seldom achieves). But I will leave this until later, and, as there is very little time, I will write down what happened today.

"Sasha's depression, I think, will now finally disappear. She already feels more cheerful today. And why? Just because Sincerity was here and later Fim Lodijensky* came.

"How sudden, unexpected, and poetic was our meeting! The moon, the balcony, the wonderful night. And how funny! . . . I had just finished singing to myself 'Come to the kingdom of roses and wine—I am waiting' and, singing this, I thought, 'How annoying it is that he hasn't come for so long,' when suddenly I heard familiar voices, and finally saw the white cap. . . . I thought that they were coming to see us, but no, they passed; finally, I guess, 'Sincerity' saw someone standing on the balcony. Well, then I asked them to come in.

"How strange it is that sometimes one somehow . . . not that one is disappointed in one's expectations, but . . . I don't know how to say it . . . one is not completely satisfied. It was that way particularly with this man when I was waiting for him. It seems to me that I now know him very well, yet when I see him I am always surprised that he is different from what I expected. And it is strange that today everything happened to the contrary—the one [Modest] who was going to make Alexandra happy and cheer her up made *me* happy. Anyway, I saw so little of 'Sincerity' that I didn't have time to ask about him, or tell him anything. And there was so much I wanted to tell him. 'Humor' not only didn't cheer up Sasha, but depressed her, while 'Sincerity' made me happy and will even more, I am sure, tomorrow. How good it is that I am to see him tomorrow! Today was just like a dream, so sudden and quick. Sometimes one desires to see more than is actually

* Anka Kalinin's brother.

[169]

true, yet one sees only what is true and this doesn't seem to be enough. I see things as they are.

"*August 31* [1870]
"If anyone, a stranger, were to read what I wrote last night, he would think, 'What nonsense!'—particularly the last phrase, which is clear only to me.

"*August 31* [1870]
"Late in the evening
"Everyone came to our home who was supposed to come. I am not quite satisfied with this evening. It is because I am not satisfied with myself. Oh, this unbearable feeling which always interferes!

"And it is all so strange. I talked a great deal with 'Sincerity,' but it seems to me that I didn't say what I wanted to say, and not the way I wanted, and not all I wanted to say. I don't know myself what I want!

"'Humor' was very charming today. He speaks so well, so cleverly, particularly when he is in his best vein. And he sang so well. I cannot understand his attitude toward Sasha. I think she interests him, and that he thinks her a fascinating, mysterious, capricious, yet strong character. [Later Nadejda Purgold changed this to:] He knows her well—just as she is, but is he capable of falling in love, of being fascinated. . . . I don't know. He is so self-centered, with such a terrible ego.

"*September 3* [1870]
"Late at night
"What shall I write about last evening? Everything was so wonderful, so wonderful—it happens very rarely. It was much better than last Monday. Nothing interfered with my free enjoyment of 'Sincerity's' music. Yes, I am more and more sure that his music is somehow closer to me than 'Humor's'; it has something irresistibly attractive and warm about it, and at the same time it has the grandeur of great beauty. I felt so happy, so gay.

"When I listen to some of my favorite pieces of his, I feel an inner rapture that I cannot control but must express with a gesture, a movement, a word. The one who has in him this spark of God should be a thousand times happy! From today's conversation with 'Sincerity,' I convinced myself again that he is very intelligent and is not so limited

[170]

as many think. . . . It is seldom that one feels as easy, as comfortable, as with 'Sincerity.' His presence never disturbs me. On the contrary, I become more free, more daring. He is so charming, and is probably a very honest and good man. I could never say that I feel as free in 'Humor's' presence; he disturbs me.

"It has been a long time since I have felt so strongly what I played. After *Goldfish** and *I believe that I am loved,*** I felt chill and it was some time before I became calm. Perhaps some people would find it strange that one could feel so intensely while only playing the accompaniment, but it does happen to me, and I feel so wonderful at these moments. How can one express such happiness in words?

"*September 23* [1870]
"In the morning

"How unhappy I am for what I said above about Korsinka [Rimsky-Korsakov]. I didn't analyze him well. It was all wrong, and not at all what I wanted to say. And why did I insult him about his intellect? It isn't at all as it seems at first. And now I am almost convinced that one could influence him in this, and I think that if he were in the society of well-educated and intelligent men—but not musicians—he would develop other interests than music. However, God should guard him from losing his musical friends, and yet he needs the other kind.

"But what made me happy is that since our return [from abroad] our relations are much better than before. We are the best of friends.

"For instance, now in examining my conduct with different people I find in myself another trait—to show off not only before others, but before myself. It is strange, but it happens. It is very fascinating, for instance, for one to imagine oneself's being in love and even letting others see it. Yet this should never really happen. One should always analyze one's relations with others, and one should be careful not to show one's feeling, whether true or false. It is lucky that Korsinka is such a rare person that no matter what one tells him, no matter how much foolishness one might repeat to him, no matter how badly one might behave, nothing evil will come of it because—I'd stake my life on it—he would never repeat it, never tell, nor imply it with one word.

* By Balakirev.
** Rimsky's song, composed in 1870 and dedicated to Balakirev.

[171]

He would behave like a noble, intelligent man. But not all are like him, and one could say that there are no more like him. Yes, truly there aren't, there aren't! . . .

"I confess now that once before I displayed my feeling for 'Power,'* which I cannot say was completely in my imagination (at one time it was very sincere and true), yet it was of the kind that, had I used a little restraint and wanted to control it, would have disappeared. Therefore it couldn't have continued, such feelings are never of any duration, and I am happy that now I can confess this to myself.

"*September 24* [1870]
"In the morning
"It seems to me that, if I consider it more seriously, this showing off comes partly from the fact that one wants to convince himself and others that one is capable of being fascinated, capable of deep feeling and love. But of course this is silly, because if in reality it doesn't exist, why should one convince oneself and others of something that isn't there? And if it is there, then there is no point in trying to convince anybody—anybody can see it.

"Of course the first thing is not to force one's nature, to be just what one is. Not everyone is capable of love, and not all are capable of the same depth of feeling. But the quality of love and its manner of expression are of course different, just as people are different. Some love quietly and warmly, and others passionately and stormily, but the two feelings are equally strong. [Later on Nadejda added: "This is wrong. I was then too young."]

"I am of the opinion that a spark of something good and a tendency toward good lies in a human being's nature, and that this spark either develops or is smothered depending on environment. I don't believe that wicked traits are inborn. I believe that human nature is essentially good, and that man is not normally wicked. One can observe this from the fact that it is very hard to corrupt a man, because this spark of good will always break through. How often we see people in the wickedest surroundings, where they are exposed to corruption, still remaining good. Perhaps there are those in whom everything good has decayed,

* Balakirev.

but I think that even in the most damned criminal, if one would search carefully, one would find at least one-millionth of the divine spark. (The word 'divine' I don't mean in a devout sense, but in an ideal.) This is why I repeat that I don't think I am so corrupt that I could not love. How far indeed has this question taken me!

"What concerns me personally is that I am very happy right at this minute. This sincere confession to myself that I am free, that I don't love anyone—that is, that I am not in love with anyone—makes me very gay. But I do love . . . well, for instance, that same Korsinka. I am so sincerely and with all my soul attached to him, I am so deeply convinced of his goodness (if I may express myself so), that I am capable of making any sacrifice for him. Of course in this case a great deal is due to his warm feeling toward me, of which I am as sure as I am of my own towards him. I have already come to the conclusion that I cannot love without being loved. I feel so at ease, so happy, so gay in his presence. Since our return, every evening when they have all been here visiting has been so happy. For instance, last Wednesday, when 'Humor' was here, I laughed and laughed, and I accompanied on the piano with so much pleasure. Last spring I revealed too much of my feeling for 'Sincerity' and was almost caught by 'Humor.' One must be oh, oh! how careful with him! Well, he was delighted, and began to hint and joke, which was very embarrassing for me. Of course I at once tried to stop him. But it now worries me sometimes lest something unfortunate may come of it. After all, there is his friendship with 'Caustic,' * and then with that woman;** and besides, I wouldn't swear that he would not say something bad about me, even perhaps just to be mean or smart. Yet it would be terrible for me if on this account my friendship were ruined with Korsinka. We spoke only a few days ago about the impossibility of our ever quarreling.

"*September 28* [1870]
"In the evening
"Even though occasionally I feel doubtful about 'Humor,' particularly since our return from abroad, owing to Sasha's anger with him for the reasons explained before, still he is probably a good man (just like the rest of our musical friends, with the exception of 'Caustic.' "

* Cui.
** Nadejda Opotchinina.

[173]

Apparently the sisters did not realize that Modest Mussorgsky was living at the time in the arms of his romantic ideal, as it were, and that what he concealed from the rest of the world was more than just a friendship with "that woman" (as Nadejda called her in the diary), for whom Modest's every dedication and remark revealed the deepest affection and respect. Whatever may have been his attempts to solve his emotional conflict with barren logic (Nadejda Opotchinina was about twenty years older than he), they were restricted to discussions between the two. The concealment of his love was the only way to keep this world of his intact. Modest was too honest; perhaps this was the only instance in his life in which emotion made him betray his frank, straightforward, and sometimes brutally direct character. Alexandra was annoyed and confused by the sophistry in Modest's speech and action. She waited with pained amazement for a cue, but he had no intention of speaking the words she wanted to hear.

The Purgold sisters knew even less about Mili Balakirev, who came only occasionally. His religious fanaticism, his piety, were slowly putting out the fire that once burned in him. A certain apathy was evident in everything he did, but only to those who knew him very well, for he still spoke and moved with verve. Stassov called his attention over and over again to Dargomijsky's *Stone Guest,* which was almost ready to be presented except for overcoming the financial difficulties involved in the terms that Dargomijsky had specified in his will. Dargomijsky had demanded that 3000 rubles be paid for the performance rights and, according to an old law, no Russian composer could receive more than 1400. Therefore it was decided to get up a subscription to provide the sum necessary to make up the difference, and in that way help the theater to purchase the performance rights of *The Stone Guest* from Dargomijsky's heirs. Cui and Stassov wrote the articles for the subscription drive, and it was decided to give a concert to raise the funds, which Mili was to conduct. But he was lukewarm toward the whole idea, and postponed it so long that the concert never took place.

He who had once been so correct in his relations with others became so negligent that he even offended a dear old friend like Ludmilla Shestakova. He promised to go with her to a performance of *Russlan* and even asked her to get him a box; but on the night of the performance he played cards instead and chatted with one of his new friends.

On his rare visits to the Purgold home, he sometimes played his own compositions or discussed with them Tchaikovsky's *Romeo and Juliet,* in which he was very much interested. It must have been on one of those evenings, when Mili's spirit again shone bright, that an outsider like Nadejda Purgold could have been so impressed by him. He praised her suggestions for revising the closing bars of *Romeo and Juliet,* which were too loud and out of the general mood of the piece, and was very eager for her to do a piano arrangement of the overture.

> *"September 30* [1870]
> "One o'clock in the morning

"Good heavens, what happened to me last night? How can one explain what there is in this man?* It is some kind of power, some invincible terrific power, that dwells in him and draws one to him. He is extraordinary; everything lights up with a strange glow as he enters the room. Wonderful rays shine from his eyes. Just one of his gentle words means more than a thousand spoken by others. In no one, not even in 'Sincerity' whom I love so, does one feel this force, this unexplainable something that is in him and in his music. And last night he was so gentle with me, so thoughtful. What more is there to wish for? I was so happy! All the past evenings are pale compared with last night when everything was made radiant by the presence of this extraordinary man. And to such a personality Fate is so unjust. Where then is justice on the earth? But I am so full of last night's happiness that I don't want to poison it with any other thought.

* Balakirev.

[175]

"One would think I was mad—such nonsense I've written. His *Tamara* drives me insane. The last stanza about the voice of Tamara could be applied to him: 'In it were combined magic witchery and invincible power.' I should like to plumb the depths of this man's soul—look at what is there. Naturally there is nothing there but good—but *what* is there?

"*October 18* [1870]

"In the evening

"This time surely, if someone were to read the foregoing pages, he would say that they were written by an adolescent girl, and a mad one at that! Good Lord, what nonsense I have written! And yet it was sincere at the moment. At the moment! Now is it possible that my character is such that I am capable of feeling one way one moment and another way the next? No, this would be too wicked. But it is terrible that in regard to this man it always happens that if I don't see him I can calmly judge and think of him, see all his faults; but when I see him, again everything is twisted, everything goes upside-down. No, there is no doubt. There is a terrible power in him.

"However, a few days ago I heard something about him that had an unpleasant effect on me. I heard that he hates women. First of all, it is just absurd. But once I realized this, I was able to explain to myself many facts. It became clear to me at last why he doesn't want to be more friendly with us, and even backs away from it. And as I myself have no small amount of pride, this can definitely change my attitude toward him. This means that I shall never make a single step toward him to become more friendly, and certainly won't give him a chance to think that I would desire this. It annoys me just to think that he doesn't consider a woman equal to him, perhaps even feels contempt for her and regards her as a lower creature. Or perhaps there is another feeling. It might be that he keeps away from women because he is afraid of falling under their spell, realizes that a woman can be clever and sly and, if she wanted to, could control him. . . . Perhaps the woman who told me this had no basis for it. Perhaps it is all nonsense.

"*November 18* [1870]

"Yes, it is hard to keep a diary. One's mood changes so often, and one can't write it all down. And it isn't right in this respect—one tends to exaggerate a passing, momentary feeling. For instance, I cannot forgive myself for what I wrote after the evening 'Power' spent with us. I was simply in a good humor and felt very gay, and not only because of his presence. I attributed it all at the time to his personality, and I have written such drivel that one would think I was in love with him. Such nonsense! I am just as far from it as I am from the stars.

"November 21 [1870]

"Lately I have been thinking so much about our musical friends—that is, I have been analyzing them as personalities, comparing them with each other—and I decided to write down my thoughts, particularly since it seems to me that the conclusions to which I have come are substantial and will remain permanent. It is as though my eyes were suddenly opened and a great deal became very clear to me. For instance, the personality of 'Bach.' * I used to imagine far more than there really is in him. Now, first of all, I do not consider him so intelligent as I once did. I think that the comparison I made was very apt: if one takes a small piece of rubber and pulls it in all directions, it will stretch and get large; but of course it will also get flat and thin. I apply this to Bach's intellect. He knows a great deal, he starts a great many things at the same time, his interests are varied, and he talks about all of it; but in reality he is, after all, a small man. All his activities are focused on small details—little things to which he gives great importance, so that, judging by his words before thinking over what he says, one could almost imagine that he moves mountains. It is precisely his intellect that is not deep.

"This expresses itself also in his small vanity and conceit, which I didn't see before. He imagines that he is far more intelligent and more active than anyone else, that his work plays an important role in the artistic world as well as the scientific, while in reality he hasn't done anything important; and he busies and spends himself mostly on trivialities that only become more pronounced when he gives them such importance.

"In a moral sense I think he is a good man, but not particularly passionate or even warm. Besides, in his attitude toward women . . . here also a few things create an unpleasant impression.

* Balakirev had given this nickname to Stassov at the beginning of their friendship.

"As he is a frightful chatterer, he becomes annoying and tiresome. He is the kind of person whom it is pleasant to see once in a while, for he has nothing repulsive about him nor could one call him wicked. But to see him often—God forbid! [Nadejda's opinion of Stassov at this moment is different from the one she was to hold in her more mature years. Only her extreme youth could have been responsible for her misjudgment.]

"What I said about 'Humor' above was all correct. But I am not yet sure he is not capable of saying something mean about us behind our backs, of cracking a joke and giving ground for gossip. He allows himself too much freedom, and sometimes forgets himself, thinking that one may say anything as long as it is in the form of a joke. Because he wants to be different, original, not like the others, he thinks that everything will be permitted him and forgiven. His behavior the other day with Sasha, for instance, could never be excused. But as he is a little off balance, I think it was due to this rather than to any meanness in him."

In December of 1870 the Purgold sisters' mother died, and for the next few months the girls withdrew from musical life. The "evenings" at their home stopped, and they saw little of their friends. When in April, owing to Ludmilla Shestakova's kindly intervention, they resumed their musical life, they learned that Mussorgsky's *Boris,* after many months of careful consideration by the Directors, had been finally rejected.

What the Directors' committee rejected was probably the greatest conception of a people's drama ever written. In its original form it had only three acts, and the opera did not contain a single feminine character. The committee completely failed to grasp Mussorgsky's idea, and based its rejection on the grounds that some of the passages were too daring in harmony, and the fact that the opera did not have a role for a prima-donna.

Contrary to everyone's expectations (because of Modest's indignation), he listened to Stassov's and Nicolsky's advice, and immediately began to work on a second version.

"Five months have passed since I have written my notes and oh, Lord, how much I have lived through since then! A terrible calamity* fell on our home and on our family, and there were besides all my personal troubles. I don't know what to compare my present mood to, but I am sure that it is terrible, and that it is coming to a head.

"I have calmed down because he [Rimsky] is very quiet and happy, but of course it is unsatisfactory to calm oneself simply by postponing the critical outcome of a situation. From his actions and words I cannot be sure that there ever was anything.

"Oh, my Lord, how difficult it is to change a relationship with someone once it is on a definite basis! He always misunderstands me. Every change in me he ascribes to my depression, and doesn't really realize what is going on. And the more seriously I think about it, the more terrifying it becomes.

"I cannot read today. I am too disturbed by the thoughts and memories of last night's conversation. It is terrible that he is so beguiled by me that he refuses to see my insignificance. Doesn't he believe that what I said last night I meant in all sincerity? Or perhaps it wasn't entirely sincere after all, because I didn't say all that could be said in my own favor. I spoke mostly in generalities and did not use concrete, convincing facts. And they are so convincing that I am afraid to confess them to myself. This is why I haven't done it. He is such an irreproachable, clean, ideal human being that he cannot see anything bad in others. He illuminates me with his own light, and he himself, without realizing it, enjoys its reflection. It is exactly as if the sun were to enjoy the moon. This comparison struck me today, and I regret that I didn't think of it yesterday. I would have told him.

"That is a very good comparison—a good comparison of my critical ability and my musical development. He says that I have developed in this respect to such an extent that one could ask me about anything and respect my opinion. But doesn't he realize or does he forget where it

* Her mother's death.

[179]

came from? It came from his circle and particularly from himself, because I am closer to him than to the others and feel his influence more than I do theirs. Therefore it is only the reflection of a light that is well known to him. It only proves that I don't bring to the circle anything new, fresh, individual, and therefore cannot exert the good moral influence about which he speaks. Oh, how mistaken he is! How clear all this is to me, and how I would like to prove it to him. Of course I am convinced that sooner or later he will come to this conclsion himself, but it should be soon—the sooner the better. No matter how terrible it is, I believe I shall have the strength to bear it.

"Concerning Sasha he is absolutely right, and in his comparison of us he is also right. But again it is terrible that he sees me suffused in his own good, warm, soft light and therefore exaggerates. But even here one can see how sad and unreal my position is in the circle, and my influence on it. Even he can't clearly specify it. It is a sort of *moral* influence. This is a very pleasant but insignificant word, denoting a quality that one can conceive of but which is not tangible or concrete. Well, from the example that I shall now use I think it will become clear. For instance, suppose I disappeared from the circle. Well, let's say I died or something like that. My going would pass without leaving a trace. It would have no effect. Perhaps for a while it might disturb their work—well, at least it would sadden them all a little just because of our personal relationship in music, particularly Korsinka, with whom we are such friends and who, I am afraid, looks upon me as more than a friend. But as for the music, my departure would leave no trace and have no effect. But if Sasha were to disappear, would it be like that? No, it would be felt a great deal. The evenings would be destroyed, no one would be able to perform anything, and there would even be less composing done because, when one knows that one will hear one's compositions performed excellently, one writes more eagerly. And finally I am convinced that some works of Mussorgsky would have never been written if there had been no Sasha. Without realizing it, he wrote his 'Kids' [*The Nursery*] on account of her and for her, because he knew very well that no one but Sasha could perform them as they should be performed. With her interpretation she inspires others, and

[180]

with her gay, vivacious, sociable nature she brings life and cheer to everyone. She is the heart of any company.

"But I don't bring an element of gaiety or anything like it into society. Here is the true difference between us. I am very sorry that yesterday I didn't remember to tell him this illustration, which I have thought of so many times. And now even if I wanted to I don't think I will tell him, because I promised myself yesterday not to return to such subjects. It's about time that my personality stopped playing such an important role in our conversations. It is unpleasant to me and I am ashamed. What is this pride—imagining that he would like to hear such self-analysis? On the whole this is a very disturbing thing, and if I could get rid of it I would be much happier. But even here he doesn't understand me. He says that such dissatisfaction with oneself, this continuous striving for improvement, is the fate of all talented, progressive natures, and that, though on account of it they are never quite happy, the unhappiness is the good thing about it. This is probably generally true, but not when applied to me. For instance, he could apply it to himself. He says that he is not contented with a single piece he has composed; but with him that is good because it isn't just fruitless. It drives him to improvement and perfection. This dissatisfaction is generally good for talent and genius, and I count him a genius. But for mediocre natures that are not very talented, like mine, it only brings unhappiness and misery. This continual thinking and analyzing of oneself brings about a realization of one's insignificance, and the constant discord between thought and action, and the impossibility of balancing these two causes a consequent depression which sometimes leads to complete despair. First of all, it paralyzes action, chills one's enthusiasm for his work, and hinders him from progressing on the road he has chosen; and second, it has a bad side in that it makes one an egotist in the narrowest sense of the word. When one sinks into oneself, it appears to others that one is cold, and that is true. On account of it one becomes incapable of feeling the needs and unhappiness of others, cannot sympathize or help with either words or action. And this is very bad. I have become convinced that the best thing in life is the conviction that one lives for others, not

[181]

for oneself, and that one is needed by those around him if one loves them and can be of use.

"And Korsinka is such a wonderful, clean, complete human being; I shall never know another like him in my whole life, and my meeting him will forever remain for me the bright ray in my life.

"June 1 [1871]

"I am so full of controversy that at times I cannot understand myself —well, just cannot understand. Therefore it is very hard for me to write down all my changes of feeling. How revolting I sometimes am in my own eyes! I know only one thing—that I am unworthy of him, that he stands so high above me that I shall never reach his stature in my own eyes, that I am not worth one of his dear glances, not one of his darling warm smiles in which he reflects all his being and which I have never seen in any other man. Just for this darling smile I am ready . . . I don't know myself what I am ready for . . .

"June 6 [1871]

"How wonderful it was last night! How happy he made me! But what delights me is that my conscience is now clear. The problem that disturbed me, and disturbed me because I didn't dare tell him, at the same time realizing that by not telling him I would be deceiving him— this problem suddenly resolved itself in a way I could never have imagined. First of all it seems that I had not deceived him because he knew all about it. I remember that once, at the beginning of our acquaintance, I mentioned it to him, but was not sure whether he had forgotten or simply hadn't understood me. And afterwards I didn't dare to speak of it because I thought, 'If he finds out, then he will be definitely disappointed in me, will lose his faith in me and in my talent.' But apparently even though he knows about it he does not consider me a mediocrity. . . . But what is most remarkable is that yesterday he came to the contrary conclusion and began to convince me of it. . . . Basing his belief on the few facts I had told him, just by chance, he began to prove to me that I was mistaken about myself and about everything that I attribute to myself. And it is true that the feeling for tonalities [in music] in me does partly exist. One couldn't say that it doesn't exist at all, yet it probably is not well developed. I don't know whether one could develop this feeling by practicing exercises, or whether it is given only by nature. I told him that I very often make mistakes in tonalities. He remarked that that happens with everyone and even with him sometimes, particularly in certain keys. Good heavens, how many times this used to bring me to despair. It seemed to me . . ."

With the beginning of this phrase the diary comes to a close.

14

ND SO THE FEELING FOR TONALITY, THE BASIS
on which a true musical nature is founded, and which distin-
guishes it from that of a mere music-lover, seemed to become the
basis for other chords that vibrated in these two young people.
Just as Borodin's love for Ekaterina was further strengthened by
his respect for her when he discovered on one of the summer
nights in Heidelberg that she could not only recognize the tonality
of a piece played at the concert but even follow its modulation, so
now Rimsky's feelings for Nadejda became, by her admission of
helplessness, even more tender.

However, a sudden change in Rimsky's life played the decisive
role in the relations of the two lovers. Azanchevsky, the new director of the Conservatory, offered Rimsky the post of Professor
of Practical Composition and Instrumentation, as well as that of
conducting the orchestra class. Rimsky, who frankly admitted to
Nadejda that his own feeling for tonalities was a far from sure one,
and who realized that his knowledge of composition, instrumentation, and counterpoint was purely instinctive and therefore too
vague for the task of teaching these subjects to others, was not

[184]

only surprised but too embarrassed at first to accept. He knew that he was utterly unprepared, and that it would be foolish and dishonest to take the position. "To be sure," he argued, "to hear and recognize an interval or a chord is more important than to know their names, the more so as those names can be learned in a day, if need be. It is more important to orchestrate colorfully than to know the instruments, as military bandmasters know them, who orchestrate by routine. Of course, to compose *Antar* or *Sadko* is more interesting than to know how to harmonize a Protestant chorale or write four-part counterpoint, which seems to be necessary for organists alone. But it is shameful not to know such things and to learn of their very existence from one's own pupils."

But his friends urged him to accept. Even Balakirev, who had shown very little interest in their general activities during the past season, was stirred by Azanchevsky's proposal. Though it was against his principle to join a conservatory (only a year ago he had refused Rubinstein's offer), and, in Rimsky's case, he knew better than anyone his unpreparedness as a teacher, he squinted his Oriental eyes and advised him to accept. Mili was guided by his personal interest in seeing one of his own men in the enemy's camp.

Cui agreed with Mili for the same reason, and wrote in one of his articles: "It is particularly significant—this invitation to Korsakov, one of the representatives of the contemporary movement of young Russian composers. It signifies that the Conservatory relinquishes its attitude of exclusive conservatism and accepts life and progress. Such a new direction could naturally be of great benefit to our musical life."

The final decision come from Rimsky himself. Here was an opportunity to change his life radically, to leave the naval service in which he had no interest and devote his life entirely to music. To these advantages no doubt was added the hope that he could make plans for his life which included Nadejda. He decided temporarily to combine the two careers and accepted the proffered position while still remaining in the naval service, giving only part of his time to his work at the Conservatory.

Still another change took place in Rimsky's life. For years he had been living by himself in a small furnished room, spending most of his time and his summers at the apartment of his brother Voin. But in the fall of 1871 his brother's health (he had suffered for years from heart disease) made it imperative for him to go to Italy, and their mother went on a visit to Moscow. With his family gone, Rimsky felt alone. His only other close attachment was to his musical friends, and as in the past few years he and Modest Mussorgsky had grown particularly close, the two decided to throw their lot together. Since both of them received very modest salaries, they moved into a furnished room in a boardinghouse on Panteleymonovskaya Street, "up the stairs along the corridor on the right, the first door to the left."

This is the only case in the history of music in which two composers have lived together in the same room, each working on his own compositions. The usual conception of a musician as a man of temperamental idiosyncrasies and petty jealousies is such that this kind of arrangement seems not so much impossible as just ridiculous. But despite the fact that the two were diametrically opposed both as composers and as human beings, they not only did not get in each other's way, but actually benefited by such close contact. They complemented each other, both in their musical creative talent and in their technical abilities. Modest perfected Rimsky's recitative and declamatory skill, while Rimsky restrained Modest's indulgence in what he considered his sometimes warped and bizarre originality, and polished his rough harmonization and his occasionally illogical construction—in a word, made Modest's compositions sound more musically acceptable for the time.

They scheduled their work so that Modest used the piano in the morning while Rimsky either wrote, copied, or orchestrated at a desk, and Rimsky used the piano in the afternoon when Modest

Rimsky-Korsakov

went to his office. Besides, Rimsky was at the Conservatory twice a week, and Modest spent many evenings at the Opotchinins'. The two lived in perfect harmony.

Stassov would come very early in the morning while they were still asleep, wake them up, help them to get out of bed, bring water and soap and hold towels for them while they washed, help them with their socks, trousers, robes or jackets, and slippers. Then they breakfasted together on tea with sandwiches and Swiss cheese, which they all loved so much that they were called "cheese-eaters." After tea they turned to their favorite occupation: they sang and played on the piano and showed Stassov, with great pride and the suppressed excitement of a gambler who plays for high stakes, everything they had written on the day before.

Borodin would drop in and drink innumerable glasses of tea while he listened to the work they had done on their operas, *Boris* and *The Maid of Pskov*. When one of the men left, Borodin would continue his musical intercourse with the other, and await the return of whichever had had to go to his more prosaic occupation. The hands of the clock would be indicating the night hours while they thought it was still day.

Or the two friends would gaily cross the short distance that separated them from Borodin's home. Borodin was composing his Second Symphony, which he began when he gave up work on *Prince Igor*. As he said to Stassov—who was much disheartened over Borodin's abrupt acknowledgement of defeat in the face of the new problem an opera presented—none of the material for *Igor* was wasted. He used it all in the Second Symphony, and in fact, it became for him his *Prince Igor*.

Even Cui came out of his sedate, warm, family corner to take part in these musical conferences. For Cui this was almost a daring adventure, for now he was the father of one child and expecting another, and he left his home more rarely than ever. It was his curiosity about Borodin's Second Symphony and the feverish productivity of Modest and Rimsky that excited his interest.

But the harmonious life in the furnished room in Zaremba's house was interrupted for a few weeks when Rimsky received news of Voin's sudden death, and was sent to Italy by the Naval Ministry to bring his brother's body home. Much saddened, Rimsky took his leave. His life with Mussorgsky was a great inspiration in his work, he had just started his courses at the Conservatory, and above all, he was unhappy over parting with Nadejda even for such a short while. From the remarks in his letters to her—that he was thinking of her all the time, and that whenever he saw anything beautiful he wished she were there to share it with him—and from Nadejda's letters to him, in which she said that she was so happy that his mother liked her, it would be fair to suppose that the two had pledged their troth before Rimsky went to Italy.

On his return a few months later Rimsky learned that the "Invincible Band" were to embark on a very original and ambitious work for which Gedeonov, the Director of the Imperial Theater, had written a scenario, *Mlada,* based on Slavic mythology. It was to be a grandiose enterprise in four acts in which opera, ballet, and pageantry were to be combined. Gedeonov chose four members of the Balakirev group to participate and approached them through Stassov, who probably suggested the idea to him. The time for such an enterprise seemed most opportune, for since their first meeting the four men had never been so close, and the Slavic background of the subject could not have been more suitable.

The work on the four-act play was to be divided as follows: Victor Krylov, Cui's former schoolmate and his close friend, who wrote the libretti for Cui's operas, was commissioned to write the libretto; Cui, who in his *Ratcliff* had shown a conventional skill in handling dramatic subjects, was given the writing of the first act; Borodin, with his thorough knowledge of ancient rites acquired while studying material for *Prince Igor,* was to compose the fourth act dealing with pagan rites, "the apparitions of dead Slavic princes, a temple engulfed by the sea"; while Mussorgsky and Rimsky were to divide between them the second and third acts. To Rimsky was assigned the composition of "folk-wise choruses, the flight of shadows, and the appearance of Princess Mlada" (around whom the plot revolved), and Mussorgsky was to compose "the big fantastic scene of sorcery and the orgies in honor of the Black God on the hill of Triglav." Moreover, Minkus, the official ballet composer of the Imperial Theaters, was to compose the incidental ballet music. The imagination of the composers was to be given complete *carte blanche*, for financial considerations would be no obstacle, according to Gedeonov.

As usually happens in such "works to order," the four members used all the manuscripts and sketches they already had on their shelves, making the necessary alterations and writing additional material to suit the score. Though they began with their usual enthusiasm, putting aside everything they were working on at the time, they soon grew indifferent because the whole plan was too vague. Modest wrote to Stassov:

"I am ashamed to take the pen into my hand to describe 'Sagala, hush!' and other rubbish written at some time, by someone, perhaps with drunken eyes and brains—I beg you humbly to be inspired by the fumes of delirium tremens! Horrors! It is not my nature to struggle along with the irritation that some little people arouse in me, but if the cause of that which gives birth to this feeling does not disappear or is not in my power to destroy, then the struggle, from a sharp pain, becomes chronic. (The simile is quite accurate; bad temper that casts a gloom over a man's life is just a sickness, and continual relapses make it chronic.)

"The treatment of the composers of *Mlada*, as though they were hired workmen, the stupid evaluation of their efforts, the complete lack of manners in the worthy entrepreneur, have the natural (and impending) consequence of a moral fiasco in our circle—this is what troubles me. My dear friend, you know that I cannot carry any such

[189]

trash inside of me and nurse it. Therefore I am taking an active position. It is simpler, it is more direct, and it is better. I have declared (as well as I can in a clean, delicate way) to Korsinka and Borodin that in order to preserve the maiden innocence of our circle and save it from being prostituted, I will be the one who will dictate the work of our hired labor, and not the one to listen. I will ask the questions, and not answer them (all this, of course, with the permission of Korsinka and Borodin), and as for the entrepreneur, let him say what he likes."

But the ambitious enterprise came to nothing because Gedeonov overestimated his financial resources, and the four members took the composed scene-sketches and plans and used them later in other works. (Cui, who was the first to finish his assignment, used the pages he composed for *Mlada* in his opera *Angelo,* on which he was already working. Later he published the first act of *Mlada* as a separate work. Rimsky used the *Mlada* music in his opera-ballet *Mlada,* in the Andante of his string quartet, and in his opera *Snegurochka* (The Snow Maiden). What Borodin wrote, he partly used in his *Prince Igor;* after his death it was orchestrated by Rimsky-Korsakov and published as a separate work entitled "Finale from the Opera-Ballet *Mlada.*" Modest, who used in *Mlada* the music from *Night on a Bald Mountain,* worked it into a separate symphonic composition and later incorporated it in his *Fair at Sorochinsk.*)

Mili Balakirev had not been asked to participate in Gedeonov's plan, and perhaps *Mlada* would have been one of the greatest products of the combined talents of the Mighty Five had they had him as their leader in the plan—that is, the Mili of previous years, not the man whose spirit was now befogged and listless.

However, Mili's battered ambition was to be kindled once again, but in his own field of conducting. After a whole season of teaching, he suddenly dropped all his pupils and decided to give a series of concerts. Perhaps the illness and consequent inactivity of

the Grand Duchess, and the sudden death of Alexander Serov—
the arch-enemies of his concertizing activities—as well as Rimsky's
joining the Conservatory, had something to do with his decision.
Most probably, however, it was because of the marriage of one of
his sisters which, along with the income from a successful teaching
season, relieved him of immediate material worries.

This sudden turn, with its complete disregard for his financial
future, plus his fanaticism and odd mode of living, led to rumors
that he had gone insane. Even Borodin, the calmest and most
rational in judgment among the Five, suspected such a possibility,
since he remembered Mili's severe suffering from headaches and
dangerous depression. It was to Borodin alone that Balakirev
turned for suggested names of psychiatrists, and it was Borodin
alone who knew of the intensive treatments that Mili had been un-
dergoing for the past year.

"Suppose he is not insane," thought Borodin. "Is the state in
which he is at present any better than insanity? I hate to think
that Mili might finish as Gogol did. His pietism is of a suspicious
quality, and does not bode any good. And now this utter disregard
for his own economic interest! What is awaiting him in the future? It is terrifying to think of."

Stassov was becoming used to the odd behavior of his old friend.
At first he had refused to accept Mili's sudden change. With his
natural frankness and more out of concern for him than from
lack of tact, he would touch the spot most painful to Mili. "Now
how can you, an intelligent human being, how can you . . ." he
would start, trying to reason with Mili about his sudden religious
mania. But now he accepted Mili's sad state of mind.

At an "evening" at Ludmilla's, Mili—who would once, from
the moment he walked into the room, have wanted to know what
was new, who was working on what, how far they had progressed, offering his help and spurring action—now sat and said
nothing. Ludmilla tried to revive his interest in music, asking him
to finish his *Tamara*. "Well, just for my sake!" But Mili only

lifted his eyebrows and looked into space. Then, after a long pause: "If I have to finish anything, it will not be this work . . . but another . . ."

"Is it your concerto?" asked Stassov eagerly.

"No, not the concerto."

That was all he said. "He certainly is not composing something in secret," thought Stassov.

Balakirev fussed and shuffled with preparations for five concerts that he planned to give with the Free Music School. If this was the "other work" he meant to finish, he was no match for the task. The concerts were like the echo of an old trumpet call. He had lost his self-assurance and his command over the orchestra men. He did not conduct well, and the concerts had no success. On April 3, 1872, he conducted the fourth concert of the series. As the last number on the program he played the Polonaise from Modest's just-completed Polish act from *Boris*.

A Polonaise is a majestic opening to a festival, and Mussorgsky's Polonaise from *Boris*—one of the greatest works by a member of the Five—should have been the fanfare to the future success of their glorious music. Instead, it was a requiem to the once close association of the Mighty Five. This was Mili's last concert. He had to cancel the fifth for lack of funds.

Balakirev resigned from the conducting desk of the Free Music School and spent the following years in self-imposed exile. At a salary of eighty rubles a month he took a position as a minor clerk in a Warsaw railroad station on the outskirts of the city, in one of the commercial offices. Stassov wrote him later that this was no time for a man in his best years to come down from his pedestal when there was still so much work waiting for him, to "close his little shop for God knows how long," and reminded him that one should neither experiment nor trifle with talent and art. Mili's answer was lifeless and sad. He said that it had not been easy for him to leave the Free Music School, but that there would be others who could do his work, and that he would rather do honestly the job he had taken on than lower the art (of music) to that of a common trade by giving piano lessons.

It is a matter of conjecture whether one should add as one more reason for the complexity of Mili's behavior the fact that Rimsky was now completely out of his life and was starting a new one on his own. Rimsky married Nadejda on June 30, 1872. Among the few guests at the Shuvalova Church was Modest Mussorgsky, who was his best man. Three months later, Mussorgsky again served as best man when Alexandra Purgold married Nicolay Molas, who was in the government service and an amateur landscape painter.

15

"OUR DEAR DOVE, LUDMILLA IVANOVNA," MUS-
sorgsky wrote to Ludmilla Shestakova, "five years ago you succeeded in your blessed desire to join the little musical circle in
your home. You were the witness of our fiery creations, our struggles, our striving, and our fights, and your heart was always alive
with response to these fights, struggles, and fiery creations. A
great deal of good was done and you deserve a tribute, by all
rights. Bright is the past of the circle—cloudy is its present: frown-
ing days have come. I shall not blame anyone of the members for
this, 'for there is no anger in my heart,' yet I cannot refrain from
honoring the circle with the words of Griboyedov: 'Some have
departed; others, you see, have been slain.' Very sad for the circle,
and no matter how I try to shoo away the annoying flea that
buzzes the mean words, 'You fell apart,' the flea is right there with
its buzz—which is like laughter, mean, wicked laughter.

"It is up to you, my dear dove, to gather the remnants of the
self-destroyed Holy Army, to fight the Chaldeans to the last drop
of blood, in the full meaning of the phrase. There will be warriors
from whose hands you could not tear the banner, and those war-

riors will come perhaps in rags, but the rags will be their own, not taken from strangers, not in women's robes and skirts as in the Holy Army of the great executioner.

"The artist believes in the future because he lives in it. And this belief has urged me to put my donation at your feet, and to confess before you. Take my Boris under your wing; let him, blessed one, start his public struggle from your hearth.

"Mussorgsky"

So wrote Modest on July 13, 1872, two weeks after Rimsky's marriage. This was the first admission by a member of the group of the beginning of the end of their collective work. He mourned Mili's defeat, and prophesied Rimsky's departure from the group while Rimsky was still on his honeymoon.

Modest's and Rimsky's last work together was on the latter's *The Maid of Pskov,* which he dedicated "To the music circle dear to me." This opera had been written during the past three years, running parallel to the development of Rimsky's happy love-affair with Nadejda, and during those pleasant days when he and Modest lived together and consulted each other on every phrase in their scores. It was so much "their" opera that Modest played and sang all the parts from memory on every possible occasion. When Rimsky finally decided to show the opera to Napravnik, Modest helped him perform it; and when Rimsky later ran into difficulty with the censor, Modest stood by his friend and accompanied him to the censor's house where he again sang and played the whole opera. The second act suggested that the republican form of government was a good thing; and it seems that this suggestion was undesirable. There was also an old law dating from the time of Nicolas I which stated that the rulers antedating the House of Romanov (1630) might be represented on the stage in drama and in tragedy, but not in opera. ("Suppose the Tsar should suddenly sing a ditty; well, it would be unseemly," they were told.) But these minor troubles were finally overcome through Rimsky's connections in the Navy and the personal intervention of Grand Duke Constantine, brother of Alexander II. The opera was accepted for performance at the Maryinsky Theater in January of the following year (1873).

But the days were gone when Modest's and Rimsky's hearts had beaten in unison as they anticipated the success of Dargomijsky's *Stone Guest,* silently watching its mild success on February 16, 1872, at the Maryinsky Theater. It had a few more performances, and then was put on the shelf with a remark very similar to that made about Bach's *Art of the Fugue:* "It is music to study, not to play." But Modest and Rimsky still considered it a masterpiece that fully expressed their idea of modern opera.

Rimsky was starting on a new path in his private as well as his professional life. A professor's desk at the Conservatory was awaiting him on his return. This occupation was to have definite consequences for him as a musician, and Mussorgsky sensed it. Balakirev was now out of sight. Cui as a composer had never been inspired by any ideology, national or other. He wrote songs and operas, but he did not strive to break new paths for future Russian music. His strength lay in his literary propaganda for the ideas of the Five, and he lived happily within the four walls of his married life, every summer writing one act, as sure as fate, of a new opera, *Angelo,* on a medieval subject that did not interest Modest. Borodin, although he composed music on Russian themes and in Russian colors, had no definite formula or ideal in music for which he would "fight to the last drop of blood." He was, as Modest put it, "drinking tea somewhere" and leading his usual life in congenial Russian disorder. Modest Mussorgsky was the only one of the Five who still believed in what had once bound them together and made them so unselfishly happy in one another's achievements. Undeterred, he held to his course, but he felt alone.

Firm and straightforward to the point of fanaticism in all his artistic beliefs, Mussorgsky did not possess sufficient will-power to stand alone in life; he needed social intercourse, and a friendly arm on which he could lean. His very existence had to be nourished by constant communication with those with whom he could discuss and interchange ideas. "If I didn't push myself, even when not asked, into every little dispute or conversation though of the smallest interest—there would be no more Mussorgsky."

He once told Ludmilla Shestakova that if she were to read in the paper that he had shot or hanged himself, it would simply mean that he had married. Yet it was home that he needed above everything, and not the short-lived companionships with which he was forced to gratify his thirst for affection and understanding. The recent marriages of the Purgold sisters (one of them to his roommate, who of course moved out of the lodgings they shared together) sharpened Modest's sense of loneliness.

"Man is a social animal"—this saying of the philosopher Spinoza influenced the thought of the Russian intellectuals in the middle of the 19th century; and Mussorgsky was a social animal in the extreme. Since the time he had lived in the "community"— his happiest days, he said—Modest had always continued his acquaintance with men in other branches of art.

Though Stassov kept his rich life well under control and seldom mixed the groups of people with whom he associated—he had a full life at home with his own family and those of his brothers and sisters; another with his associates at the library where he worked; another with the musicians of the Balakirev group; still another with painters, writers, and sculptors whose works he promoted—he introduced Mussorgsky to all these distinct circles, for Mussorgsky was the only composer of the time who showed a lively interest not only in music but in all branches of art and knowledge, in literature, old or new, foreign or Russian, in history, astronomy, sociology, and science. He was well versed in everything that Kant, Beneke, and Locke had to say on associationist psychology; he knew the Baconian method of studying natural phenomena; he was eloquent in discussing Descartes' rationalistic theories in ethics and his belief in the supremacy of mind over passion; he was familiar with Leibniz treatises on immorality, idealism, and innate ideas, and with Fichte's *Sturm und Drang*. Therefore discussions with Modest were particularly interesting and informative, and stimulating because of his original approach to everything he read and observed.

"Despite the naïve beliefs existing today in regard to the elegant delicacy of the contours of naked Venuses, Cupids, and fauns, with and without flutes, with fig leaves or 'just as mother brought them into the world,' I declare that the antisympathetic (I mean to say antique) art of the Greeks is vulgar. The Lilliputians are urged to believe that Italian classical painting is perfection; I think it is deadly and revolting like death itself. In poetry there are two giants—vulgar Homer and refined Shakespeare. In music there are two giants—meditative Beethoven and ultra-meditative Berlioz. If one could add to these four giants their generals and field-adjutants, we should have a pleasant company. But what did this adjutant company do? Just hopped and danced on the paths that were marked by the giants. But 'very forward,' terrifying!

"And ours? Glinka and Dargomijsky, Pushkin and Lermontov, Gogol and Gogol and again Gogol (there is no one to equal him)— all great generals, and they lead their artistic armies to conquer good lands. Since their time their artistic heirs have been busy fertilizing the ground of the land they did not conquer. And the land is so rich that it doesn't need fertilizer any more.

"Darwin confirmed in me my dreams, which I approached with a sort of stupid shyness. Artistic expression of pure beauty in its material sense is the vulgar playing of children—it is the childhood of art. The finest characteristics of human nature in the mass, the continuous stubborn digging in these little-known lands and conquering them—here is the real call for an artist. 'On to new shores! Fearless through storm, shallow water, and reefs—on to new shores!'

"Man is a social animal and cannot be otherwise. In human masses just as in individual human beings, there are fine characteristics that have not been fathomed, fine features that have not been touched. To discover them and to study them in reading, observation, and speculation with all one's guts, so to speak, and to feed all this to humanity as a healthy meal which has not been tasted—this is the aim! What rapture! What real delight!

"Sculpture in white or dark is unsatisfactory. Painting, despite the richness of colors, is more or less unsatisfactory. There should be sculpture in color, and for this one would have to invent a special material that would be able to take the finest touch. If Antokolsky could do his *Inquisition* in such a medium, particularly with the right lighting, Lord, what depths would appear in his composition!"

Small wonder that the musical circles, which even Nadejda Rimsky-Korsakov had considered very limited, left Modest unsatisfied. He turned to the group of young Russian artists who, like himself influenced by the trend of liberal tendencies, were creating their own new Russian art. He became friends with Vereshchagin, Repin, Antokolsky, Gornostaev, Ropet, and Hartmann. Among them the most remarkable were Ilya Repin, who had just been awarded the Gold Medal for his painting *The Daughter of Jairus* and who later became Russia's most famous painter; Mark Antokolsky, who aroused public interest with his monumental sculptures of Ivan the Third and Fourth, the bas-relief *Inquisition,* and his statue *Christ before the People,* which later brought him Europeon fame when he received a medal for it at an exposition in Paris; and Victor Hartmann, the architect who two years before had caused a sensation in a competition for works to commemorate the event of April 4, 1866—the day Tsar Alexander II escaped assassination in Kiev—with his design for the great gate of Kiev.

In no other circle could Modest have found so much kinship in thought and belief. "He only is an artist," said Antokolsky, "who loves humanity as passionately as he loves his art—who dedicates his whole life to art for the sake of humanity. Only in such favored beings is the divine spark to be found, bright and unquenchable; and that, in art, is the one thing needful, for when the soul ceases to lend its sympathy, the death of art begins."

[199]

Mussorgsky brought into the new group the vivacity, excitement, and pathos of creation, with which he stimulated everyone. Later Repin wrote modestly that he could not understand why Mussorgsky was so attracted to him since he was not a musician, and he attributed it to the fact that Mussorgsky must have been touched by Repin's enthusiasm over Modest's musical genius, which was then far from being recognized. To Repin, Modest was a nugget from the Russian soil, and his looks reminded him of the giants in Russian fairy tales.

Thoughts and plans were fermenting day and night. Often, when Repin was visiting him, Stassov would awaken him at three in the morning and make him sit up and listen to the new plans and ideas for Modest which Stassov had discovered among old manuscripts in the cellars of his library. He often unfolded his newly discovered treasures to Repin even before Mussorgsky knew about them.

Thus under Stassov's warm patronage a new friendship grew up among Antokolsky, Repin, and Mussorgsky which Stassov christened his favorite "audacious Troika" (the traditional Russian three-horse carriage).

As it happened, in the summer months of 1872 Modest was alone in St. Petersburg. Stassov and Antokolsky were in Moscow at an exposition, and Repin was in Paris. "So here is how it is, my dear glorious shaft horse," he wrote to Repin. "Though the Troika has temporarily dispersed, still it pulls where it should pull." He was writing this while sitting in Stassov's apartment studying Repin's latest portrait of their friend and admiring the masterpiece. "He actually crawls out of the canvas into the middle of the room. What will happen when you go over it once more with shellac? What life! What power!

"The painter has known for a long time how to mix his paints and does it freely, if God has given him sense. But our brother the musician first thinks, then measures, and once he has taken

the measure he thinks some more—childhood—utter childhood
—a baby!"

"Why is it, tell me please [Modest asked Stassov], that when I listen to the conversation of our young artists—painters and sculptors—I
can follow the trend of their thought and their aims, and seldom hear
about technique, except perhaps in case of necessity? And why, when
I listen to our musical brotherhood, do I seldom hear an alive thought
but see only the school bench, technique, and the musical alphabet?

"Is musical life so immature because it is created by the half-witted?
How many times, not purposely but just as though by silly chance
(from around the corner), I have started such a conversation with the
brotherhood! Either I would be reproached, or else I wasn't clear, but
most probably I was just not understood. Well, let's suppose that I am
incapable of presenting my thoughts clearly—to present my brains, so
to speak, on a tray with my thoughts impressed on them (as in a tele-
gram).

"And what about themselves? Why wouldn't they start? Apparently
they have no desire. You, Generalissimo, are the only one who understands me, and moreover you prod me in the right places with a sure,
courageous hand.

"Am I perhaps afraid of technique because I am so bad at it? I am
sure there are some who will come to my defense. I, for instance, cannot bear it when the landlady, who is baking a pie, particularly a good
pie, says that a million pounds of butter, 500 eggs, a whole row of cab-
bages, 150 and 1/4 pieces of fish . . . went into the pie; for when one
hears about the kitchen, one begins to imagine that either the landlady
or the cook is dirty, one sees the head of the capon lying on a bench,
a fish ripped open in the middle lying on another bench, and sometimes right next to it some guts peeking from the sieve (as though
the cockroaches had paid a visit); and even oftener one imagines a
greasy apron on which the cook has blown his nose—the same apron
with which he later wipes the edge of the pie-plate so that it will be
good and clean. . . . Well, the pie becomes less appetizing. In a mature
artistic creation there is always that side of virginal purity which, if
one starts touching it with dirty paws, becomes revolting.

[201]

"Truly, as long as the artist does not reject the diapers, suspenders, and leggings, there will reign the symphonic priests who put their Talmud of the first and second edition as the Alpha and Omega in the artistic life. Their little brains feel that the Talmud cannot be used in a live art where there are people, life—that there is no place in it for prescribed paragraphs and chapters. Well, naturally they scream: 'The drama, the stage, are in our way. We need space'; and to flatter their brains they declare that the world of sound is limitless. But their brains are limited. So what could there be in the world of sound? One has the space they talk about when lying on a lawn and following the flight of the clouds in the sky. First one sees a little lamb, then an old grandfather, then nothing, then suddenly a Prussian soldier. I don't blame Polonius for not agreeing with Hamlet about the cloud. The honorable cloud is very unsteady, and in a second can turn from a camel into Laroche.* I am not against symphony. I am against symphony composers, the incorrigible conservatives. So don't tell me, my dear Generalissimo, that our musicians talk about techniques more than about aims and historical problems because of the fact that—and so on.

"I am disturbed as to why Ivan the Fourth and the Third, and particularly *Yaroslav* of Antokolsky, and Repin's *Boatmen,* are so alive, so alive that when one is introduced to them one feels like saying: 'Well, it is exactly you that I would like to see.' Why is it that everything that is written in our contemporary music, in spite of its excellent quality, does not live like that? And when one hears the music, one feels like saying: 'Oh, yes, but I thought that you . . .' and so on. Please explain this to me. But put aside the limits of art. I believe in them only partly, because the borderlines in the religion of the artist are equal to a standstill. What does it matter whether some great brains did not reach the limit and other brains thought about it a great deal and finally did? Where then is the borderline? Relatively speaking—yes! Sounds cannot be a chisel or a brush; this, even children know."

Those who are familiar with Tolstoi's *What Is Art?* will find a striking similarity in the views expressed by the two Russians.

* H. A. Laroche, a St. Petersburg music critic.

Tolstoi and Mussorgsky did not know each other, but both were undoubtedly influenced by the writings of Drobolubov and Chernishevsky, the two champions of artistic realism. It is interesting to note that when Tolstoi, at the age of seventy, in the closing paragraph of his book prophesied that "the artist of the future will be free from all the perversion of technical improvements concealing the absence of subject matter, and who, not being a professional artist, and receiving no payment for his activity, will produce art only when he feels impelled to do so by an irresistible inner impulse," he did not know that such an artist had died in his own country almost two decades before.

"Pull, shaft horse, pull, without fatigue," Modest wrote to Repin. "And I, as the side horse, am also pulling somewhere so that there will be no trouble—I am afraid of the whip. And I feel in which direction I should push, and I carry and pull my burden. . . . This is what it is: I want to do people; when I sleep I see them, when I eat I think of them, and when I drink they appear before me as a whole—big, without any paint or tinsel. Well, if I succeed, thanks; if not, I will be very sad. But you won't get the people out of my head. Oh, no, don't jest. You won't."

Modest was speaking of his plans for a new subject for his next opera. While Modest was still working on his second version of *Boris,* Stassov, ready with suggestions for new work, called his attention to one of the gloomiest and most dramatic periods of Russia's history—the early years (1682-89) of the reign of Peter the Great, which were marked by an internal struggle, both class and religious, and by the court intrigues aroused by the young Tsar's European innovations.

"Khovanchina" was Peter's contemptuous name for the uprisings of the archers (Streltzi), the fierce and undisciplined regiment led by Prince Ivan Khovanski. When Peter was only a boy of ten, Khovanski gained powerful support at court through intrigue and became so brazen that he planned to marry his son Andrei to one of the Princesses and himself become the Tsar. At least this was what he was accused of, and for which he and his son were sent to the gallows. The conspiracies between two families, the Narishkins and the Miloslavskys; the struggle between the religious group of fanatical Old Believers and the new reformers; the story of the common people who suffered from all of it—all this constituted rich material for Mussorgsky's conception of a great people's drama.

With his characteristic enthusiasm, he plunged into research, into all the annals, memoirs, and history books that treated the period. As he learned more about the subject, he gradually veered away from Stassov's idea of an individualized, personal drama until finally he saw the struggle between old and new Russia at the time of Peter the Great as akin to the analogous struggle in his own epoch. As in the original version of *Boris*, he again wanted the people to be his principal hero. He asked Stassov:

". . . And what if Mousorianin slams at Mother Russia! It is not the first time that I have dug into the black earth, and not in fertilized earth, but directly into the raw; I long not just to become acquainted with people, but to become intimate with them, like brothers. It is terrifying! But it is good!

"What then? Why was a Russian fooled by heresy? Don't I know how to give the answer? Don't I know where the force is hidden, where the truth lies? . . .

"The black earth force will show itself when you dig to the bottom, and to dig the earth one should use a tool of a strange kind. And didn't they dig Mother Russia at the end of the seventeenth century with such a tool so that at first she didn't understand what they were digging with and began to croak? And then she accepted, the dear one, all sorts of privy councillors, and they didn't give her, the dear suffering one, a chance to come to herself and think: 'Where are you shoving?' The ignorant and the confused were executed. Power! Strength! But the prison still exists, and the police are the same. Only the time is different. The privy councillors don't allow the black earth to breathe.

"To put the past into the present—that is my task.

[204]

" 'We went ahead!' You are lying. 'We are still where we were!' On paper, in books, we went ahead—but we are still where we were. As long as the people cannot examine with their own eyes what is being done to them, as long as the people do not decide for themselves that this or that should be done to them, we shall remain where we were. All sorts of public benefactors are ready to gain great honors and to record them in documents, but the people are groaning, and so as not to groan they drink, and then groan all the more. 'We are still where we were!' "

It was only natural that, at that time particularly, discussions of technique and the purity of music were of little interest to Mussorgsky. "All these last days I have been forced to mingle with admirers of absolute musical beauty," he complained to Stassov, "and I have experienced a strange feeling of emptiness in talking with them."

Modest spoke of the only two meetings he had with Tchaikovsky, who happened to be in St. Petersburg on a short visit in connection with the production of his new opera, *Oprichnik*, and Cui invited him to a Sunday morning musicale to play it for his friends. Tchaikovsky came, but he neither brought his score nor played. Instead he listened to what Cui and his friends had to offer.

According to Modest, Tchaikovsky liked only parts of *Mlada*. He asked to see Modest's *Detskaya*, about which he had heard so much from Balakirev some years ago.

" 'They' [Tchaikovsky] were not in accord either with the nature of the composition or with its aim," related Modest; "and 'they' declared that though the author's performance gained the listener's favor, on the whole it was just rot." Then Modest was asked to play something from *Boris,* and as he performed it he watched Tchaikovsky out of the corner of his eye. Tchaikovsky was half asleep, "probably dreaming of sherbet or Moscow dough," thought Modest, and soon "he even looked like a piece of dough." In fact, Modest expected him at any moment to start fermenting. He even saw "small bubbles which grew and popped with a dull, lazy, not very pretty noise." Modest could hear the bubbles saying: "Powerful man. . . ." ("He means me," thought Modest.) ". . . But the strength is scattered. . . . It would be good for him to occupy himself . . . with a symphony. . . ." (*"En forme,* of course," thought Modest.) The "strong man" thanked Tchaikovsky. And that was all.

The next day Mussorgsky met Tchaikovsky again at the home of Bessel, the music publisher. This time Modest played the Polonaise from *Boris.* Tchaikovsky did not care for it. Russia's two greatest composers had very little respect for each other.

Tchaikovsky's attitude toward the Five was marked by the condescension of the professional toward the amateur. "Balakirev is the greatest personality of the entire circle, but he relapsed into silence before he had accomplished much," wrote Tchaikovsky in one of his letters to his friend Nadejda von Meck, only a few years after this visit. Tchaikovsky wrote his letters very carefully, for he expected them to be published some day, and therefore it is fair to credit him with having weighed his opinions very carefully before writing them down. He said that Cui "is a gifted amateur. His music is not original, but graceful and elegant; it is too coquettish—'made up,' so to speak. At first it pleases, but soon satiates us. That is because Cui's specialty is not music but fortifications. . . . Borodin, aged fifty, Professor of Chemistry at the Academy of Medicine, also possesses talent, a very great talent which, however, has come to nothing for the want of teaching, and because blind fate has led him into the science laboratories instead of a vital musical existence. He has not so much taste as Cui, and his technique is so poor that he cannot write a bar without assistance. . . . The one exception in latter days has been Rimsky-Korsakov, the only one among them to discover that doctrines preached by the circle have no sound basis, that their mockery of the schools and the classical masters, their denial of authority and of masterpieces, is but ignorance." He had more hope for Rimsky-Korsakov, who now began to study with such zeal "that the theory of the school soon became to him an indispensable atmosphere."

As for Mussorgsky—though Tchaikovsky admitted that, "with all his ugliness," he spoke a new idiom, that "his very original talent flashed forth now and again, and that his gifts were perhaps the most remarkable of all the Five"—still Tchaikovsky thought that "his nature is narrow and he has no aspirations towards self-perfection. He has been too easily led away by the absurd theories of his set and the belief in his own genius. Besides which, his nature is not of the finest quality, and he likes what is coarse, unpolished, ugly. He is the exact opposite of the distinguished and elegant Cui."

"Mussorgsky plays with a lack of polish, and even seems proud of his want of skill, writing just as it comes to him, believing blindly in the infallibility of his genius."

But above all, Tchaikovsky differed with Mussorgsky in his art credo. "I have never come in contact with anything more antipathetic and false than this unsuccessful attempt to drag truth into the sphere of art, in which everything is based on falsehood, and 'truth' in the everyday sense of the word is not required at all."

Modest had utter contempt for Tchaikovsky's religion of pure beauty of sound. "It isn't the music we need, nor the words, nor a palette, nor chisel—no, the Devil take you liars, hypocrites, *e tutti quanti!* Serve us some live thoughts, carry on a live discussion with people no matter what subject you choose for this conversation with us! You can't fool us with pretty sounds, like a well-to-do lady passing around a box of chocolates!"

And Modest could not forgive Tchaikovsky for catering to public taste in order to make a name for himself, and considered it shameful that he used art to further his personal aims. But the two men never engaged in a real discussion of their beliefs in art but only exchanged polite, meaningless words which left Modest with a "strange feeling of emptiness."

"This strange feeling was succeeded by another even stranger," he said to Stassov, "which I do not know how to describe: it is akin to that aroused by the loss of a very close and dear friend with whom, as one might say, 'one shared the days and shortened the nights.' Like spring beating out of the earth, so was life with such a friend, and one passionately wanted to live; the dear friend is gone and it is as if in a deep forest at night one heard only strange, inhuman, dead sounds that made one fearful."

Modest was probably referring to Rimsky, whose life was tending toward just that absolute musical beauty for which he was laying a foundation in his work. From the time of his first lecture in his theory classes, Rimsky realized the amount he would have to learn before he could teach others, and with the most admirable will-power he set out to study thoroughly "from the beginning." Rimsky, the composer of *Antar* and *Sadko*, sat next to his own pupils in Johansen's classes. Meanwhile, in his own classes, he had to pretend that he knew everything and was often forced to resort to general remarks. Time was a good friend to him. As a rule, the pupils did not suspect that he was as ignorant on the subject as they, and by the time they began to suspect, he had learned something. As he said, he was possibly the very best pupil in the Conservatory. Besides, how could anyone doubt his ability in the face of the success which his new opera, *The Maid of Pskov,* had on the first of January, 1873? But the ten performances that followed the première did not turn Rimsky's head nor swerve him in any way from his resolution to continue his thorough study at the Conservatory.

As though Providence were looking after his musical education, Rimsky received a new appointment from the Ministry of the Navy Bands throughout Russia. Besides giving him substantial financial support, this order put him into civilian rank and he could therefore take off his hated officer's uniform. When Azanchevsky asked him to conduct the orchestra class he had accepted without knowing how to go about it, for he had never conducted an orchestra in his life. Now, through this new appointment, he had a chance to learn about the orchestra and its instruments at close range.

His duties were to supervise the bandmasters, their appointments, the choice of repertory, and the quality of the instruments, and to act as intermediary between the Navy Department and the Conservatory. The new occupation aroused in him the desire to write a complete and detailed textbook on instrumentation and, in connection with this ambitious work, he busied himself "with various outlines, memoranda, and drawings having reference to a detailed explanation of the technique of the instruments." As he said later in his memoirs, he was eager to tell the world no less than all on this score. In studying the material for this textbook, he eventually got completely lost in the maze of information advertising various instruments of different makes, each make offering special advantages and disadvantages. Though after several years of work Rimsky finally abandoned the project, he learned a great deal about what, as he said, any German military bandmaster knows, but what, unfortunately, the artist-composer does not know. With characteristic thoroughness he began to practice on various instruments, such as the trumpet, clarinet, and flute, much to the horror of his neighbors.

During this time he often visited Borodin, who became his willing partner in all these practical studies. Borodin had just returned from a trip to Kazan. No one had told him that the convention of scientists and doctors which he went there to attend had been postponed for three weeks, and so he had found himself in the strange city with nothing to do. He occupied his time by visiting friends in the country. But at long last his colleagues arrived, and for two months they attended conferences of the most serious nature during the day and spent their evenings in school-boy fashion, eating too much caviar, crab, and watermelon, drinking "Bruderschafts" and champagne, and singing *Gaudeamus* with many "Hurrahs!" while drunkenly supported on each other's arms. Botkin and Mendeleev were there. It was once again as in the old days in Heidelberg. Mendeleev walked naked about the rooms before breakfast drinking *kvass,* and Botkin sang heart-rending songs. Two chamber-music concerts were arranged with the local musicians, just to please Borodin. "Oh yes, Little Father," his scientist friends said to him, swaying on their legs and pointing their forefingers at Borodin. "We have heard of your little sins in that field." It was another world, where there was no mention of Balakirev's madness and Modest's weary struggles, or of *Prince Igor, Boris,* and *Sadko.*

Borodin returned to St. Petersburg alone. Ekaterina was again in Moscow under treatment. The state of Borodin's home life had changed very little during the years. The heating system was improved, but, since there was no way of controlling it, the rooms were unbearably hot. The plumbing had at last been put in order, but now there was a stench from the water that had washed into the ground floor of the building during a recent flooding of the Neva. In Borodin's apartment some curtains were lying about that had been taken down for replacement and repairs, and pieces of furniture that had been sat through were waiting to be taken to the upholsterer. Borodin was going to attend to it all "presently," but so far he had not found time. The cats lay sunning themselves on window sills and furniture in the most frivolous postures, forgetting their age and disregarding the social position of their master.

Borodin heard that his songs had been published, and wrote to his wife asking if she had seen them, since he had forgotten to ask for copies. His brother Mitya was living with him, and the samovar as usual never left the table.

Rimsky was appalled to see that to the usual disorder of Borodin's life there was now added another disturbing element. Borodin had always been interested in reforms that would allow women the right to study at the universities and to practice the professions on an equal footing with men. He now had scores of women about him taking up his time with committee meetings, conferences, pleas for help, and benefit performances, while the score of *Prince Igor* lay forgotten and the Second Symphony progressed at a snail's pace.

I will leave to my readers' imagination what Borodin's home must have been like when, in the midst of his "routine," he and Rimsky practiced their exercises on brass and wind instruments. Rimsky would bring along a *Flügelhorn* (the signal horn used in army orchestras), a bassoon, or a clarinet of special make. These sessions at which they explored the vast possibilities of brass instruments, besides affording pure fun for Borodin, were responsible for the excessive use of brass in his Second Symphony which he was then orchestrating at odd moments.

Mussorgsky had no part in this new association of the old friends. At this phase of his lonely life, while still living alone in the room Rimsky had once shared with him, Modest struck up an acquaintance with a young man which grew into such a close friendship that the two shared their lodgings together for the following two years. Twenty-four-year-old Count Arseny Golenishchev-Kutuzov was a distant relative of Modest's and, like him, belonged to the remnant of impoverished Russian nobility. He was then just making his début in the literary world as a poet. With typical enthusiasm, Modest placed the talent of his new discovery in the same class with that of Pushkin and Lermontov, though the young poet showed no real promise, nor did he eventually fulfill Modest's expectations. However, Modest was at first genuinely impressed by the young man's ability—more, probably, by Kutuzov's devotion to him.

Kutuzov roomed at the same boardinghouse where Mussorgsky lived, and the proximity of a friend brought him much comfort and happiness. Living alone was almost unbearable for Modest, and he confessed to Kutuzov that he was actually afraid of being alone.

Modest introduced Kutuzov to Stassov, who also lavished encouragement on him, and Modest sincerely hoped to add to the Troika a fourth member so that there would be a poet as well as a painter, a sculptor, and a musician in the group. Kutuzov's outlook on life kept him remote from any troubling ideas. He lived within the small world of his own emotions. In his poetry he still spoke of the old, beautiful feudal world he saw crumbling about him. He accepted life as an endlessly boring experience, gloomy as a graveyard, in which death was the only possible solution to all problems. Under his influence, Mussorgsky for the first time became introspective.

Their friendship was mutually beneficial, but though Kutuzov, inspired by *Boris,* wrote *Vasily Shuisky,* an epic poem based also on court intrigue, it was far from great artistic creation that Modest achieved in his music based on Kutuzov's two cycles of pessimistic poetry: *Sunless* and *The Songs and Dances of Death.*

In the summer of 1873 Victor Hartmann died suddenly in Moscow from a heart attack. Modest had not suffered such a blow since the death of his mother. It was even more poignant because he was affected by Kutuzov's pessimism and lack of hope in the future. In Hartmann, Modest had found not only a close and entertaining companion, but also a man of vision who was capable, in Modest's opinion, of transforming Russia's architecture. His death at the age of thirty-nine aroused Modest to a helpless wrath.

"The wise ones console us, the fools, that though 'he' is gone, everything that he had time to create will live, and 'how many are so fortunate as not to be forgotten?' This hamburger (with horseradish for tears) is a product of human ego. To hell with such wisdom. If 'he' has not lived in vain but did create, what kind of scoundrel would one be to reveal in the thought that he can create no more? No, there cannot be any peace nor any consolation. This is a lot of flabbiness. If nature is only coquetting with me, I have the honor of meeting a cocotte and therefore trusting her less—that is, I should trust her less and watch her carefully, for at odd times she might lure me to such a degree that even the sky would seem a mere nothing. Or should one rather, like a brave Hussar, charge into the thick of life and choke to death, but first enjoy it to the full? Enjoy what? The flabby cold earth which now, not with coquetry but with true desire, accepts into her horrible embraces each 'King of Nature,' no matter who he is, like an old, worn-out hag for whom anyone is good enough since she has no choice."

Stassov was in Paris at that time, and—both to console his friend and to pull him out of the gloomy state into which Kutuzov was dragging him—he suggested that Modest come to visit Liszt. As much as Stassov liked the young poet, he did not wholeheartedly approve of the introspective side road that Modest's creative ability had taken. Liszt was the man for Modest to see, and Stassov urged Modest to join him. Just for a moment, a bright ray of hope passed through Modest's weary mind as he thought of the possibility of seeing Liszt, a man with whom he could discuss art in a language that he felt his Russian musical brethren did not understand. "What new worlds could be opened in his talks with Liszt! What far corners, unseen by other eyes, could they look into!" But he was only a government clerk, he reflected, condemned to an office where his work could be done much better by others. Stassov repeatedly invited him, and even asked his brother Dmitri to place at Modest's disposal the salary due him from the library so that he could feel free to leave his job and join him. But Modest refused, excusing himself by saying that he could not leave his superior officer who had been so good to him for so long but who had now fallen ill, and that he had "six thousand documents to attend to." These excuses were by now of a usual pattern, and meant only one thing to those who knew him as well as Stassov did.

Borodin's friends reported that they had seen Modest in the

[213]

suburbs of the city engaged in such a noisy brawl that the police had to be summoned. Borodin heard that Modest suffered from hallucinations and that he would disappear for days at a time.

One month passed before Stassov heard from Modest, who usually wrote him almost every day when Stassov was in St. Petersburg. Rumors reached him in Paris that Modest was selling most of his belongings and even his clothes, about which he was so meticulous, that he had been put out of his apartment because he could not pay his rent, and that no one knew where he was lodging. In the spring of that year, Modest had confessed to Stassov that he suffered from fits of what he thought was insanity, and this only added to Stassov's anxiety.

For weeks Modest, dressed in forlorn clothes, his hair disheveled and his face sunken from lack of sleep, had been seen in disreputable places in the company of dubious characters. Modest was drinking.

16

THE GREATEST OPERA IN RUSSIAN LITERATURE, and a drama equal to those of Shakespeare, Mussorgsky's *Boris Godunov* had to travel a steep and twisting road. It was rejected twice by the Opera committee; then, after a private hearing at the home of Vladimir Purgold, it was decided to present three scenes from the opera on the stage. A year later on the 6th of February, 1874, the curtain rose at the Maryinsky Theater for Modest's people's drama.

"The opera was finally presented on the stage with stupefying success. The impression it created on the audience, the artists, and the members of the orchestra was astonishing. Its success was a complete triumph for the author," wrote Modest Mussorgsky in his autobiographical sketch.*

This flamboyant account of his success was true so far as it concerned the actors and the members of the orchestra. And it was true that for once the public appreciated what the "learned" critics failed to see. But even before the criticisms came out in the

* This sketch, written in the third person, was intended for Riemann's musical dictionary, but Mussorgsky never finished it.

press, Modest's triumph was marred by an occurrence insignificant in itself, but which caused him much grief and anxiety.

Four young ladies had sent him a wreath, decorated with ribbons on which they had embroidered flowery inscriptions and their favorite motives from the opera. This was to be handed to the composer on the stage. (Russians have always been very romantic in their expressions of admiration for an artist.) However, owing to the theater's regulations, the wreath was not presented publicly to the composer, but brought to him backstage. Mussorgsky's admirers were hurt, and Stassov, the chief instigator of the affair, was not willing to allow the matter to drop there and remain forgotten.

"I implore you, don't give the press the story of the wreath. It might bring consequences which you desire least of all. *Boris* may never be performed again. I beg you, I implore you by the strength of your love for me . . ." Mussorgsky wrote these few lines in haste to Stassov. He saw the success of his new opera crumbling on account of the silly incident.

But the journalist Stassov betrayed the Stassov whom Modest called friend. Signing it with the initials of the young ladies' names, he wrote an open letter to the editor of the St. Petersburg *Gazette,* telling the whole story. When Modest read the letter in the paper he became almost hysterical. He wrote an apologetic letter to Napravnik, whom Stassov blamed in his letter for refusing to present the wreath on the stage; and he made the mistake of writing another letter to the editor of the paper, explaining his innocence in the whole affair. These unfortunate letters served as additional material for the critics to use in ridiculing Mussorgsky: they accused him of using the incident to talk about himself in an important newspaper, so as to add a journalist's laurels to those of the musician and poet. To the great surprise of all, Cui made no exception. It pained Modest to read the lines in his column, for Cui had already flayed *Boris* with the most unjust criticisms.

[216]

Cui's part in the spiteful, adolescent derision, which in the style of a cheap scandal-sheet mocked and ridiculed his friend (who was obviously in distress), might perhaps be explained by that lack of any sense of values which often marks the journalist when personal matters are concerned; but there is far less excuse for his unfair criticism of *Boris*. Cui's attitude might have been the result of professional jealousy because his own first opera, *Ratcliff*, had been a failure. Or perhaps he thought it would not be good for Modest to realize success with his first stage offspring—that it might make him too proud and haughty. Cui's criticism was very cleverly compacted of the praise due to Modest's talent, and the most annihilating statement of Cui's own disapproval.

"There are two principal defects in *Boris*," said Cui in summing up his elaborate verdict: "choppy recitative and the vagueness of scattered musical ideas which make the opera a potpourri." He pointed to the "slender musical interest in many of the scenes, and the preference for coarse splashes of color in the tone-painting." He finished by saying that "these defects are due to immaturity, the author's lack of self-criticism, haphazard self-complacency, and a slap-dash way of composing which brings the same sad consequences to Messrs. Rubinstein and Tchaikovsky."

Cui's criticism fell like a hammer on Modest's head. "Complacency!!! Slap-dash way of composing!!! Immaturity!!! . . . Whose . . . whose, I would like to know!" exclaimed Modest. "It took the production of *Boris* to reveal myself to others, and to expose their true selves to me," he reflected. Losing what little faith he had retained in the old circle, and with the reserve of a proud man who has been hurt, he drew even farther away from it.

Despite press criticisms, however, *Boris* appealed particularly to the Russian youth, who found their own revolutionary ideas embodied in it, and who sang the most daring excerpts from the opera in the corridors of the universities and even in the streets. This had its effect on the government officials, and after ten successful performances in that year, a most ruthless and inartistic cutting of the opera was forced upon Mussorgsky by Napravnik, who in turn had been coerced by the government officials, until only a skeleton was left of the already revised version of the first performance. *Boris* survived another ten performances in the following years, and then was suddenly taken off the repertory of the Maryinsky Theater because, so it was said, it displeased the royal family.

Cui was not Modest's enemy, and *Boris* was all that the Invincible Band could ever have hoped to achieve in expressing its principles. It was just that during the past few years so much had happened, so much had affected and changed them, that when the call came for the final test it came too late. They were no longer friends-in-arms, champions of liberty.

"You have doubtless heard of the disruption of our school," Borodin wrote to a friend. "It is not astonishing. It is in the natural order of things. So long as we were eggs laid by one hen (and that hen Balakirev), we were all more or less alike; but when the young chickens came out of their shells, each one clothed himself in different feathers, and when our wings had grown, each one flew away in a different direction."

Rimsky accepted another musical position in addition to those he already held as a professor at the Conservatory and as Inspector of Navy Bands. In the fall of 1874 he became the Director of the Free Music School, which had practically ceased to exist since Balakirev's departure. Rimsky decided to reorganize the school, put it on a sound financial basis, and not expend its small funds on great plans for concerts à la Balakirev. Since the Free Music School was essentially a vocal institution, he divided the pupils into two classes. The beginners were taught elementary theory and solfeggio, while he coached the more advanced students in preparation for public concerts.

Two concerts a year were all that the school could afford at the beginning, and as for the programs, Rimsky's choice was very

Stassov

different from Mili's. His recent years of study in harmony and counterpoint, as well as his teaching at the Conservatory, had radically changed him as a musician. In his study of counterpoint he learned to admire and honor the great genius of Bach—although in his younger days, as he said, "without even a proper acquaintance with the master" he used to repeat Balakirev's words and call Bach a "composing machine" and his works "maids of beauty, frozen and soulless." Looking back on his early friendship with Balakirev and the circle, he said that he had not understood then "that counterpoint had been the poetic language of that composer of genius, and that it was just as ill-judged to reproach him with his use of counterpoint as to upbraid a poet for using verse and rhyme instead of employing free easy prose," and that he had had no idea at the time of the historical evolution of the civilized world's music and had not realized that "all of modern music owed everything to Bach." It was then that he saw how foolish it was of Berlioz to say that "Palestrina was only a series of chords," a bit of nonsense repeated in the circle. Rimsky recalled that Stassov had once been such an ardent worshiper of Bach that he was even nicknamed "Bach," and that he too had once admired Palestrina and the old Italians, but that later, influenced by his Slavophil tendencies, he had thrown all this aside.

Besides, in choosing his programs Rimsky had to take into consideration the fact that because of limited funds the school could afford only a very modest orchestra which could play only comparatively easy pieces. And finally, he had to consider his own inexperience as a conductor. He preferred to start at the beginning, as he said, and not at the end. Modern orchestral pieces would have been as far out of his own reach as they were out of his men's. His programs therefore consisted so predominantly of classical music that one critic remarked: "The most modern composer on the program was Haydn."

This choice of programs by a member of the "unruly band" of modernists was considered a definite sign of Rimsky's desertion of his old colleagues. Borodin was the only one who reasoned about it calmly. "Many people have been distressed to see Korsakov take a retrograde step and give himself up to the study of musical archeology. For myself I can quite understand it, and it does not trouble me. Korsakov's development was the reverse of mine. While I began with the classics, Korsakov began with Glinka, Liszt, and Berlioz."

Of the Five, only Borodin was capable of this sober, detached reflection and of understanding the inevitable consequences of the final break within the circle; for, despite the fact that his friends considered him a musician primarily, he was a scientist first and a musician afterwards and remained so until his dying day. To Borodin, music was not the matter of life and death that it was to Modest, nor was he absorbed by any such artistic vision as possessed his younger friend. When, on laying aside the score of *Prince Igor,* Borodin said that he would compose what came into his head and not bother with great ideas, he spoke his credo. Years passed before he gave another thought to *Prince Igor,* which, had Borodin been Mussorgsky's artistic and intellectual equal, could have become another *Boris* or *Kovanchina.* But since he was not concerned with expressing any "idea" in the opera, he allowed the unfinished score to lie on the shelf and gather dust, as he would any of his songs.

An old friend, an army doctor, came to visit him after a long absence from the capital. In the course of their reminiscences, Borodin casually mentioned the forgotten *Prince Igor,* and the doctor convinced him of what Stassov and the rest of his musical friends had tried for years to make him see—that is, that *Prince Igor* was worthy of his talent. Although the next day he hurried to Stassov to announce the resurrection of this opera, and they embraced happily and shed tears, he worked on the *Prince Igor* score only when the few arias he had written became known in musical circles.

The way he treated his compositions proved what he himself had said so many times. "Did you ever see that sign over the store on Litenaya near Nevsky?" he once asked Ludmilla Shestakova, who was always urging him to work on his music. "It says: 'Work and Fun.' Well, it is so with me. Science is my work, and music is my fun." He repeated this idea again and again.

"For my colleagues in music it is their chief business, their occupation and aim in life. For me it is a relaxation, a pastime, which distracts me from my principal business, my professorship. I do not follow Cui's example. I love my profession and my science. I love the Academy and my pupils. My teaching is of a practical character, and for this very reason takes up much of my time. I have to be constantly in touch with my pupils, male and female, because to direct the work of young people one must be always close to them. I have the interests of the Academy at heart. If, on the one hand, I want to finish my work, on the other hand I am afraid of devoting myself to it too assiduously and of throwing any scientific work into the shade."

Despite the implications at the beginning of that passage, Cui was as conscientious and sincere in his work as professor and instructor at the Military Academy as he was in his interest in music. He combined the three vocations of army man, music critic, and composer in a routine as smooth as a calendar's. His home life moved at an even pace, he was the father of two children, and his was on the whole a life in which nothing extraordinary was likely to happen. He was at work on his new opera *Angelo,** a work which certainly, neither in its style of composition nor in its ideology, could be considered in any way akin to *Boris*. His few cutting remarks about the new trend in Rimsky's musical interests did not imply at all that he was ready to condemn him as Stassov was, who when he learned from Mussorgsky that Rimsky had written sixty fugues and fourteen canons shrugged his shoulders and said, "De mortuis aut bene, aut nihil."

* *Angelo* is based on Victor Hugo's play *Angelo, Tyrant of Padua*. Ponchielli used the same subject for his opera *La Gioconda*.

Modest was the only one who still called "On to the new shores!" And Rimsky's musical attitude destroyed completely his hope for the circle. In Modest's farewell to it he wrote:

"When I remember certain artists who are now behind a fence, not only sorrow overcomes me but also a sort of slush, for their whole desire, their aspiration, is to drizzle, drop after drop, and all the drops such even, beloved ones. It pleases them, but to a real man it is a bore.

"For God's sake, can't you let yourselves go, my dear ones, as live people do? Show whether you have claws or fins, whether you are beasts of prey or just amphibians! Without any sense, without any will, they have bound themselves, these artists, by tradition, yet imagine they are still doing things.

"All this would be of very little interest and merely unpleasant if they, these artists, had not once taken up another banner and tried 'to lift it up proudly before human society.' Caught up in the middle of the road by the iron fist of Balakirev, they began to breathe with his mighty lungs (though not to the full size of his giant chest). They challenged tasks that have troubled great minds. Then Balakirev's iron fist loosened, and they felt that they were tired, that they needed rest; where could they find this rest? In tradition, of course. 'As our fathers have done, so will we do.'

"They put the glorious fighting banner in a safe place, hid it carefully, and locked it with seven locks behind seven doors. They have rested and rested. Without the banner, without aim, without the desire to look into the future, they pore over what was done long ago and no longer wants them. And so from time to time the critical frogs, puffing contentedly in their inherited rotten swamp, present these artists with their praise. How else? The Mighty Five have hatched into a horde of soulless traitors; their scourge has become a child's toy whip."

When Modest bade farewell thus to the Invincible Band, his rightness of judgment, his belief in himself and his intellectual vigor and clear moral perception, seemed to him to be just as indubitable as they had always been. But his voice was no longer heard. His closest friends turned away from him, and a contributing reason was the sort of life he was leading, abandoning himself for weeks at a time to drink and only spasmodically appearing in a presentable state. If they realized what was causing this gradual disintegration, this complete loss of self-possession leading to a life without sails and rudder, they offered him no support. Except for Stassov. He was still capable of pulling his friend out of the depths into which he would sink when Stassov was absent from the capital, and then Modest would again "boil" with a new work.

To commemorate the painter Hartmann's death, Stassov arranged an exhibition of his pictures in January of 1874. Not until the summer of that year did Modest pay his tribute to Hartmann: a suite for piano, repainting the pictures through his own medium of sound. Modest chose the piano for his orchestral work, probably influenced by Liszt's boldness in showing the kinship of piano and orchestra in his *Danse Macabre*. With astonishing rapidity Mussorgsky finished his *Pictures at an Exhibition,* which (as had been the case with his songs based on Kutuzov's verse) his masterly dramatization put far above the level of the work that had inspired it.

For a while it looked as though the happiness he had found in this work would sustain his ardor and keep him busy on *Khovanchina,* the magnum opus on which he was working, even though spasmodically.

A year after Hartmann's death, almost to the month, Nadejda Opotchinina died. What Modest's reaction was it is impossible to tell, since there is here a gap in information just as there is for the time when he lived in her house while working on *Boris.* Modest, who wrote letters constantly, left no letters dated after her death in which there was any mention of her name or any sign as to what had occurred. And there is not the slightest hint of it in any of the letters of his friends. Modest's grief found its expression in an epitaph dedicated to her memory which he wrote in the form of a song:

"Mean, cruel death like a vulture's talons attacked your heart and killed you. Executioner, damned by all the ages, has snatched away even you. Oh, if all those to whom my lament may seem insane could have only understood your soul! Oh, if they could have listened to you in conversation, or in a heated argument! Perhaps with a lofty thought I could draw for these people your serene image illumined by your love of truth, your inquisitive mind looking calmly at people. You broke away in time from the glitter of society, from 'the ties of habit'; you parted from it all without anger, and with a clear understanding you learned a different life."

Again, as after Hartmann's death, Modest disappeared for many weeks, and when he returned his mood was somber. His mind was too preoccupied with death, the master of all living. The most dramatic songs in his two cycles *Sunless* and *The Songs and Dances of Death* are connected with the period he had spent with Kutuzov. And now he did not realize that his happy life with the poet to whom he was so attached was also coming to an end.

On one summer night he found himself locked out of his apartment. Kutuzov had just left for the country place where he spent his summers, and he had taken the apartment key with him. Had Modest wanted to he could have forced the door, as Kutuzov's brother did the next day, but he was afraid to be alone. He walked most of the night along the banks of the Neva, and finally he wearily climbed astride a stone lion at the entrance to an empty mansion to rest. Looking across the Neva, he suddenly remembered that near by there lived an old friend, Naumov, a man who led a bohemian life and on whom anyone could call at any hour. When Mussorgsky walked into Naumov's house, he entered on the last stretch of his turbulent life.

Paul Naumov, at one time a naval officer, was a bon-vivant who in his youth had managed to squander the money he inherited from his parents, and later the fortune of his wife, by whom he had three children. When Modest called on him, Naumov was living with his youngest son, Sergei, in the house of his sister-in-law, a woman with a sizable fortune, in the role of her husband. He kept open house for his friends, former army and navy officers as well as actors and singers who were in search of free dinners and liquor. However, to give Naumov his due, one must admit that he was a well-educated man, a great music and drama enthusiast, and (according to Stassov) not a drunkard of the low type that Modest associated with at Maly Yaroslavetz (a restaurant with a bohemian reputation). His devotion to Modest was that of a genuine friend, but he was unable to restrain him from his dangerous passion. On the contrary, this was actually encouraged by the warm and affectionate care with which all the members of the family surrounded Modest, overpraising him and gratifying his every wish, "petting and spoiling" him, as he himself said, as well as by the general bohemian atmosphere of Naumov's home.

Modest's nocturnal call on Naumov would not have developed into a permanent visit had Kutuzov—like his other room-mate Rimsky—not made plans of his own. Modest wrote to Stassov:

"December 29-30, at night.
"Here is what happened, my dear. A lad became confused by all sorts of desires, and he who did this is no other than Count Arseny Golenishchev-Kutuzov. And here is how he did it: he thought up a marriage, and not just for fun, but in all seriousness.

"Here is another who goes home on a furlough, never to return. Good heavens! Here am I, spending my time with all sorts of bureaucratic nonsense, trying to grasp an idea (and happy when I catch it), while people who don't have to do this get married to take a burden on themselves! I cursed Arseny in plain language, and was even rude to him. Let come what may, to lie is not for me. He invited me to meet his betrothed (I don't know her). I won't go; otherwise I would be lying. I don't like what he is doing—and I won't go. That's all there is to it. He says that he loves her—I still won't go. There's no need for it.

"Such things drive me to work even more. I shall be left alone—and alone I shall stay. I shall have to die alone—I can't expect everyone to go with me. It's annoying, Generalissimo, about Arseny."

17

"YOU PROBABLY DON'T KNOW," WROTE BORO-
din to an old friend in January 1877, "the very pleasant news we
have. Dear Balakirev, the talented Balakirev, is in the process of
resurrection as regards music."

Like a ship returning to its home port, Mili Balakirev began to
send out signals of his approach. The earliest light to appear on
the horizon was ignited by Rimsky's becoming the director of
what had once been Balakirev's own Free Music School. First
Mili sent a letter of congratulation to Rimsky, following this with
a letter in which he upbraided him for his poor choice of programs. Later, when he began visiting Stassov, Mili—who during
the past four years had refused to listen to music because it was
such a painful subject, claiming that all the disasters of his life
had been due to his preoccupation with music—was now eager for
all the news and seemed interested, although he still refused to
see anyone. And finally, when Ludmilla Shestakova decided to
have her brother's operas published and asked Mili to edit them,
he docked at the pier, as it were.

Four years of seclusion under the influence of his religious mania had left an ineradicable mark on Mili. Though he had only just passed his fortieth birthday, the fiery enthusiasm and the meteoric flight of his fancy which had made his personality so magnetic, so irresistible, were no longer apparent. The same ardent believer in his two favorite tonalities—B minor and D-flat major, he had lost interest in everything new, had become suspicious and even hostile toward it. If he himself had "thawed out," as his friends called it, his taste remained frozen. He wanted to pick up his musical life where he had left it, while his friends had gone ahead. The source of his inspiration had dried up and he could only "sing unfinished songs" and perfect ideas that were the dead ashes of his once spontaneous inspiration.

When Balakirev finally saw Borodin, he was not interested in either *Prince Igor* or Borodin's Second Symphony, but only in the First Symphony, which he himself had once blue-penciled but now wanted Borodin to rewrite, restoring to the score all the fragments he had hitherto censored.

His despotism and rough language remained unchanged. He still treated Mussorgsky as though he were a "driveling idiot." However, he was pleased to find that Modest, contrary to Rimsky's warning that he had become haughty after the success of *Boris,* was properly humble and was even thinking of studying with Rimsky. This pleased Balakirev, and he himself gave him some homework to do on *A Night on Bald Mountain,* about which they had disagreed some seventeen years ago.

Mili actually promised Ludmilla to finish his own *Tamara;* though not until a priest in his recently acquired circle of acquaintances told him that such was God's will did Mili put one bar of *Tamara* on paper.

Stassov, spurred by Balakirev's return, was ready with plans, great plans for him to take up again his position as the leader of the circle and to "shepherd the flock." With the persistence of a pregnant woman's craving for something, he continually urged Mili to save Mussorgsky from a physical downfall, and Rimsky from a moral. Rimsky, after two years of theoretical study, was losing faith in his own creative powers. He was actually on the verge of believing that perhaps after all he was only what Mili thought him to be—a man capable of developing other people's ideas, but incapable of anything original of his own. But Balakirev was not concerned about the two men. He moved slowly and cautiously. He told Stassov that if he had kept his job with the railroad, he eventually could have reached a position that would have enabled him to live comfortably so that he would not have to run from house to house giving piano lessons. He said he had been forced by circumstances to leave his job, but he never told the circumstances to anyone. He earned a meager income as supervisor of music in a girls' school and by giving the private piano lessons that he so resented. Mili remained close to the new friends to whom he was bound by his religious fanaticism, and did not wish to collaborate with the old circle. He preferred to remain a spectator and a critical adviser, the role which he never abandoned but which was the least desired by his former pupils.

Both Ludmilla Shestakova and Stassov tried to bring the group together again as it had been in the old days. They arranged musical evenings for them, for they believed that the break was not serious, that it was just a "temporary cooling off," that their evenings were "unique in history," and that "surely these great, talented men were not going to drop all this on account of trivial things that had come between them." From time to time Ludmilla Shestakova succeeded in bringing two or three of them together, but they no longer met and worked as they had in the late sixties. The old spirit was not there. Even the one youngest in his enthusiasm, their host and source of inspiration, Stassov, was showing weariness, and he certainly could not grow excited over the frivolous theme that Borodin, Cui, and Rimsky were collaborating on—paraphrases on a polka that Borodin had written for fun.

Chopsticks (or Dog's Waltz, as it is called in Russia), known to everyone who ever touched the piano keyboard, originated with one of Borodin's adopted daughters, Gania. She had asked Borodin to play duets with her, and when he remarked that she did not know how to play the piano, she thumped out what is universally called *Chopsticks* with the two forefingers of each hand. This amused Borodin so much that he set out to write variations on the theme, keeping the original theme in the upper register of the treble so that it could be played by anybody who has two fingers, while for a real pianist there were variations to be played at the same time. He wrote an amusing polka, a requiem, and a funeral march in the same comical vein, and when he showed it to his friends they were so enthusiastic that they joined in composing their own variations.

Naturally, Balakirev had no interest in this, and Mussorgsky's interest lasted only for a while. Mili was indignant that they should waste time over such utter nonsense, and felt that they should be ashamed of even showing it to anyone, much less consider publishing it. As for Modest, he wrote a Gallop for it, but, since they objected to his changing the theme in the development, he refused to go on with it. To replace him they acquired a new collaborator—Anatol Liadov, Rimsky's pupil. (Curiously enough, it was this shallow piece that first found its way westward into Europe, rather than any serious work of the Mighty Five. Liszt was so enchanted by it that he too made his contribution to the piece by adding his own variation.)

Yet Ludmilla clung to her belief in her friends. To force Borodin to finish work on his Second Symphony, she asked Napravnik to perform it during the approaching season, and presented Borodin on his return from the country with the *fait accompli*. This threw him into a panic, for besides the fact that the symphony was unfinished and he had not written a single bar on it in the past year, he discovered that he had put the scores of the first movement and the finale in such a safe place that he could not find them. The rehearsals were already scheduled, and each time that Napravnik sent a request for the needed parts, all the papers and books, the maps and newspapers, the linen and even some furniture, were set in motion at Borodin's home. But the scores were nowhere to be found. To make matters worse, Borodin fell ill, and it was while in bed with his head wrapped in compresses that he rewrote in pencil the score of the Second Symphony. But his copy was not ready in time, and the performance had to be postponed to the next concert.

"Thus my two symphonies will both be performed in the same week. Never before has a professor at the College of Medicine and Surgery found himself in such a position."

Borodin never said a truer word. The performance of the sloppily written score, with mistakes in the orchestral parts, was not a success, and Borodin returned to writing *Chopsticks* and occasionally working on fragments of *Prince Igor,* which by now was losing its last thread of continuity as a whole, as well as the dramatic tension it had had in its original libretto.

"I am an enemy of dualism and dualistic theories in chemistry, in biography, in psychology, and in philosophy, as also in the Austro-Hungarian Empire; yet, as if it had been done intentionally, everything in *Prince Igor* came in pairs like the animals in Noah's Ark.

"Two Khans—Kontschak and Gsak; two Vladimirs—Galitzky and Poutivlsky; two women in love—Yaroslavna and Kontschakovna; two fools—Skula and Eroshka; two brothers—Igor and Vsevolod; two love affairs, two outrages on the princely dignity, two captive princes, and two victorious armies of the Polovtsi."

Rimsky rightly remarked that had it not been announced that fragments from *Prince Igor* were to be played on the programs of the Free Music School, the fate of the opera would have been different. With his usual "Anon, sir, anon, sir" attitude, Borodin postponed the orchestration of the Polovetsky Dances until Rimsky finally insisted on his bringing the untouched piano version to his house. There Borodin and Rimsky, with the help of Liadov, set out to orchestrate and copy parts. The work had to be done in such great haste that to save time they wrote in pencil, spraying the finished sheets of the score with liquid gelatin and hanging them up to dry like wash on lines in Rimsky's study.

Modest was seen less and less with his old friends. Though after Nadejda Opotchinina's death he clung to Ludmilla Shestakova's responsive friendship and gentle, motherly care, he was conscious of the criticism that his mode of life evoked among his musical friends. In his naïve way, Modest wanted to bring the Naumovs into the old circle. As with Arseny Golenishchev-Kutuzov, he now wanted to introduce the young Sergei Naumov to Stassov, and the Naumov family to Ludmilla Shestakova. He spoke of his new friends in the most flattering terms, hoping that once the others knew them as well as he did they would understand his liking for them. But neither Stassov nor Ludmilla cared to make their acquaintance.

In all this there was a glaring ambivalence. His theoretical conception and its actuality; his mind's final verdict and his heart's love that lagged behind; even the principle of his own moral existence—all came into question.

Modest was deeply wounded, but he understood. He could not, as Mili had done, find relief from his misery in a world of mysterious reconciliation, to be deceived by the flattery that religion pays to the human heart, and mix philosophical conceptions with an arbitrary symbolism that could not come out into the open field of logic.

Nor could he face his dilemma alone. Inwardly crushed, Modest lived through days when each word of sympathy, each tear from another's pain, and each curse that sprang from the same hatred as his, bound him in a sense of intimacy. For a wound heals more quickly when it is like another's wound.

For all his old friends' compassion and their occasional "If we could only save him from Naumov," they did not seem to understand what it meant for him to tear out by the roots his most cherished convictions. Nor could they see that he, who never lost his faith in principles, but rather in men's will to apply them, must surrender because he had to endure the restrictions of the civil servant, and that his shabby coat stood in the way of the recognition of the man who wrote *Boris Godunov*. They who suffered only from external causes did not understand the gnawing despair into which Modest was sinking. To them it was only weakness and caprice.

It almost seemed that they thought he should be saved from his new friends so that he might devote more regular attention to his clerical job—as though this would set everything right! What Modest had said at the age of twenty—that he could not combine army life with the only work he felt himself destined for—was even more pertinent now, in his maturity. The futility of the hours he spent daily at a desk while his whole being was craving for his own work gave him such a sense of degradation, of humiliation, with no hope whatever for the future, that he sank into "sadness, sadness, and tears," from which only drink could provide a release.

Life had given Mussorgsky so many opportunities for suffering, so few for happiness. Misfortunes wear out the strongest character. Fear of tomorrow's uncertainty pervades the whole being and undermines the assurance without which no worth-while work can be done. Modest's difficulty was financial; he was too proud, too sensitive, ever to appeal to anyone for help, and his friends did not seem to realize his need until it was too late. Once Modest became the slave of his passion, he could no longer claim mastery over his own life.

It was easier for him to be with those who did not touch on the "Holy Thing," who, if they did not understand, were willing to listen, would not argue or judge, scold or comfort him. Oftener and oftener he was seen at the restaurant Maly Yaroslavetz, where he was not treated as a stranger but even enjoyed generous credit. At a table covered with bottles, the writer Sergei Maximov would

[232]

regale the guests in his hoarse voice with stories of Siberian life, of hard labor, of the "unfortunates" who were sent there. Or the opera bass Vladimir Vasilyev would complain of the difficult times: "Napravnik is fierce! He keeps you tight as a string. Try to miss a rehearsal, and he will peck you to death. Only Saturdays are left."

Modest would be sitting not too firmly in his chair next to Garbusov, the talented actor, and swaying from side to side. He would be holding a newspaper in both his hands, but from the way his bleary eyes moved from one edge of the sheet to the other, and his occasional loud snorts, one knew he had not read a line. Now and then he would lift his head, startled by the roar of Vasilyev's voice, hearing the familiar name of Napravnik. Then his head would fall back on his chest while Vasilyev went on: "Brothers, I love Lent. Then all you do is sing 'God bless you' in church, with no Napravnik to watch you or smell your breath." With this he would noisily empty a tea-glass of vodka.

Modest had heard it all so many times. He would still be sitting quietly, still holding the paper and leaning against the back of his chair. Someone would walk over to see that he did not fall off. "Don't bother him. You'll knock him over."

It would get late. His friends would leave and gradually even the last-comers would rise from their tables. In the corner of the room someone would be finishing a funny story. The waiters swept the floors, but they did not bother Modest. They lowered their voices to a respectful whisper when referring to him, and leaning on their brooms would remark significantly, "His music has been played at the Maryinsky Theater. Yes, sir."

One of the waiters would approach Modest when it was time to close the restaurant. Modest would say to him confidentially, "When I die, you will remember my name with pride." And the waiter would nod.

Or sometimes—this would be earlier in the day—Modest would confront some young musician. "You youngsters, in your Conservatory, never see any farther than cantus firmus. To you the minor is the sin of your grandfathers, and the major is the redemption. Do you think that tranquillity, excitement, and tranquillity again solve everything? No, my dear lads. I say, if you must sin, then sin! If there is excitement, there is no return to peace. But on, forward, crushing everything in the way!"

Two glasses of liquor were sufficient to make Modest drunk, for his nervous system offered no resistance to alcohol. As is often the case with alcoholics, he acted more drunk when he was sober. His language became confused, and he behaved in a very queer manner. When he attended one of the last rehearsals of *Boris,* he assumed dramatic poses while listening to the orchestra, becoming quite ecstatic over the execution of various instruments, often at utterly unimportant points. He would either drop his head in deep thought on his chest or toss it proudly into the air, shaking his hair and lifting his hands theatrically. When at the end of the scene the timpani played pianissimo the phrase that represents the distant sound of the monastery bell, Mussorgsky stood up, straightened himself and, crossing both his arms on his chest, bowed deeply to the drummer.

His irregularity and degraded appearance endangered Modest's job. He spoke in a shaking voice of the intrigues being planned against him. But they did not matter—"*Khovanchina* is going well," he said. Then he drank and was ill again. He was sinking rapidly to the bottom. Stassov begged Balakirev to save him by using his influence among his new friends who had power in the Government and the Church. "Mussorgsky is a corpse," remarked Mili; "there is no use doing anything for him." But he did something: T. I. Philipov, Mili's friend, gave Modest a small clerical job at the Office of the Imperial Comptroller, of which he was the head. It was only due to Philipov's prominence and his connections with the highest officials of the Government that Modest was tolerated there at all. His "work" consisted merely in his turning up on payday to collect his salary. But his conscience disturbed him. He himself realized that he could never again count on leading a regular life, but he still hoped to earn his living as a musician, wanted to give himself entirely to art. Was this not enough reason to be granted a living? Had he not proved that his one aim was to serve art?

Through his contacts at Naumov's home, Modest was constantly being invited by young students to participate as accompanist at various student benefit performances. Though he was at that time as poor as any of the needy students, he contributed his services gratis. These performances gave him new hope. "If worst comes to worst," he wrote to Stassov, "I can earn a living by tapping the keyboard."

The opportunity was not long in offering itself. A friend of Naumov's, Daria Leonova, at one time a fine singer, asked Modest to go with her as her accompanist on a tour through southern Russia. His old friends were opposed to this proposition. They had very little respect for Leonova and thought she was using Modest's name for the sake of publicity. Even Mili, who was not in the least disturbed by Modest's condition, wrote to Ludmilla Shestakova asking her to do everything in her power to prevent Modest from going on the trip. "How can Leonova take on such a responsibility? What will she do if the blood suddenly pours out of Modest as it did at your home?" But Modest expected to gain complete financial independence from the receipts of this tour, which he thought would bring him a thousand rubles, and he accepted. The tour was a failure, although Modest spoke of its great artistic success.

When Mussorgsky returned, it was clear that he could not earn his living by playing the piano. If he did not realize this himself, the critics mercilessly told him so. Only at times was great playing heard. He had not played for many years and, besides, he had never had a concert repertory. As for accompanying he was too unreliable for anybody except Leonova. It was unanimously affirmed that as accompanist Modest knew no equal; he brought

[235]

the art to heights unknown at the time. But even the students, who always used him for their benefit performances, knew that they must call him at the last moment, for there was no knowing whether he would be sober or not.

Fortunately, two groups of friends independently collected some money, and each supplied him with eighty rubles a month, supposedly for the purpose of making it possible for him to finish *Khovanchina* and *The Fair at Sorotchinsk*. He began work on the latter for his friend Petrov, the famous singer, but never finished it.

Modest's creative ability was dulled by now. His verve had slackened. He was too tightly held in the grip of financial destitution to do anything worth while. Now he decided that he must finish quickly all the works he had started. Without any definite plan, he was chopping *Khovanchina* to pieces, throwing out characters and scenes, and cutting whole acts. He hurriedly made piano arrangements from *Boris* for Bessel, the publisher, so that he could get some money.

He no longer lived at Naumov's, but in a small, miserable room that was called "furnished" on Offizerskaya Street. According to the poet A. N. Maikov, who called on Mussorgsky once at two o'clock in the afternoon, he found him, dressed in a frock coat, asleep in an armchair next to a dirty table covered with remnants of food and a couple of empty bottles; there was nothing else in the room.

Mussorgsky was more comfortable during the following summer at Leonova's home in Oranienbaum, where he "finished" *Khovanchina*. There he and Leonova made plans for and opened a joint music school. Once again Modest's enthusiasm was aflame. "He coached students and even taught theory," said Rimsky scornfully, remarking that the exercises Modest wrote for his students were full of mistakes. The school had only a few pupils at the beginning, and though Modest's faith in its success never wavered, the misery of his existence dragged him back into Maly Yaro-slavetz for longer and longer periods.

His last public appearance was on the 28th of January, 1881, the day of Dostoevsky's death, at a club where Dostoevsky's picture, swathed in black crape, was brought to the stage. Mussorgsky went to the piano and improvised a funeral march that sounded like his bells in *Boris*. As he played, the audience rose to listen to Modest's farewell to another man who had spoken out for "the insulted and the injured," and his own farewell to all living.

Two weeks later he came to Leonova in great excitement and told her that he had no money and no way of earning any, that he was facing starvation and would have to go on the streets to beg. She comforted him as much as she could, promising to share with him everything she possessed, and then later in the evening took him along to a party where one of her pupils was singing. Leonova remarked that when Mussorgsky accompanied her he was very nervous; either he was moved by the young girl's singing, or there were other reasons. An hour later Modest had a fit and fell unconscious to the floor.

When he recovered consciousness, Leonova took him to her carriage and prepared to drive him home, but on the way he begged her to let him stay at her house; he was afraid to be alone. The next morning he breakfasted with his hostess and seemed in good spirits, but as he got up from the table he suddenly fell again. Leonova summoned his friends, and it was decided to put him in the Military Hospital under the care of Dr. Bertensen, an old admirer of Modest's. Since Mussorgsky had been retired from the Army for so many years, he had to be entered in the hospital books as Bertensen's hired servant.

While in the hospital he at times showed signs of recovery. He even spoke of a trip to Constantinople or Crimea that he would like to take. But his fate was sealed. His brother Philaret visited him and left him some money. The two attendants were under strict orders not to buy any liquor for Modest, but "the heart is not a piece of stone" and they bought him a bottle of cognac.

On the 16th of March, 1881, his forty-second birthday, the one whom he had hated and mocked, whom he had made sing and dance in his music, came for his soul. He died of delirium tremens, and it was believed that the fits were epileptic. Whether or not he was actually insane during the last two months of his life has never been ascertained.

*   *   *

After his student days in Heidelberg, Borodin went abroad three more times. In 1877 he took two of his students to Jena to enroll them in the University where they were to take their doctor's degree. While in Jena he visited Liszt in Weimar which was, as he said, "as far as Tsarskoe Selo is from Petersburg." Liszt was always the ambassador-at-large for all young composers the world over, and his residence was a mecca to all musicians.

From the time of Liszt's visit to Russia in 1842 when he met Glinka, he had been interested in Russian music and, since Wagner had said his last word in *Parsifal*, Liszt's interest turned particularly to the development of Russian national music which he considered the only "vitalizing stream" in music at that time. He was well acquainted with all the important works of the Five, and a great admirer of Borodin.

Liszt thoroughly enjoyed his unique position in the musical world, and like a king bestowed his favor on all who flocked to him. He greeted Borodin with a princely welcome, clasping his hands with his iron fingers as in a vice, and took him directly into his life. For days Borodin lived as though in a dream, spending all his time with Liszt, taking meals with him, attending his classes, accompanying him to rehearsals and concerts, always surrounded by Liszt's adoring pupils, admirers, and patrons of art from the nobility. The atmosphere reminded Borodin of his early association with Balakirev, except that Liszt's life had more glamour.

[238]

Liszt praised Borodin's First Symphony, telling him that the first movement was perfect, that the Andante was a *chef-d'œuvre,* and that the Scherzo was enchanting. And then he began to pick (*"picorer"*—Borodin recalled Mussorgsky's picturesque expression) with his fingers on the piano the passages that particularly impressed him. Talking incessantly in both French and German, Liszt caught his hand and held him down to the sofa for a long, detailed interrogation on everything that was going on in music in Russia. First of all he wanted to know what success Borodin's work had had at home, what his plans were, whether he had a good publisher. He asked about Rimsky, whom he esteemed very highly and whose *Sadko,* despite its failure at the first performance in Vienna, he admired very much. He asked about Mili Balakirev. *Islamey* was lying on his piano; he played it himself and made his students study it. And he spoke to Borodin about Cui's book, *La Musique en Russie,* which contained an exposition of the views of the Five which Liszt had read with great interest. He talked to Borodin about the essence of future music. "You know, in Germany they compose a great deal. I'm lost in a sea of music which threatens to entirely submerge me. But heavens, how flat, how insipid it all is! Not a single living idea." This sounded like an echo of Mussorgsky. Liszt wanted to have Borodin's Second Symphony performed immediately, and Borodin telegraphed his publisher for the score.

Later Borodin took time from the third meeting of the Naturalist Society in Marburg (at which Hegel, a disciple of Darwin, read a paper on "Polynemes and Medusæ") and from visiting collections and museums and all the gatherings of students and professors, to go back to "Venusberg, where Liszt was the Venus." Liszt performed his Second Symphony the day after the score arrived.

Borodin went on to Bonn and Aix-la-Chapelle, and planned to go to Strasbourg and Munich to see Erlenheimer. But he intended to pay one more visit—this time neither as scientist nor as musician, but as a devoted husband to the place where his romance had been born: Heidelberg. He had not been there for seventeen years, and the vivid memories of his youth swelled his heart uncomfortably but pleasantly. As he rode from Mainz along the River Rhine he watched from his window "all these Beneheims, Hennenheims, and the other heims" and scanned every hill, house, village, and footpath where once he and Ekaterina had spent their happiest moments. He jumped into an omnibus and rode to the Badischer Hof, the hotel where he had stopped for the first time in 1859. As he rode, he watched all the familiar streets. As one does in a dream, he felt that he was looking at places he had seen long ago and that now he knew beforehand what would come next. There was the Hauptstrasse, next would be the Darmstädter Hof, then Derara, then the Goldner Engel. At the hotel, he unconsciously sat down at the same table in the dining room where he had sat seventeen years ago. The cane chair was extremely comfortable; it felt like "his" chair. And the guests at the table seemed like old friends, though he saw them for the first time. It was the same table d'hôte, and the dishes tasted exactly as they had seventeen years ago. They tasted very good to him.

He wanted to go to Hofmann's pension, where he had met Ekaterina for the first time, to the little house with the old, worm-eaten staircase, but he did not dare to ask about it. "What if the little house has been destroyed, razed to the ground? What if the name of Hofmann is forgotten?" He walked by St. Peter's Church where he had played in the orchestra, passed the museum where he used to rehearse, the little confectioner's and No. 12 Friedrichstrasse where he had shared a room with Mendeleev before his marriage.

He turned to the right and found himself in front of Kapfengasse 6, where Erlenmeyer's laboratory had been. Borodin went into the courtyard. The laboratory no longer existed, but the buildings were intact. He saw the window of the room where he had worked. Then two doors away he saw No. 2, his little lodgings with "the linen closet." He wanted to go in, but he hesitated; an old woman was sitting at the window, knitting in German fashion with one finger in the air; and he didn't dare to go in.

He could hear his own heart beating as he started on the road to Wolfsbrunnen. It was as familiar to him as the five fingers of his hand, but it looked as though it had been swept and widened—perhaps for his coming, he thought. At Wolfsbrunnen everything was the same, except that a covered gallery had been added. He sat down opposite the pool in which trout were swimming. The water was still flowing in four streams from the wolves' mouths, just as it had flowed "then." "It has been flowing like that for seventeen years!" A young waitress of fifteen came up to him, smiling pleasantly. He was sure she was going to say, "At last you have come to see us. Why have you been away so long?"

"Will you have a beer, or something else?" she asked.

He looked in vain for the stones on which Ekaterina and he had sat, and the rock near the gate of the town where he had seized Ekaterina like a lunatic and knocked down her umbrella. "The ruthless hand of progress has destroyed these relics and planted a railway line all along the river," Borodin reflected.

In a little street crossing the running Bergheimerstrasse he found Hofmann's pension. "Does Herr Professor Hofmann live here?" Borodin asked.

"The Herr Professor died a fortnight ago."

It was short and to the point, thought Borodin.

"The Frau Professor is at home. Shall I announce you?"

Sophie Petrovna appeared, dressed in black, and was glad to see him. In a few words she gave him the details of the death of her husband, who had succumbed after an attack of apoplexy. She spoke of her children. Little Mary was married in London and was already the mother of another little Mary. Little Heinrich had been living in Hamburg for some time. . . . Borodin squinted his eyes trying to remember Heinrich—he must be the one who had been thrown into a water tank by one of the students. . . . Charlie, the little Charlie whose life Borodin had saved by extracting a piece of glass from his throat, was finishing his studies at the university.

In the little dining room of the old pension everything was the same. The same misses and madams from the British Isles who boarded at the pension sat "preserved like conserves," decorously and ceremoniously sipping their coffee.

Sophie Petrovna asked about Ekaterina, and introduced him to her little English niece Lulu. Borodin raised his eyebrows at the name. Lulu, young and pretty, was born and raised in Moscow but educated in Heidelberg. The delicate young lady was engaged to a Russian doctor named Bedriaga, who soon made his appearance. The young doctor of philosophy at the University of Jena was a Muscovite, a passionate music-lover, a good pianist, and ("Fancy—of all things!") a nephew of Rimsky-Korsakov. He knew Borodin by name. Now he was studying zoology and going through the stage of Wolfsbrunnen and Schloss—long walks under the trees and through the dark arcades at night with his fiancée, with whom he was in love up to his ears. Borodin had no difficulty in understanding the young man.

In the summer of 1881 while in Magdeburg, Borodin met Liszt again, and with him listened to Rimsky's *Antar* Symphony conducted by Nikisch. Seated next to them was Gille, Liszt's intimate friend since 1840, an enthusiast for modern music whose vivacity, brusqueness, and freedom of sarcasm reminded Borodin of Stassov.

He visited Liszt once again in Weimar. On the day of Borodin's arrival, Liszt urged him to make a four-hand arrangement of his *Steppes of Central Asia,* the score of which he had just received. "Here, here, wait! I will get you some paper." Liszt wanted the work done by the next morning. "Spiridon," he called to his servant, "bring me some music paper." But before Spiridon had a chance to move, Liszt was already writing "Primo, Secundo" on a sheet of paper that he found in the cupboard. Liszt talked as

Mili used to talk, and Borodin remained Borodin. On taking his leave, he forgot the paper. This was the last time Borodin saw Liszt. His third visit to Europe was to Belgium.

It was purely by accident that the Countess Maria de Mercy-Argenteau, a wealthy Belgian and a patroness of art, became acquainted with the music of the new Russian school. In the fall of 1882 a young Belgian musician, Théodore Jadoul, with whom she often played duets, brought her the score of Napravnik's *Danses nationales.* She was so much impressed by the ingenious and colorful manner in which Napravnik had introduced the folk-themes into his pieces that Jadoul wrote to the composer asking him about his other works as well as those of other contemporary Russian composers. Napravnik replied that he knew only one Russian who was remarkable—Tchaikovsky. But though Tchaikovsky's compositions impressed the Countess with their "feminine grace," she found them rather monotonous and plaintive. Then in 1883 Jadoul sent her Borodin's *Steppes of Central Asia* and Cui's *Polka for Piano,* and these revived her interest in Russian music. She wrote to Cui, and when the latter sent her his book, *La Musique en Russie,* which mentioned not only Napravnik and Tchaikovsky but also several of their contemporaries—Balakirev, Mussorgsky, Liadov, Rimsky, and Borodin—she felt that she had found a "real gold mine."

To understand their vocal compositions better, she studied Russian and translated their available songs into French. In connection with this work she corresponded with Cui. He told Borodin about her, told him that she liked his *Steppes.*

"What of it?" shrugged Borodin. He was nursing his cat Vasily, who was old and ill.

Then the Countess wrote to him herself, asking him if he did not know that he was a great composer, and why he did not compose more. Borodin did not reply immediately. He had not answered his friends' letters for almost a year. Ekaterina had just returned for a short visit, and the whole house was upside-down. The two adopted girls had grown up. They were marrying Borodin's pupils. Lectures, committees, and examinations at the Academy kept him busy.

"My dear Madame," he wrote finally to the Countess de Mercy-Argenteau, in answer to a letter that had been lying for more than six months on his desk. "I am flattered and touched by your kindness . . ." and so on.

But the capricious Countess was not going to allow his Slavic inertia to stand in her way. With the art of a woman of the world she adjusted her correspondence in such a way that two months later Borodin was writing to her: "You are to me what the good Princess is in the fable . . ." This sounded more to the Countess' taste. Three months later Borodin addressed her as "Dear, good mother," and closed with "I reverently kiss your little hands, which you must keep on me." He spoke of himself as "a white bear from the steppes of a barbarous land covered with snow, a bear who feeds on church candles," and referred to the Countess as a "supreme being." ". . . You are extraordinary."

"No, it is you who are extraordinary," repeated the Countess, as in a duet.

And Borodin corrected her translations of the arias and choruses from *Prince Igor*, cautioning her that it was a Russian opera for Russians.

In her enthusiasm, the Countess decided to propagandize Russian music in her own country, and began by giving, during the winter of 1885 in Liége, three concerts whose programs were exclusively devoted to the Russian school. Once her enterprise proved successful, particularly with Borodin's First Symphony which had to be repeated at each concert, she decided to arrange concerts at the International Exhibition that was about to open in Antwerp.

Borodin, interested in the exhibition as a scientist, and pleased by the success of his symphony in Liége, accepted the invitation to come to Belgium. Belgian hospitality, which surpassed anything Borodin had hitherto known, made him feel as though he were "living in clover," as he said. The organizers of the Antwerp Exhibition requested his presence at a concert of Russian and Slavonic music. As had been Balakirev's experience in Prague, the German colony did everything in its power to prevent the performance of Borodin's Second Symphony. However, both symphonies, his *Steppes,* and his songs created such a furor and he made so many friends that he promised to come back for performances of his works in Brussels.

The indefatigable Countess persuaded the directors of the Liége theater to accept Cui's first opera, *The Prisoner of the Caucasus,* which she had translated herself, and the performance was scheduled for the Christmas holidays of 1885 so that Cui could come and take part in the final rehearsals. Other concerts, scheduled by the Société d'Emulation, were to include Borodin's Second Symphony at public concerts in Brussels and at the Liége Conservatory.

Thus it was the two least revolutionary members of the Mighty Five who came to witness the success abroad of the new Russian school. The Countess de Mercy-Argenteau was "all joy, agitation, and emotion," and like a "true-bred hen" kept her protégés by her side—one on her right and one on her left. Perhaps the reason for her close surveillance of Borodin was that in the short time of her acquaintance with him she had learned that Borodin would never do today what could be done tomorrow.

Enjoying the hospitality of the Countess at her old chateau, the two musicians spent a month in a whirl of activities. The newspapers heralded their arrival, and music shops displayed their music, as well as Rimsky's. They attended rehearsals and concerts both in Liége and in Brussels where their music, as well as Rimsky's *Antar* and fragments from *The Maid of Pskov,* were performed. Success and applause followed them from one city to another.

Cui's opera *The Prisoner of the Caucasus* had great success despite the fact that the performance was very much like that of *A Life for the Tsar* which Balakirev had witnessed in Prague. "The choruses were pitiable," Borodin commented. "As for the dances, the deuce knows what they were like! The costumes were laughable. The Cherkess costumes, with their cartridge bags and fur caps, were all right, but the rest were the very devil. The women were dressed neither like Russians, nor Tatars, nor Georgians. The prisoner himself was dressed like a coachman without sleeves." But the enthusiasm of the audience knew no bounds. Cui was presented with a gilded lyre and recalled with fervor. His success was so great that negotiations were soon under way for a performance of his *Angelo*.

But the height of their success was reached at two concerts given in Brussels. The first concert was performed in the Salle de la Grande Harmonie on Saturday, chiefly because the English would not listen to profane music on Sunday. Then on Sunday the performance was repeated at the Théâtre de la Monnaie for the Belgians. At the close of the Russian concerts, at which Borodin's Second Symphony created a furor, the two composers bowed from their box as the Belgians shouted, *"Vivent les Russes! Vive la Russie!"* The host of celebrities, musical, theatrical, and literary, who attended the performances, invited the two to so many parties that, had they accepted the invitations, they would have had to spend another two months abroad.

Borodin had witnessed the complete success of his musical work. As he journeyed home, he realized that in the past few years he had become recognized as a composer, and had gained a solid reputation abroad. His first symphony had achieved success in festivals and concerts at Baden-Baden, Leipzig, Dresden, Rostock, Antwerp, and Liége. His second symphony had been performed at popular concerts in Brussels, Liége, and Sondershausen. But the most successful of all was *The Steppes of Central Asia*. It had gone the rounds of Europe from Christiania to

Monaco. In spite of its patriotic and national tenor, it was played in Vienna and Paris. His Quartet, which had been performed repeatedly in Europe, traveled across the ocean to be played at a concert of the Philharmonic Society in Buffalo, New York.

Back home once more, Borodin, stimulated by his success, was eager to start on new work. But Ekaterina was ill, and he spent most of his time with her in Moscow. Then he returned to Petersburg to his university work. "Do you know that I have the embryo of the Third Symphony? But it will be long before it will see the world. I still have so much work to do on *Prince Igor*, which progresses very slowly," Borodin wrote to Ekaterina on February 3, 1887.

Twelve days later Borodin was entertaining guests at a costume party arranged by the Academy students and professors. Dressed in the Russian blouse and high boots, he danced and joked with his friends. While talking with one of these, he suddenly fell to the floor. At first the guests thought Borodin was joking, imitating somebody, as he had done earlier in the evening. The pairs were still dancing to the raucous piano music when Borodin stopped breathing. He had died instantly of a heart attack. Very few people had known of his heart ailment.

* * *

As far back as 1884, Rimsky had written to a friend in connection with the revision of his First Symphony: "What a disgraceful composition! Not so much in its adolescent ideas as in the complete technical ignorance it betrays. Oh, new Russian school! Oh, Stassov! Oh, Balakirev! whom we all loved so and in whom now I am more and more disappointed both as musicians and as men."

A new life was starting for Rimsky. Its story does not belong in this volume—the story of his loss of faith in himself due to his theoretical studies; his gradual rebirth as the artist the world has admired for the past half-century as the composer of *Snegurochka*, the *Capriccio espagnol, Le Coq d'or,* and *Scheherazade;* and his leadership of another group of young musicians in a circle known as the "Belaievs." *

As concerns his association with the Five, Rimsky is responsible for the present versions of Mussorgsky's operas *Boris Godunov* and *Khovanchina,* and Borodin's *Prince Igor,* which he edited and completed with the help of Glazunov, who wrote out the overture from what he could remember of Borodin's own playing. Immediately after Mussorgsky's death, Rimsky set out to organize and revise as well as rewrite all the *Khovanchina* material. When Rimsky's version of the opera was presented to the Directors of the Maryinsky Theater, it was rejected; the dominant influence on their decision being Napravnik's view that one revolutionary opera was enough. (*Boris* was still considered part of the repertory, though no longer performed.) In 1911 *Khovanchina* was resurrected and made immortal by Chaliapin. According to Diaghilev, who presented the opera in 1913 in Paris, Rimsky's version left "not one stone on another of the original Mussorgsky."

Boris fared even worse at Rimsky's hands. Out of the 258 pages of Rimsky's score, hardly twenty conform to the original text. Rimsky cut, altered modulations and harmonies, and—besides all the retouching and embellishing—actually took the liberty of changing the order of the last two scenes, thus distorting the essence and the psychology of the drama. What Rimsky did to *Boris,* artistically, will be clear only when Modest's first version of the opera (the one rejected by the Directors) is allowed to speak for itself. But that *Boris Godunov* is known to all is due to Chaliapin's first performance of it in 1904.

Rimsky's friendship with Mili lasted until the early nineties. They worked together on Glinka's scores at the Free Music School and at the Imperial Chapel; but, because of the continual friction in connection with their work, their friendship disinte-

* A circle of musicians fostered by M. P. Belaiev, music publisher and patron of art.

grated first into a cordial relationship and then into a final break. Rimsky, who was nearing fifty, would no longer tolerate Mili's despotic attitude or his weird behavior.

Nor could Rimsky forgive Cui's criticism of his operas *May Night* and *Snegurochka,* and the relationship between the two became that of two mere acquaintances. Whether Mme. Cui's remark to Rimsky, after a performance of *Snegurochka,* to the effect that at last he had learned to compose an opera meant *"We* think so," or was just a tactless blunder of her own, it certainly did nothing to warm Rimsky's feeling toward the circle on which he had turned his back.

His friendship with the old "combatants" was so weak that petty incidents sufficed to destroy it completely. He was no longer so close to Stassov. When in the first months of 1887 Anton Rubinstein planned a series of Russian operas to be financed by funds from the concerts of the Russian Musical Society, and to that end invited Rimsky to conduct in the following season, Stassov, always suspicious of Rubinstein's "Russophilism," accused Rimsky of betrayal and treachery to the future of Russian music by making himself, as he said, a hired workman for Rubinstein. "Let Cui," wrote Stassov, "who would do anything in his ambition for fame, fall for such bait."

Nadejda Rimsky-Korsakov answered the letter for her husband:

"Your letter has made me very angry. I am furious and feel I must tell you so. All your lion's pronouncements are irrelevant and ridiculous. You are fighting windmills. What right have you to suspect my husband of being a base renegade and devil knows what? You should write your mean letters to those who gossip with you. And I hope that Nicolas does not need anyone's advice to act honorably and honestly. Nicolas and Rubinstein made no mention of the concerts you spoke of. Nicolas agreed to conduct the regular concerts of the Russian Musical Society orchestra only if he could have complete freedom in choosing the programs, and I see no reason why this should bring more harm to the future of Russian music than when Balakirev conducted the orchestra and everyone was so delighted. As for 'hired workmen,' my husband has never been that to anybody and never will be. Goodbye."

In all fairness to Nadejda Rimsky-Korsakov it should be said that, though she was the closest collaborator in all her husband's creative work, she had never lost her individual critical ability, and expressed it freely to Rimsky. Of the two, it was she who remained loyal to the basic ideas of the Mighty Five. She was interested in new thought and not in "the same but said differently."

*   *   *

Balakirev outlived his popularity, outlived what he had stood for and what his call had been in the field of art. When in 1881 he became the Director of the Imperial Chapel, he reached the position of a middle-class employee which guaranteed him a steady income, with a comfortable life free from immediate material worries and with the security he had needed ever since his arrival in St. Petersburg in 1857. It was the lack of this security (except for the brief period when he had conducted the Russian Musical Society) that had caused the failure of all his projects. But when Mili reached this position after his years of pious religious mania, he was no longer the eagle that Stassov called him.

Balakirev's six-room apartment was divided by a corridor into two parts of three rooms each. He occupied the front rooms while Adrian, his servant, butler, private secretary, handyman, and expert in meat pies and strawberry preserves, shared the back rooms with the cook. The large sitting room with three windows facing the garden was kept in semi-darkness. Heavy curtains prevented the sunshine from penetrating into the apartment. Between the windows were old-fashioned glass shelves on which sat two bronze candelabra. An autographed portrait of Liszt hung above a delicate model of a harmonium under a glass bell; it had been presented to Mili by admirers. Next to it lay a marble hand of Liszt holding a gold pen, a piece of sculpture for which, according to Stassov, Balakirev's admirers had combed the art shops of Europe. A heavy bronze clock, also under a glass bell, stood on a little table that was covered with albums containing pictures of Prague, Berlin, and Warsaw. The soft divans and armchairs, upholstered in blue silk, were spread with white sheeting during weekends. On the walls hung portraits of Glinka, Beethoven, and Mozart, and a large set of shelves containing beautifully bound volumes of music stood next to the two grand pianos. Balakirev cherished the three top shelves particularly, for these contained Chopin's and Liszt's works which he rewrote, rearranged, and edited—and considered better than the original. A large etching of John Hus' triumphal march to death stood on one of the pianos. Presiding over all this in one corner was a large image of the Virgin. The entire icon was studded with small pearls, and a little oil lamp burned under it day and night.

On New Year's Day and Easter, Adrian would hang about the walls the wreaths and laurel leaves decorated with gold-inscribed ribbons that betokened Balakirev's public successes, thus giving the room an even gloomier appearance, until it suggested a graveyard. But as time went on, this ceremony was canceled because it only awakened painful memories.

No one was allowed to enter Balakirev's bedroom, his holy of holies. The small room was kept in darkness except for the light from the candles and oil lamps that burned before the icons on the walls. Portraits of patriarchs and high dignitaries of the Russian Church, dressed in their robes and with large silver stars and crosses on their breasts, looked down severely from their heavy frames. A few soiled shirts and underclothes and an old odd pair of trousers lay around in disorder. In this room Balakirev slept and prayed.

For his work, Balakirev used the dining-room table, which was covered with small objects necessary for letter-writing, as well as a heavy iron cross that he had brought with him from Prague in memory of John Hus. He never believed in using the telephone, and answered every letter by hand. Nor did he believe in electricity, but insisted that kerosene lamp light was better for his eyes. Instead of a lounging robe, he wore an old-fashioned caped coat that served him as raincoat and overcoat as well.

He lived ceremoniously. Adrian had to announce his visitors by bringing their cards to his master on a small silver plate and then stand at the door and wait for Balakirev to order, "See him in." When bringing in a letter, Adrian had to serve with it a small silver knife with which Balakirev opened the envelope.

He did not like to mix his company, and had different days for his friends. The meals were served with old-fashioned etiquette. Adrian would appear at the door as master-of-ceremonies and announce: "Dinner is served, sir," then stand back of Mili's chair throughout dinner to observe his every order. The table was always laden with all sorts of hors d'œuvres, fruit, and a large fruit cake. Occasionally wine was served, but Mili did not indulge in either drinking or smoking and did not approve of them. Otherwise he was a very hospitable host. At the table he wanted his guests to have plenty of everything. He always urged them to have more, and if they refused he would shake his head and say, "You don't behave very well today," and then would himself make an extra sandwich of whatever was on the table and offer it impaled on the end of a knife.

Balakirev had his own musical evenings on Tuesday. Women were not invited, and of his old friends only Cui came, and but once or twice. It was an entirely different group of people: colonels from the Cossack regiments, critics from the most reactionary papers, occasionally a priest, and a few pupils among whom was Serge Liapunov, a talented young composer who was the only worthy visitor at these gatherings. They usually discussed the latest articles that had appeared in musical magazines, generally of foreign publication, because Mili looked with disdain on anything written in Russia and considered it a disgrace to be praised

[252]

by a Russian. He was particularly interested in the writings of Calvocoressi, the more so when he learned that the man was of the Greek Orthodox Church, which made Mili feel a spiritual kinship with him. They would play Liapunov's latest work, and occasionally Mili would go to the piano to illustrate one of his own ideas. These gatherings, however, resembled midnight services more than they did the old Balakirev meetings at which Stassov and his former pupils clashed in their beliefs as to what the new Russian school should strive for.

The young musicians who surrounded him at the concerts, although they called themselves "Balakirevs," were not the men whom musical circles and critics had feared but admired in the late sixties. When after a performance Mili would storm into the greenroom and scream, "Who composed that garbage?"—or when he refused to play on a Bekker piano because he no longer enjoyed the friendship of the owner of the firm, saying that the piano was "just a frying pan"—no one was seriously impressed. Mili was a haughty, contemptuous, bitter, and lazy old man, and by his unrestrained language alienated all his friends. Of the old circle he preferred not to speak, and usually changed the subject if it was mentioned. When Rimsky's memoirs were published, Mili said he was not interested in seeing them.

During the ten-year period in which he held the position of Director of the Imperial Chapel, he composed almost nothing. "It is not God's will," he explained to Ludmilla Shestakova. Instead, he took a real interest in reorganizing the Chapel, and the reconstruction of the building and the concert hall was due to his initiative.

Balakirev's attitude toward his students was always that of a benevolent father. He fed the poor pupils, helped whole families financially, and refused to accept any payment of debts owing him even at the time when he was not too well provided for. Adrian would shake his head: "You need new shirts and clothes, and yet you still give away money!"

[253]

Owing to his close association with the high officials and clergy connected with the Imperial Chapel, Balakirev's views became even more reactionary. He was such a great admirer of the absolute monarchy of Alexander III that when Nicolas II ascended the throne Mili resigned from his position. He had utter contempt for the official ministers close to the young Tsar; and, as for the Grand Dukes, they were "walking barefoot in the clouds and nothing good can come of their influence."

In 1898 he appeared for the last time in public as a conductor. This time he presented his own symphony, his First Symphony, which he had been composing for forty years. From then on he worked on various compositions that he had always wanted to finish, wrote a piano concerto, and composed his Second Symphony.

Balakirev lived by himself during his last years, almost forgotten by everyone, and in 1910 died of a heart ailment. His companions at the end were two stray cats. When at his burial someone wanted to make a speech at the grave, Serge Liapunov stopped him, saying that Mili's wish was to "let the voice of the Church speak last for me."

*　　*

Cui, as though preserved by his regular, uneventful life, lived to be eighty-three years old. He taught the art of fortification to seven Grand Dukes, including Nicolas II, and to scores of Russian military heroes. In his military career he reached the rank of General, and as a musician he became the president of the Imperial Russian Musical Society. He no longer saw much of Balakirev, nor did he follow Rimsky into Belaiev's circle. Cui composed on his own and, if he was influenced at all, it was by his friendship with Countess de Mercy-Argenteau, with whom he spent his summer vacations. His compositions became more lyrical, more romantic, and more French. He wrote several operas but, though they were produced both in Russia and abroad, they never created enough interest to remain in the operatic repertory. As a composer, Cui was a miniaturist, and his work would always be most successful in the drawing room.

He himself wrote that the failure of his *Ratcliff* did not discourage him, and that his unpopularity did not disturb his spirit. "I face calmly the fate of my compositions, for it is in their creation that I find complete satisfaction."

Cui's chief service in the cause of the Mighty Five lay in the clear analysis of their aims which he gave to the public in the articles he wrote when "the pot was boiling," and when he waged war against the old Moscow school. "Many years later," he wrote, "when my aim was reached and my comrades-in-art had been recognized in the world, I laid aside my pen with the feeling of complete satisfaction." A great deal of ink as well as nervous energy had been spent in this fight, with no apparent victory at the time for either side. History has shown that the victor was Russian music.

In 1915, when he was past eighty, César Cui finished Mussorgsky's *Fair at Sorochinsk,* and it was presented in October 1917 during the turmoil of the Russian Revolution. He died six months later, in March 1918. His death passed unnoticed, for Russia was afire. The tocsin was calling to all citizens: "On to new shores! Fearless through storm, shallow water and reefs—on to new shores!"

* * *

Bibliography

BOOKS, ARTICLES, AND PERIODICALS CONSULTED
IN THE PREPARATION OF THIS BOOK

Mihail Ivanovich Glinka

"Polnoe sobranie pisem Mihaila Ivanovicha Glinki." Izd. Nik. Findeizenom. In *Russkaya muzykal'naya gazeta*, 1908, Vol. 2.

Pisma M. I. Glinki. In *Russki Arkhiv*, Moscow, 1869 and 1890.

"Pisma i programmi po povodu opery 'Russlan i Lyudmila.' " In *Russkaya Starina*, St. Petersburg, 1877, Vol. 5.

Abraham, Gerald—The Foundation-stone of Russian Music. In *Music and Letters*. London, 1937, Vol. 18.

Abraham, Gerald—Glinka. In *Studies of Russian Music*. Scribner, New York, 1939.

"Zapiski Mihaila Ivanovicha Glinki." Izdanie *Russkoi Stariny*, St. Petersburg, 1871.

Baskin, V.—"Izd. pisem M. I. Glinki." In *Prilogenie k Nive*, 1908, Fevral.

Bulgakov, M. A.—"Vospominaniya o M. I. Glinke. In *Russkaya muzycal'naya gazeta*, St. Petersburg, 1899.

Calvocoressi, M. D.—"Tvorchestvo Glinki. In *Niva*, Prilogenie, St. Petersburg, 1911.

Calvocoressi, M. D.—*Glinka*. In *Les Musiciens Célèbres*. H. Laurens, Paris.

Engelgardt, N. A.—"Davnie Episody." In *Istoricheski Vestnik*, St. Petersburg, 1912, #9.

Findeizen, N. F.—*M. I. Glinka*. Gosudarstvenaya Philarmoniya, Petrograd, 1922.

Findeizen, N. F.—"Biografiya Glinki: Detstvo, otrochestvo i yunost." In *Egegodnik Imperatorskikh Teatrov*, St. Petersburg, 1896-97, Vol. 2.

Findeizen, N. F.—*M. I. Glinka: Ocherk evo gizni i muzykal'noi deyatelnosti*. Moscow, P. Yurgenson, 1903.

Findeizen, N. F.—"Pushkin i Glinka." In *Russkaya muzykal'naya gazeta*, St. Petersburg, 1899, #4.

Fried, S. B.—"Rodonochal'nik Russkoi Muzyki." In *Vestnik Znaniya*, St. Petersburg, 1912, #2 and #4.

"M. I. Glinka." In *Russkaya muzykal'naya gazeta*, St. Petersburg, 1894, 1895 i 1903.

Glovacheva (Panayeva), A.—"Vospominaniya." In *Istoricheski Vestnik*, St. Petersburg, 1889, Vols. 35, 36, 37, 38.

Insarskii, V. A.—"Iz Zapisok." In *Russkaya Starina*, 1894, b. 1-3.

Karmalina, L. I.—"Vospominaniya 'Glinka i Dargomijsky.'" In *Russkaya Starina*, St. Petersburg, 1875, Vol. 13.

Kashperov, N.—"Vospominaniya o Glinke." In *Russki Arkhiv*, Moscow, 1869.

Kern, A. P.—*Vospominaniya*. (Including a supplement: "Pisma Glinki k A. P. Kern.) Leningrad, *Academia*, 1929.

Krasev, A.—"Mihail Ivanovich Glinka." In *Vsemirni Vestnik*, St. Petersburg, 1906, Vol. 2.

Kuznetzov, K. A.—*Glinka i evo sovremeniki*. Gosudarstvenaya Academia Khudogestvenykh Nauk, Moscow, 1926.

Laroche, G. A.—"Glinka i evo znachenie v istorii muzyki." In *Russki Vestnik*, Moscow, 1867, Vol. 10.

Montagu-Nathan, M.—*Introduction to Russian Music*.

Montagu-Nathan, M.—*History of Russian Music.* Scribner, New York, 1918.

Montagu-Nathan, M.—Glinka. In *Masters of Russian Music.* London, 1916; Duffield, New York, 1917.

"Neizdanye pisma Glinki (1851-55)." In *Russkaya muzkal'naya gazeta,* St. Petersburg, 1897.

"Novye materialy dlya biografii Glinki: Pisma k nemu K. A. Bulgakova, A Gedeonova, N. Kukolnika i Ya. Yanenki." In *Russkaya muzykal'naya gazeta,* St. Petersburg, 1896 and 1897.

Shestakova, L. I.—"Zapiski Glinki." In *Russkaya Starina,* St. Petersburg, 1870, Vols. 1 and 2.

Shestakova, L. I.—"Byloe M. I. Glinki i evo roditelei." In *Egegodnik Imperatorskikh Teatrov,* St. Petersburg, 1892-93.

Shestakova, L. I.—"Poslednie gody gizni i konchina M. I. Glinki." In *Russkaya Starina,* St. Petersburg, 1870, Vol. 2.

Rieseman, Oskar von—*Monographien zur russischen Musik.* Drei Maskenverlag, München, 1923-1926, Vol. 1.

Stassov, V. V.—"M. I. Glinka: Novye materialy dlya evo biografii." In *Russkaya Starina,* St. Petersburg, 1889, Vol. 61.

Stassov, V. V.—"Novye materialy dlya biografii M. I. Glinki." In *Egegodnik Imperatorskikh Teatrov,* St. Petersburg, 1892-93-94.

Stepanov, P. A.—"Vospominaniya o Glinke (1825-55)." In *Russkaya Starina,* St. Petersburg, 1877.

Strugorschikov, A. N.—"Vospominaniya o M. I. Glinke." In *Russkaya Starina,* St. Petersburg, 1874.

Tzetlin, M. O.—*Pyatero i drugie.* Novyi Gournal, New York, 1944.

Alexander Sergeivich Dargomijsky

"Avtobiografiya i perepiska." V. G. Kastrioto-Skanderbek i V. V. Stassov. In *Russkaya Starina*, St. Petersburg, 1875, Vols. 12 and 13.

"Avtobiografiya i pisma A. S. Dargomijskavo." In *Artist*, Moskva, 1894, #35, #37, #39.

"A. S. Dargomijsky." In *Egegodnik Imperatorskikh Teatrov*, St. Petersburg, 1903-1904.

"A. S. Dargomijsky: Po povodu 25 letiya so vremeni smerti." In *Russkaya Starina*, St. Petersburg, 1894, #2.

Brando, E.—"O Kamennom Goste Dargomijskavo." In *Apollon*, St. Petersburg, 1916, #1.

Cui, C.—"K Kharacteristike Dargomijskavo." In *Egegodnik Imperatorskikh Teatrov*, St. Petersburg, 1909, Vol. 3.

Findeizen, N. F.—*Alexsander Dargomijsky: Ocherk evo gizni i muzykal'noi deyatelnosti.*

Fried, S. B.—"Russkaya Muzyka." In *Vestnik Znaniya*, St. Petersburg, 1912, #6.

"Alexsander Sergeivich Dargomijsky." In *Russkaya muzykal'naya gazeta*, St. Petersburg, 1894.

Karatygin, V.—"Wagner i Dargomijsky." In *Apollon*, St. Petersburg, 1913, #8.

Karmalina, L. I.—"Vospominaniya: M. I. Glinka i A. S. Dargomijsky." In *Russkaya Starina*, St. Petersburg, 1875, Vol. 13.

Korzukhin, I.—"Alexsander Sergeivich Dargomijsky." In *Artist*, Moscow, 1894, otzyvy o Dargomijskom v. pechati, #33, and continued in subsequent volumes.

Kurdyumov, Yu.—"A. S. Dargomijsky kak opernyi compositor." In *Russkaya muzykal'naya gazeta*, St. Petersburg, 1904, Vol. 4.

"Novye materialy dlya biografii A. S. Dargomijskavo." In *Russkaya muzykal-naya gazeta,* St. Petersburg, 1896.

Riesemann, Oskar von.—*Monographien zur russischen Musik.* Drei Maskenverlag, München, 1923-1926, Vol. 1.

Sololov, V.—"Alexsander Sergeivich Dargomijsky v 1856-69." In *Russkaya Starina,* St. Petersburg, 1885, Vol. 46.

Timofeyev, G.—"A. S. Dargomijsky evo sem'ya, evo pervye shagi na compositorskom poprishe." In *Muzykalnyi Sovremenik,* Petrograd, 1917, #7-8.

Timofeyev, G.—"Dargomijsky i Znachenie evo tvorchestva." In *Vestnik Evropy,* St. Petersburg, 1913, #3.

Trifonov, P. A.—"A. S. Dargomijsky po evo avtobiografii, pismam i proizvedeni'yam." In *Vestnik Evropy,* St. Petersburg, 1886, Vol. 6.

Zvyerinski, A.—"K biografii A. S. Dargomijskavo." In *Sovremenik,* St. Petersburg, 1913, #9-10.

Mili Alexeivich Balakirev

"Iz perepiski M. A. Balakireva s P. I. Tchaikovskim." In *Vestnik Evropy*, St. Petersburg, 1912.

"Perepiska M. A. Balakireva s N. A. Rimsky-Korsakovym (1862-1908)." In *Muzykal'nyi Sovremenik*, Petrograd, 1916-17, and continued in subsequent volumes.

"Perepiska M. A. Balakireva s V. V. Stassovym." Vol. 1, 1858-69, Moskva, Ogis-Muzgis, 1935.

Bulitch, S.—"M. A. Balakirev." In *Vestnik Evropy*, St. Petersburg, 1910.

Findeizen, N. F.—"Biografia M. A. Balakireva." In *Russkaya muzykal'naya gazeta*, St. Petersburg, 1895.

Glebov, V. P.—"M. A. Balakirev." In *Istoricheski Vestnik*, Petrograd, 1916, 3, 12.

Karatygin, V.—"M. A. Balakirev." In *Apollon*, St. Petersburg, 1910, #10.

Karenin, V.—"M. A. Balakirev." In *Russkaya Mysl*, Year 31, Vol. 7, Moscow, 1910.

Liapunov, S.—"M. A. Balakirev." In *Egegodnik Imperatorskikh Teatrov*, St. Petersburg, 1910, Vols. 7 and 8.

Newmarch, Rosa—*The Life and Letters of P. I. Tchaikovsky*. John Lane Company, New York, 1906.

Prokofiev, G.—"M. A. Balakirev." In *Moskovski Egenedelnik*, Moscow, 1910, #21.

Rimsky-Korsakov, N.—*My Musical Life*. Alfred A. Knopf, New York, 1942.

Lakond, W., ed.—*The Diaries of Tchaikovsky*. W. W. Norton, New York, 1945.

Timofeyev, G.—"M. A. Balakirev." In *Russkaya Mysl,* 1912, Vols. 6 and 7.

Timofeyev, G.—"Balakirev v Prage." In *Sovremenyi Mir,* St. Petersburg, 1917, Vol. 6.

Bunimovich, V. T. (Muzalevsky, V.)—*Balakirev.* Leningrad, 1938.

Abraham, Gerald—*M. A. Balakirev.* New York, Scribner, 1939.

Stassov, V. V.—"Sobranie sochinenii: 25 let Russkavo isskustva." Isskusstvo v XIX veke, 25 letie Besplatnoi shkoly.

Weinstock, Herbert—*Tchaikovsky.* Alfred A. Knopf, New York, 1944.

Chernov—*Muzykal'naya Letopis,* Vol. 3.

Bowen, Catherine Drinker—*Free Artist.* Random House, New York, 1939.

Tzetlin, M. O.—"Pyatero i drugie." Novyi Gournal, New York, 1944.

César Antonovich Cui

Braudo, E.—"César Antonovich Cui." In *Apollon,* St. Petersburg, 1917. #8-10.

Cui, C.—"Neskol'ko slov o sovremennikh opernykh formakh." In *Artist,* Moskva, 1889, Vol. 4.

Cui, C.—"Iz moikh opernykh vospominanii." In *Egegodnik Imperatorskikh Teatrov,* St. Petersburg, 1899-1900, prilogenie 2-e.

Cui, C.—"Pervye compositorski shagi." In *Egegodnik Imperatorskikh Teatrov,* 1910, Vol. 1.

"Cui, César Antonovich." In *Egegodnik Imperatorskikh Teatrov,* St. Petersburg, 1892-93.

Cui, C.—*La Musique en Russie.* Krehbiel Collection, 1880.

Mercy-Argenteau, Countess de—*Memoirs.*

Findheizen, N. F.—"C. A. Cui." In *Russkaya muzykal'naya gazeta,* St. Petersburg, 1894, Vol. 1.

Kubileyu—"C. Cui." In *Russkaya muzykal'naya gazeta,* St. Petersburg, 1903.

Krechetov, K.—"Compositor o compositorakh." In *Severni Vestnik,* St. Petersburg, 1896, #6.

Krylov, V.—"C. A. Cui, Ocherk." *Prosaicheskiya sochineniya.* Leont'ev, St. Petersburg, 1908.

Tzetlin, M. O.—Pyatero i drugie. Novyi Gournal, New York, 1944.

Hazets, Alfred—*Borodin and Liszt.* Digby, Long and Company, London.

Rimsky-Korsakov, N.—*My Musical Life.* Alfred A. Knopf, New York, 1942.

Modest Petrovich Mussorgsky

"Avtobiograficheskaya zapiska M. P. Mussorgskavo." In *Muzykal'nyi Sovremenik*, Petrograd, 1917, #5-6.

Abraham, Gerald—"Mussorgsky's 'Boris' and Pushkin's." In *Music and Letters*, London, 1945, v. 26.

Platonova, Yu—"Novye Materialy dlya biografii Mussorgskavo." In *Russkaya muzykal'naya gazeta*, St. Petersburg, 1895.

"Neizdanye pisma Mussorskavo k L. I. Shestakovoi i P. S. Stassovoi." In *Muzykal'nyi Sovremenik*, Petrograd, 1917, #5-6.

"Neizdanye pisma Mussorskavo i Borodina." In *Russkaya muzykal'-naya gazeta*. St. Petersburg, 1897, Vol. 4.

Pisma k A. A. Golenishchevu-Kutusovu. Moscow, Gos. Muz. Izd. 1939.

Asaf'yev, B.—*M. P. Mussorgsky: Opyt kharacteristiki.* Moscow, Gos. Izd. 1923.

Baskin, V.—"M. P. Mussorgsky. Biograficheski ocherk." In *Russkaya Mysl*, Year 5, Vols. 9 and 10, Moscow, 1885.

Findeizen, N. F.—"Mussorgsky: Evo detstvo, yunost i pervyi period Muzykal'novo tvorchestva." In *Egegodnik Imperatotskikh Teatrov*, St. Petersburg, 1911, Vols. 1 and 2.

Fiodorov, V.—Mussorgsky: *biografie critique.* H. Laurens, Paris, 1935.

Fried, E.—*M. P. Mussorgsky: K 100 letiyu evo rogdeniya.* Leningradskaya Philarmoniya, Leningrad, 1939.

Karatygin. V.—*Mussorgsky.* Izd. biblioteki Gos. Acad. teatra, opery i baleta, St. Petersburg, 1922.

Karatygin, V.—"Nazionalnyi Muzykal'nil genii." In *Vseobschshi Egemesyachnik*, St. Petersburg, 1911, Vol. 11.

Karatygin, V.—"Rodoslovnaya M. P. Mussorgskavo po mugskoi i genskoi linii." In *Muzikal'nyi Sovremenik*, Petrograd, 1917, #5-6.

Komarova, V.—"Iz detskikh vospominanii o velikikh lyudyakh. Mussorgsky." In *Muzykal'nyi Sovremenik*, Petrograd, 1917, #5-6.

Lapshin, I.—"M. P. Mussorgsky." In *Muzykal'nyi sovremennik*, Petrograd, 1917, #5-6.

Montagu-Nathan, M.—*Moussorgsky. Masters of Russian Music*, Duffield and Company, New York, 1917.

Rieseman, Oskar von—*Monographien zur russischen Musik*. Drei Maskenverlag, München, 1923-26. Vols. 1 and 2.

Rieseman, Oskar von—*Moussorgsky*. Trans. from German by Paul England, Alfred A. Knopf, New York, 1929.

Sabaneyev, L.—"O Mussorgskom." In *Sovremennye Zapiski*, Paris, 1939, Vol. 68.

"M. P. Mussorgsky: K 100 letiyu so dnya smerti stat'i i materialy." Gosmuzizd, Moscow, 1932.

"M. P. Mussorgsky: Pisma i dokumenty," collected and edited by A. N. Rimsky-Korsakov. Gosmuzizd, Moscow-Leningrad, 1932.

Lukash, I.—*Bednaya Lyubov Moussorgskavo*. Knigoizd, Vozrogdenie, Paris, 1940.

Rimsky-Korsakov, A.—*H. A. Rimsky-Korsakov: Gizn i Tvorchestvo*. Vols. 1-4, Ogiz-Muzgiz, Moscow, 1933-37.

Rimsky-Korsakov, N.—*My Musical Life*. Alfred A. Knopf, New York, 1942.

Findeizen, N. F.—"Iz neizdannykh pisem. H. A. Rimsky-Korsakova." In *Egegodnik Imperatorskikh Teatrov*, St. Petersburg, 1913, Vol. 5.

Stassov, V. V.—"M. P. Mussorgsky." In *Vestnik Evropy*, St. Petersburg, 1881, Vol. 3.

Stassov, V. V.—"Pamyati Mussorgskavo." In *Vestnik Evropy*, St. Petersburg, 1886, Vol. 23.

Trifonov, P.—"M. P. Mussorgsky." In *Vestnik Evropy*, St. Petersburg, December, 1893.

Wolfurt, Kurt von—*Mussorgsky*. Deutsche Verlags-Anstalt, Stuttgart, 1923.

Tzetlin, M. O.—*Pyatero i drugie*. Novyi Gournal, New York, 1944.

Nicolay Andreivich Rimsky-Korsakov

Rimsky-Korsakov, A. N.—*N. A. Rimsky-Korsakov: Gisn i tvorchestvo*. Musgiz Ogiz, Moscow, 1933-37, Vols. 1-4.

Rimsky-Korsakov, N.—*My Musical Life*. Alfred A. Knopf, New York, 1942.

Findeizen. N. F.—"Iz neizdanykh pisem N. A. Rimskavo-Korsakova." In *Egegodnik Imperatorskikh Teatrov*, St. Petersburg, 1913, Vol. 5.

Karatygin, V.—"N. A. Rimsky-Korsakov." In *Egegodnik Imperatorskikh Teatrov*, St. Petersburg, 1909, Vol. 1.

Karenin, V.—"Pisma V. V. Stassova i N. A. Rimsky-Korsakova." In *Russkaya Mysl*, Moscow, 1910, Year 31, Vols. 7, 8, 9.

Montagu-Nathan, M.—*Rimsky-Korsakov*. In *Masters of Russian Music*, London, 1916.

"Perepiska M. A. Balakireva i N. A. Rimsky-Korsakova." In *Muzykal'nyi Sovremenik*, Petrograd, 1917, #7-8.

Stassov, V. V.—"N. A. Rimsky-Korsakov." In *Severnyi Vestnik*, St. Petersburg, 1890, Vol. 12.

Yastrebzev, V.—"Moi vospominaniya, Petrograd, 1915-16." Vols. 1-2, issued as supplement to *Russkaya muzykal'naya gazeta*, 1915-16.

Tzetlin, M. O.—*Pyatero i drugie*. Novyi Gournal, New York, 1944.

Alexander Porfiryevich Borodin

Pisma Borodina. Moskva Gosizd, 1927-36, Vol. 1 (1856-1871), Vol. 2 (1872-1877).

Abraham, Gerald E. H.—*Borodin the Composer and his Music.* London, 1927.

Berberova, N.—*Borodin.* Metropolis, Berlin, 1938.

Braudo, E.—"Borodin: K 30 letiyu evo konchini." In *Apollon,* St. Petersburg, 1917, #2-3.

"Koe chto novoe o Borodine." In *Russkaya muzykal'naya gazeta,* St. Petersburg, 1899.

"K portretam otza i matery Borodina." In *Russkaya muzykal'naya gazeta,* St. Petersburg, 1897, Vol. 4.

Khubov, G.—*A. P. Borodin.* Moskovsk, Gosudar, Izd. 1933.

"Neizdanye pisma Mussorgskavo i Borodina." In *Russkaya muzikal'naya gazeta,* St. Petersburg, 1897, Vol. 4.

Stassov, V. V.—"A. P. Borodin." In *Istoricheski Vestnik,* St. Petersburg, 1887, Vol. 28.

Stassov, V. V.—*A. P. Borodin.* St. Petersburg, 1887.

Timofeyev, G.—"Borodin: Gizn, tvorchestvo, neizdanye pisma." In *Sovremennik,* St. Petersburg, 1912, #8 and #9.

Trifonov, P.—"A. P. Borodin." In *Vestnik Evropy,* St. Petersburg, 1888, Vols. 5 and 6.

Tzetlin, M. O.—*Pyatero i drugie.* Novyi Gournal, New York, 1944.

Habets, Alfred—*Borodin and Liszt.* Digby, Long and Company, London.

Rimsky-Korsakov, N.—*My Musical Life.* Alfred A. Knopf, New York, 1942.

Principal Works of the Mighty Five

Balakirev

ORCHESTRAL MUSIC

Overture on a Spanish Theme (1857-58)
Overture on Three Russian Themes (1857-58)
Overture on Czech Themes (rev. in 1906 as In Bohemia, symphonic poem)
Overture to King Lear (1858-59)
Tamara, symphonic poem (1881)
Russia, symphonic poem (1882)
Symphony in C major (1897)
Symphony in D minor (1909)

PIANO MUSIC

Islamey
6 Mazurkas
3 Nocturnes
3 Scherzos
4 Waltzes
Spanish Serenade on a Theme by Glinka (1890)

VOCAL MUSIC

2 volumes Art Songs (1858-59)
2 volumes Russian Folk Songs (1861)

Borodin

CHAMBER MUSIC

String Sextet (1859-61)
String Quartet No. 1 in A major (1877-79)
String Quartet No. 2 in D major (1881-87)

OPERAS

The Bogatyrs (1867)
Prince Igor (begun 1869; completed posthumously by Rimsky-Korsakov
and Glazunov)

ORCHESTRAL MUSIC

Symphony No. 1 in E-flat major (1862-67)
Symphony No. 2 in B minor (1869-76)
In the Steppes of Central Asia, tone poem (1880)
Scherzo in A-flat major (1885)
Symphony No. 3 in A minor (1885-86; unfinished; two movements
orchestrated by Glazunov)

PIANO MUSIC

Polka, Requiem, Marche Funèbre, Mazurka (1880)
Petite Suite (1885)

VOCAL MUSIC

Songs

Cui

CHAMBER MUSIC

String Quartet in C minor, Op. 45 (1893)
Second String Quartet, Op. 68
Sonata for Violin and Piano, Op. 84
Third String Quartet, Op. 91 (1913)

CHORAL MUSIC

Two Choruses, for mixed voices and orchestra, Op. 4 (1860)
Seven Choruses, for a capella female voices, Op. 28
Five Choruses, Op. 46
Six Choruses, Op. 53
Two Choruses, for male voices, Op. 58
Seven Vocal Quartets, or Choruses, Op. 59
Les Oiseaux d'Argenteau, for children's voices

OPERAS

The Captive in the Caucasus (1859; rev. 1881)
The Mandarin's Son (1859)
William Ratcliffe (1869)
Angelo (1876)
Le Flibustier (1894)
Feast in Time of Plague (1901)
Mademoiselle Fifi (1903)
The Captain's Daughter (1911)

ORCHESTRAL MUSIC

Marche Solennelle, Op. 18 (1881)
Suite Concertante, for violin and orchestra, Op. 25 (1883)
Suite No. 2, Op. 38 (1887)

Suite No. 3, A Argenteau, Op. 40 (1887)
Suite No. 4, in Modo Populari, Op. 43
Bolero (1881)

PIANO MUSIC

Suite, dedicated to Liszt, Op. 21
Four Pieces, Op. 22
Valse Caprice, Op. 26
Two Polonaises, Op. 30
Three Valses, Op. 31
Three Impromptus, Op. 35
Six Small Pieces, Op. 39
Nine Pieces, Op. 40
Valses Movements, Op. 41
Five Pieces, Op. 52
Four Pieces, Op. 60
Theme and Variations, Op. 61
25 Preludes, Op. 64 (1904)

VOCAL MUSIC

Songs, Opp. 3, 5, 7, 9, 10, 11, 13, 18, 19, 27, 33, 37, 44, 48, 49, 55, 57, 62, and 86.

Mussorgsky

CHORAL MUSIC

The Rout of Sennacherib, for chorus and orchestra (1867)
Joshuah, for chorus and orchestra (1874)
Four Russian Folk Songs, for a cappella male choir (1880)

OPERAS

The Marriage (1868)
Boris Godunov (1868-69; rev. 1871-72)
Khovanchina (begun 1873; left almost completed; orchestrated and completed by Rimsky-Korsakov)
The Fair at Sorochinsk (begun 1874, and left unfinished; completed versions by Cui, Tcherepnin, and Shebalin)

ORCHESTRAL MUSIC

A Night on the Bald Mountain (1867)
Turkish March (1879)

PIANO MUSIC

Scherzo in C-sharp minor (1858)
Intermezzo (1861)
Memories of Childhood (1865)
Duma (1865)
La Capricieuse (1865)
La Couturière, scherzino (1871)
Pictures from an Exhibition (1874)
On the Shores of South Crimea (1879)

VOCAL MUSIC

Songs

Rimsky-Korsakov

CHAMBER MUSIC

String Quartet in F major, Op. 12 (1875)
String Sextet in A major (1876)
Quintet in B-flat major, for piano and wind (1876)
String Quartet in G major (1897)

CHORAL MUSIC

Choruses, Opp. 13, 14, 16, 18, and 19
Alexey, the Man of God, for chorus and orchestra, Op. 20 (1877)
Slava, for chorus and orchestra, Op. 21
Svitezyanka, cantata, for soprano, tenor, and mixed chorus, Op. 44 (1897)
Strekosy, for three-part women's chorus, Op. 53
Song of Oleg the Wise, cantata for men's chorus, Op. 58 (1899)
From Homer, prelude-cantata, Op. 60 (1901)

OPERAS

Maid of Pskov (1868-72; rev. 1876-78; rev. 1889-93)
May Night (1878)
Snow Maiden (Snegurochka) (1880-81)
Mlada (1889-90)
Christmas Eve (1894-95)
Sadko (1894-96)
Mozart and Salieri (1897)
The Tsar's Bride (1898)
Tsar Saltan (1899-1900)
Servilia (1900-01)
Kaschei the Immortal (1901-02)
Pan Voevoda (1902-03)

[273]

Kitezh (1903-04)
Le Coq d'Or (1906-07)

ORCHESTRAL MUSIC

Symphony No. 1 in E-flat minor, Op. 1 (1861-65; rev. in E minor, 1884)
Sadko, symphonic poem, Op. 5 (1867; rev. 1869; rev. 1891)
Fantasia on Serbian Themes, Op. 6 (1867; rev. 1888)
Symphony No. 2, Antar, Op. 9 (1868; rev. 1876; rev. 1897)
Overture on Three Russian Themes, Op. 28 (1866; rev. 1879-80)
Piano Concerto on a Russian Theme, Op. 30 (1882-83)
Symphony No. 3 in C, Op. 32 (1873-74; rev. 1885-86)
Fantasia on Russian Themes in B minor, for violin and orchestra, Op. 33 (1886)
Capriccio Espagnol, Op. 34 (1887)
Scheherazade, symphonic suite, Op. 35 (1888)
Russian Easter Overture, Op. 36 (1888)
Musikalische Bilder, suite from Tsar Saltan, Op. 57
Suite from Pan Voevoda, Op. 59
On the Tomb, in memory of Belaiev, Op. 61 (1904)
Dubinushka (1905)

PIANO MUSIC

Piano Pieces, Opp. 10, 11, 15, and 17

VOCAL MUSIC

Songs, Opp. 2, 3, 4, 7, 8, 25, 26, 27, 39, 40, 41, 42, 43, 45, 46, 50, 51, 55, 56
Duets, Opp. 47 and 52
2 Collections of Russian Folk Songs

Index

[276]